RISING FIRE

VOLCANOES AND OUR INNER LIVES

JOHN CALDERAZZO

THE LYONS PRESS
Guilford Connecticut
An imprint of The Globe Pequot Press

for SueEllen

for teachers who were also great friends:

Wesley Ford Davis
Hans Juergensen
Willie Reader

The Lyons Press is an imprint of The Globe Pequot Press.

10 9 8 7 6 5 4 3 2 1

Printed in the United States of America

ISBN 1-59228-389-6

Library of Congress Cataloging-in-Publication Data is available on file.

CONTENTS

And for all this, nature is never spent;
There lives the dearest freshness deep down things

—Gerard Manley Hopkins,
"God's Grandeur"

PROLOGUE

Rock moves. It moves all the time, everywhere, in big ways and small, through deep time and fast forward, on the surface of the earth and far below it.

And in and around volcanoes, rock flies—at times faster and farther than any bird. Or it flows like tar, or water. It floats on water, burns on water. Glowing rock chunks the size of bowling balls bob and hiss in the South Pacific, the Gulf of Alaska, the Caribbean, the Mediterranean. Earth, Air, Fire, Water: the four classic elements that form the world, all jumbled up, none of them acting the way you think they should.

Over the long arc of time, volcanoes heave themselves up into high, holy mountains and haunted summits, burst apart, erode back down. Their lavas leap and turn with the grace of sandhill cranes in their mating dance; they breathe, roar, and sing. And singing, volcanic rocks and fires can deeply affect the way we see and act in the world, the stories we tell about the world.

A man who told many stories about the same volcano was the great eighteenth-century artist Katsushika Hokusai, who understood that to look at nature in just one or two ways is to diminish it. From the middle to the end of his long and prolific life, Hokusai created endlessly inventive perspectives of Mount Fuji, Japan's most sacred mountain. Among his *One Hundred Views of Fuji* is a woodblock print of a curving, luminous-orange slope of the volcano, rendered in such close-up that it fills half the sky. Other views include a perfect cone in the middle distance viewed through slanting arrows of rain over a lake; and a tiny, snow-tipped summit visible from sixty miles through the bustling cityscape of Edo, today's Tokyo. Fuji as dominating spirit. Fuji as one of many dynamic parts of nature. Fuji as hope, a far-off snow-dream to shopkeepers on a crowded street. So many Fujis and stories of Fuji!

And on the canvas of the enormous three-dimensional world, so many other volcanoes: about 550 that have erupted in historical time, perhaps 1,450 that are potentially active—not counting hundreds more in our solar system. Each can be viewed in many ways, a metaphorical 100: a channel through which the planet's rising fires move from inner to outer space, embers turning to glittering stars; a source of the newest earth on earth; a doomsday machine monitored by satellites and seismographs and shamans; an inspiration to painters and writers and spiritual seekers. Of these "mountains *alive*," as volcanologist Maurice Krafft liked to call them, fifty-five or so are in eruption each year. In all, about 600 million people—one in ten on the planet—live in their shadows. Every one of us lives in their arc of influence. In far more ways than I was once capable of imagining, I do, too.

About ten years ago, as I sat in my basement study in northern Colorado, I took the first steps in my personal journey to Volcano Land. It all started innocently enough: I simply picked up my ringing telephone. It was an editor, friend, and former student, Randy, calling to talk me into something. He had conceived of a series of science books for children aged eight to twelve, and I was the right person, he thought, to write the first volume.

Each book, Randy explained, would offer 101 questions and answers about a particular landscape or aspect of the natural world—deserts, reptiles, hurricanes. The questions would be the kind that kids really ask about nature, not just what grown-ups think are good for them. "This way we appeal to a child's sense of wonder," he said, knowing very well that he was appealing to mine, too. A few years earlier, when he had taken one of my nonfiction writing workshops at Colorado State University, one of the first things he had heard me say in class—because I really believe it and say it often—was something like this:

The world is filled with wonderful things. They float all around us, all the time, and as a nonfiction writer it's your job, and privilege, to find them.

"I love the concept," I told Randy, though I was not quite ready to sign up. Experience had taught me to enter all writing projects warily. But as I held the phone to my ear and stared at my white basement wall, I saw an alligator take form and swim across my favorite Florida river, Tampa's Hillsborough. *How long can a gator hold its breath?* I wondered, thinking that a book on swamps would be great fun to research. For me, nonfiction writing has always meant travel, whether or not I actually leave the house. Finally I said, "Do I need to pick my topic now?"

"Hold on. I'll FedEx you a list of possibilities. Look them over and then we'll talk."

Two days later, back in my study, I ran my finger down Randy's list.

Bears

Glaciers

Gulf Beaches

The Sierras

And a couple of dozen more, each one a different window onto the world. Somewhere in there, for no reason that I could see, my finger stopped at Volcanoes.

I tapped the word. Volcanoes?

Like my wife SueEllen, who also writes and teaches at CSU, I had traveled widely and roamed even farther thanks to books about nature. We had camped and hiked all over SueEllen's native Colorado and the Rocky Mountain West, and I had researched and written environmental and travel stories in China, Thailand, Mexico, and Switzerland. But somehow, I had never seen a volcano erupt or even smolder. I didn't know if there were any hot ones within a thousand miles of our small valley in the foothills outside of Fort Collins. Until it exploded into the national consciousness in 1980 (when I was living in the Gloom Belt of northwest Ohio), I had never even heard of Mount St. Helens.

Moreover, I was wary of geology. Mostly dead rocks and dust, or so it had seemed to me. I had never even cracked open the Colorado roadside geology book we kept in the car unless SueEllen asked me to when she was driving. The breadth of my ignorance was striking. In fact, now that I thought about it, it was almost embarrassing, and it made me consider something else that I was always telling my writing students, especially the younger ones.

Write what you know. Or, what you WANT to know.

Meaning: get out there and learn some stuff about the world that carries meaning beyond your relationship with your girlfriend, your boyfriend, your divorced parents, your unfortunate fondness for video games, drinking games, bongs, et cetera. The world is a lot bigger than that, and endlessly various. Far more often than not, the students take up this challenge.

So then, how much did *I* want to know about volcanoes? While I mulled this over, something that I hadn't thought about in years suddenly popped into my head. I was seven or eight years old and sitting cross-legged on the cool linoleum floor of my elementary school library on Long Island, staring at a book. It was open to a drawing of a Mexican farmer, who was dashing so quickly across a cornfield that his sombrero had just flown off. Behind him was something that didn't make any sense to me, at least not in a supposedly true story: rocks and smoke were shooting out of a crack in the ground. These were the birth pangs, I now recalled, in the life of a brand-new volcano, which soon came to fill up that man's field. How that could have happened, and with what consequences to the people who lived nearby, I had no idea.

But now I had an excuse to find out. Plus, I told myself, this would not be one of those all-consuming projects that takes years to complete. It was only a kid's book. I looked up from Randy's list of possibilities and stared at my basement wall. I saw the geysers of Yellowstone shooting high into the air. I saw Vesuvius exploding and throwing ash over ancient Pompeii.

The book that I eventually wrote for Randy really did emerge from the curiosity of children. To build a master list of questions, I grilled some of SueEllen's nieces and nephews and the sons and daughters of friends. Then I called up the U.S. volcano national parks and monuments whose names Randy had sent me, places like Yellowstone, Washington's Mount St. Helens and Mount Rainier, northern California's Devils Postpile. During spring break, SueEllen and I drove to New Mexico's Capulin National Monument and climbed the dead cinder cones rising out of the cholla-strewn desert. I asked the park rangers what it was that kids asked them.

Will my dog start barking if this crater is about
to erupt?
Can a kid run faster than lava?
Are Volvos named after volcanoes?

Then I began to research the answers to these and more commonplace questions. Digging into the material raised even more questions. *Did volcanoes kill off the dinosaurs? If so, how did they manage to do that on a global scale?* Soon my master list was large enough to fill three or four children's books.

The questions that I eventually started the book with reflected something that struck me as important and touching: the fear and uncertainty that the park rangers had noticed in children who were confronting, sometimes for the first time, an immense and unaccountable violence in the natural world. At the same time, my opening questions came from my own list, which I realized had begun to form long ago, perhaps as I sat on the cool linoleum floor of my elementary school library.

Could a volcano erupt in my backyard?
Yes.

What could be done to stop it?

Nothing.

Nothing?

Oh, you could grab your shoes and run. That's
what a farmer in Mexico did one afternoon when a
volcano suddenly—

And so forth. At first, I exaggerated a bit for the sake of
drama and play, but then I got around to soberly explaining the
probabilities. If you live in the American Midwest, the South, the
East Coast, or most of the other places, like southern Australia,
that are far from the ragged borders of the planet's great crustal
plates, the chance of lava burbling up through your flower beds
is just about nil. For the most part, heat-driven volcanoes shoulder up through preexisting cracks in the earth's crust.

Nevertheless, *at some point* during these last few hundred million years of drifting continents, at least three-quarters of the
earth's surface above and below the sea has been formed or affected by volcanic action. That amazing fact had come to me
fairly early in my research, and I'm not sure if I ever got over it.
I learned, for instance, that as un-mountainous a place as Florida
rests largely on a foundation of sunken volcanoes. Over thousands of centuries, they have been ground down by erosion and
covered by a thick layer of limestone formed from coral, which
has itself been built, death by tiny death, from the skeletons and
shells of marine creatures. There were even volcanoes (or at least
significant volcanic action) near New York City, my childhood
home. The rising heat of the earth in the form of now cool and
hardened lava had created the Palisades, the sheer cliffs along the
New Jersey side of the Hudson River that once gave their name

to a well-known amusement park. I sometimes saw the park's cliff-top roller coasters from the backseat of the family car as my dad drove on the West Side Highway.

As I wrote my little children's book, I learned enough about volcanoes and planetary restlessness not just to confirm but revel in the fact that the world really was filled with wonderful things. The Mush Zone, for instance. That's an informal term I heard a scientist mention once for the border between the earth's fantastically compressed iron and nickel core and the mantle that surrounds it. Recent studies suggest that the core revolves slightly *faster* than the rest of the earth, completing an extra revolution every few hundred thousand years. Thus, a ball of rock more than a thousand miles in diameter actually spins inside of the gigantic rock ball of the earth. As a little boy I was told in school that bedrock, a name I loved, anchored all of Manhattan's skyscrapers. I know now that the word generally means unweathered, solid rock often found under unconsolidated or looser rock, but back then I assumed it was simply the hardest natural material there was and that it ran from the basement of the Empire State Building straight down to the unmoving, eternal core of the planet. Well, so much for bedrock.

I discovered that other worlds in our solar system feature some wonderful things, too. Io, one of Jupiter's twelve moons, contains huge volcanoes whose eruptive plumes in some cases shoot almost 200 miles above its orange surface. Photographs of Mars taken by the *Mariner Nine* satellite show a volcano, called Olympus Mons, that's fifteen miles high and the width of Ohio. It's easily the biggest mountain so far found in the universe.

But "wonderful" in this sense does not always mean just awe inspiring or terrific, amazing, nice, cool. "There is nothing so surreal as a fact," says the poet Adrienne Rich. And soon enough I found myself confronting questions that either didn't fit into a short book or deserved a deeper, more complicated consideration appropriate for adults.

For instance, the surreal fact of ritual sacrifice. Why did people in so many places—in ancient Mexico, Peru, Nicaragua, Hawaii, Sumatra, and probably Italy and elsewhere—make human and other sacrifices to volcanoes? What other demands have dynamic and striking mountains made upon the human spirit, and what gifts have they offered in return? As new research is starting to suggest, could life on the planet really have started within inches of thermal vents in pitch-black abysses several miles beneath the surface of the ocean? Given that landscape seems to have influenced human culture in so many profound and enriching ways, why do we keep treating the natural world and its creatures so badly? Questions like these kept poking at me.

Along the way, I also began to develop new eyes. Deep time eyes. For example, during the six years that I had lived and taught in Colorado, SueEllen and I had often driven west up the wriggling Poudre River Canyon and out into the wide, windy expanse of North Park, one of the more isolated places in the Rocky Mountain West. Off in the distance, in the direction of Steamboat Springs, I always noticed the rock formation that had given Rabbit Ears Pass its name. The long "ears" of twin dark towers, each fifty to one hundred feet high, stuck up from the top of a wide mountain. *Nice rocks,* I'd think as we drove closer. And that's about all I'd think.

But then one afternoon, everything changed. From miles away, I "saw" in the air above the mountain the outline of a bigger, more symmetrical mountain—an ancient volcano. Rabbit Ears, I suddenly realized, was the fractured top of a plug, a remnant of old, old lava that had stopped rising in the neck of that volcano. Eventually the lava cooled and hardened. And as centuries and centuries of erosion whittled away the softer rock and soil around it, it emerged. Rabbit Ears, it turned out, was one of many volcanoes that had erupted in this part of Colorado tens of millions of years ago, and suddenly I had accumulated enough knowledge to see it.

Soon, almost everywhere I looked, I was noticing the bones of a much older planet poking through. A cabin we owned a share of in southern Colorado's San Juan Mountains sat in a narrow valley whose sheer walls rose hundreds of feet high. The walls revealed themselves to me as many layers of ash and cinder fallen from huge volcanic eruptions thirty to thirty-five million years ago. Wyoming's Devil's Tower was one of the world's largest plugs of ancient lava, an 865-foot-tall monolith with long, columnar ridges—a common pattern for cooling lava that you can see at places like Devils Postpile National Monument in California. A Native American legend held that the Devil's Tower striations were caused by a giant grizzly bear trying to claw his way toward seven little girls who'd sought refuge on top. The tower was so high that the girls soon entered the sky, and today we see them sparkling down on us as a cluster of stars: the Pleiades. I've often wondered if Steven Spielberg had that story in mind when he gave the tower its starring role in *Close Encounters of the Third Kind*. A brief trip to Yellowstone National Park let me glimpse the shattered, forested-over, and eroded remains of a thirty-five-mile-wide crater formed by a volcanic explosion 600,000 years ago. The eruption was powered by the same forces that still keep the park's geysers fuming—by far the world's largest concentration of them, a wondrous fact that helped Yellowstone become the world's first national park. I also learned to my surprise that the explosion was one of three gigantic Yellowstone eruptions that over the last 2.2 million years blanketed the entire middle of the United States in inches and sometimes feet of ash, helping to build the topsoil that would eventually make the Great Plains so fertile. Measurable amounts of Yellowstone ash, spirited east and south by high-altitude winds, fell as far away as the Gulf Coast of Louisiana.

Years of writing personal essays and especially memoirs had already prompted me to roam freely across the decades of my corporal life. But now I was beginning to feel unmoored in the immensity of geologic time, the 4.3 billion years of our planet's existence. I was starting to experience an infinitely larger and more pliable universe than the one I was accustomed to inhabiting. Dead rocks began to come alive.

There was also something comforting about wandering through such long corridors of time, beyond the reach of homo sapiens and the consequences of their abundance and growing needs. Everyone but the brain dead has seen so many natural areas and our "living companions on the planet," as Paul Ehrlich calls them, diminished or pushed close to or over the edge of extinction—redwood groves, the Florida panther, the California condor. Since the 1930s—just seven decades out of our cosmic home's age of 4.3 billion years—the human population of the earth has more than tripled, from two to six billion-plus, and our resource consumption has increased twentyfold.

SueEllen and I had been taking this personally and very hard, and I had developed a physiological response to the continuing bad news of the world. A TV or newspaper headline about the plight of West Indian manatees or crashing populations of mountain gorillas caused my throat to constrict and my spirits to plunge.

My writerly research in the field could make matters even worse, because there was no denying the magnitude of destruction that I think even worldly and literate people still, too often, refuse to believe or can't comprehend from a distance. In Thailand to write a magazine piece about ways in which Buddhist principles were being used to help fight environmental battles, I walked around for a hot and sun-blasted afternoon on a gigantic clear-cut outside of Chiang Mai. Only a few years before, it had been a cool and ancient hardwood forest that ran for miles, home to great hornbills, barking deer, and panthers, not to mention a village of people who enjoyed its fertile soil, shade, and abundant water. Combined with other deforestation—*70 percent* of the country's forests cut down in the last thirty years—this loss had actually changed the weather, causing unheard of drought. As I stood in the sun surveying the destruction, my chest tightened, and it stayed tight for months. Of course, I knew that letting my thoughts roam over the long arc of deep time offered no solution to such a crescendo of loss. There was a tremendous clash of widely differing time scales at work here. But telling myself that volcanoes created brand new earth, a terrain of new beginnings and fresh habitats, helped my state of mind.

So did coming to understand—no, feel—that very large parts of the world operate according to rhythms separate from *me*. This was something else that I had not foreseen when I spoke to Randy on the telephone. In 1985, a year before I moved to Colorado to teach at CSU, I had gone to a doctor in Ohio for a case of poison ivy that I at first found almost as amusing as it was irritating. As an outdoor guy, I should have known better than to wade with a hedge trimmer into some backyard bushes without really looking. After the chatty dermatologist had me strip down, he looked at my chest and said, "Yup, yup, you got it—classic!" Then he had me turn around and he suddenly grew quiet. I felt a cold finger press into my back below my right shoulder blade.

"What's this?" he said finally. "This I don't like at all." It was a black spot among some moles that somehow SueEllen and I had not noticed. Melanoma, it was soon confirmed. Malignant— a word that I never thought I would hear applied to me. I was still in my thirties.

After I had it cut out, along with a hand-sized chunk of my skin, the biopsy showed "clean margins" and therefore no need for chemo or radiation. But the surgeon warned me that the cancer, having penetrated fairly deeply into my skin, could still have spawned a rogue cell or two that managed to escape his knife. Only time would tell, he concluded, though if the melanoma showed up in my lymph system or somewhere else . . . well, it would be better not to think about that.

So of course I thought about it all the time. More than five years later, with no return and statistics piling up on my side, I still sometimes woke up at 3 A.M., staring at the ceiling and wondering if a pinprick of darkness was growing inside me, a death star sailing through the infinity of my body. SueEllen sometimes woke, too, groaning or kicking back at me, but then finally suggesting that I picture some peaceful corner of the wilderness that we had recently hiked or canoed or cross-country skied through. That helped. But I found another comfort in lying there and meditating about long-term geothermal forces, the sliding of continent-sized plates, currents of stone welling up from the depths of the planet over millions of years. Compared to all that, my time on the earth was so fleeting. Volcanoes were helping me find solace in the liquid nature of rock, in the impermanent nature of everything, including me.

ANCIENT FIRES
VESUVIUS, STROMBOLI, MOUNT ETNA

Here are presented to thee . . .
the most wonderful, most prodigious,
and even miraculous Operations of Nature

—Athanasius Kircher,
Mundus Subterraneus

By the time I finished my slender book for children, I had "traveled" in more new ways than I knew existed. And I was growing hungrier for more. When I mailed Randy the completed manuscript, the school year was winding down and a number of happy coincidences were converging on me. I had just won a CSU teaching award that by some miracle came with enough cash to fly me almost anywhere I wanted to go. Then I read in the *Denver Post* that Sicily's Mount Etna was erupting, as it had many times over the centuries. It wasn't blowing its top in highly fatal, world-shaking paroxysms, but smoking and pushing out sludgy rivers of lava. Some were clinking downhill at a rate of just a few feet per day, but threatening, as Emily Dickinson once wrote, to "eat villages for breakfast." I decided it was time for me to walk some of the landscapes I had been writing about. After all, except for the mud pots and geysers of Yellowstone, I hadn't actually seen or heard even a geothermal burp. I could also take in Vesuvius, which along with Mount Fuji was probably the world's most famous volcano. Since antiquity, Mediterranean volcanoes had inspired the imaginations of the Greeks, the Romans, and visitors from the worlds of literature, art, philosophy, natural history, and religion.

Virgil, the national poet of Rome, was one of many writers who were clearly impressed by the charismatic mountains of the Mediterranean. As he wrote in the *Aeneid:*

> Aetna here thunders with an horrid noise,
> Sometimes black Clouds evapoureth to Skies,
> Fuming to pitchy curls, and sparkling Fires,
> Tosseth up Globes of flames; to Stars aspires:
> Now belching Rocks; The Mountain's Entrals torn:
> And groaning, hurls out liquid Stones thence born
> Through th' Air in showres . . . .

Yes, I needed to get as close as I could to essential fire.

When you're on a volcano, do as the volcanologists do. That's what I joked to myself as I stuffed my backpack with almost nothing but books and clothes suitable for hiking over rugged lava fields: leather gloves, plaid shirts, and dorky, wide-brimmed hats—I still often thought of the cancer-causing sun as my enemy. I also threw in a pair of faded white Nikes and decided to wear my aged but trusty hiking boots on the plane. In my excitement, I forgot that I was first going to spend a couple of days in Rome, sightseeing.

That turned out to be a mistake. As I clomped over the cobblestones of the Eternal City (which suddenly didn't seem so eternal given my new understanding of geologic time), I noticed that a lot of impeccably dressed Romans seemed to be frowning at me. They would look me up and down, then stare in outright horror at my feet. Ah, my dusty boots. Suddenly I was even more of a fashion felon than I was at home, except that none of my friends or students were around to laugh *with* me. And SueEllen had passed on this trip.

Hey! I wanted to yell to all the snazzy dressers, *I'm Italian, too!*

Yet even if I'd known enough of the language to announce this 50 percent truth (my dad's parents had left Italy in 1899 for Brooklyn), the Romans would probably have snickered at me for mangling the accent. Or loathed me for being one of those other Italians, the overseas kind, or maybe worse, one of the culturally impoverished southerners, the Calabrians. In pestilential heat and humidity that didn't seem to bother anybody else, I sat alone at a sidewalk café on the Via Something-or-Other, drinking a bottle of wine and imagining what I'd say to SueEllen if she were sitting across from me. *Snotty Romans! Sure, they look refined, but what have they accomplished in the last two or three centuries?*

I decided to escape the city a day early. I jumped on a train, rocked south past fields of poppies in full bloom, and after a few hours, with the hazy bulk of Vesuvius growing clearer and larger in the distance, I stepped into the much more comfortable anarchy of Naples.

A few days later, I took a cab to Vesuvius. You can do this in Naples. (*"Go left at the black lava river,"* I imagined saying to my driver, *"then proceed directly to the gates of hell."*) The volcano had erupted more than fifty times since the famous Pompeii blowout of 79 A.D., but it didn't seem to be doing much as I approached on a sunny afternoon. Still, this was about to be my first climb of a living volcano, and I didn't know what I'd find. A witch's brew of lava soup simmering at the bottom of the crater? The rock under my feet palsied with tiny earthquakes? Except in the vicinity of man-made tremblors like a Colorado freight train or the Brooklyn el, I had never felt the ground actually shake. Would the path to the top be hot enough in places to soften the soles of my boots? The cab zigzagged up the lower slopes of the mountain, following a ribbon of asphalt that had been laid over mounds of jagged black rock with low green bushes poking through.

The road began to climb more steeply, and we switchbacked up a more barren slope, the flank of what was called the Great Cone (or, in Italian, *Vesuvio*). Partway up the cone was a parking area. I got out and looked up: nothing but a pile of small red stones, like something I might see in New Mexico or Arizona, rising maybe another 1,000 feet. The summit lay out of sight.

This cone had not even existed when the volcano was busy burying Pompeii. In fact, this newest of many Vesuvius summits—one often growing out of another, as numerous eighteenth-century engravings and paintings make obvious—had taken form only during World War II. This occurred shortly after the U.S. Fifth Army arrived to liberate Naples. On March 18, 1944, watching the volcano's sudden sparks and hearing it rumble, an editor from the military newspaper *Stars and Stripes* composed this headline for the next day's edition:

Vesuvius Awakes for Joy
at Being Reunited
with His Old Friends from America

Apparently, Vesuvius awoke with far too much joy, because a few days later ash and lava bombs rocketing out of the crater destroyed eighty-eight B-25 Mitchell bombers that the Allied forces had parked at nearby Poggiomarino. The eruption was not catastrophic, however, killing "only" twenty-seven people, including two who died when lava hit a water tank, shattering the leading edge of the scalding rock flow. A newly remodeled Vesuvius now stood a bit taller than before—4,200 feet above the Bay of Naples.

A dusty indentation in the pebble-covered slope indicated my path to the top. I paid the cabbie, and off I trudged, happy and alone, far from snooty Romans and the insanity of Naples' traffic and other irritations of a much too-crowded world. Red-roofed towns and cities fell farther and farther away as I climbed. I could hear the wind up here. How ironic, I thought, to find peace and quiet on terrain born of such terrible violence. The sun on my shoulders and the back of my shirt felt . . . good.

It seemed odd, though, to see no one else on the slope with me. One of the books in my daypack informed me that a great tourist industry had sprung up around Vesuvius in the late eighteenth century and flourished into the twentieth century, a highly eruptive period in the volcano's long life. For years at a time, several of its vents spit out flames and lava in a relatively low-key way, drawing visitors from cold and gray, volcano-deprived northern Europe, especially. In the early days of the volcano's popularity, clumps of tourists led by local guides, all of them preceded by young boys carrying torches, often set out for the upper mountain at night, when the fires were most spectacular. Moving uphill through vineyards and olive groves, men in top hats and long coats and women in flowing dresses and plumed caps rode horses or sat in sedan chairs carried by two men or two mules. When the slopes finally grew steep and hot in places, the visitors walked, closely following their guides across the treacherous terrain with ropes or leather thongs tied about their waists.

Often they stopped partway up for refreshments at a hut where a man (or series of them) wearing a black eye patch and calling himself a hermit had them sign *The Album of the Hermitage of Vesuvius*. This album and subsequent volumes eventually became a collection of celebrity signatures: Goethe, Lord Byron, Alexandre Dumas, Flaubert. After a visit in 1787, Goethe wrote at length in *Journey to Italy* about several climbs he took to "this peak of Hell which towers up in the middle of paradise." The adventures clearly thrilled him, and helped him conclude that "Nature is, indeed, the only book whose every page is filled with important content."

Later on, various toll roads and then a funicular cableway were added to help tourists. On three occasions the tracks were destroyed by lava, the last time in 1944, when Vesuvius greeted its old friends from America.

After that blast, Vesuvius dropped into a very quiet phase from which it has still not really awakened. For this reason, I wasn't expecting to see any major pyrotechnics. But when the path ended, I was shocked by the size and steepness of the crater that suddenly opened before me. None of it had been visible from below. It's fortunate that I'm not given to vertigo, because the rim I was standing on was no more than ten feet across and much narrower than that in places. I caught my breath, sat down, and peered in.

A pit several hundred yards wide and unbelievably deep yawned in front of me. How deep it was, I really couldn't tell because the bottom swirled with vapors. The interior walls were lined with strata of burnt red, brown, and black rock. Here and there on the walls, a crack or black hole rimmed with yellow or orange stains of sulfur (once known as brimstone) hissed with steam.

Although I had learned a good deal of earth science writing the children's book, my research was much more sketchy than comprehensive, and I still didn't know enough geology to read even a quarter of what lay before me. Yet any fool could see the scars of a great inferno. Fifty years after the last eruption, the planet was still scorched here, and this crater was obviously a breakthrough place between worlds. At only 17,000 years old, Vesuvius was a youngster among volcanoes. It was also a place where someday, with two million people living within a radius of ten or fifteen miles, apocalypse would certainly threaten again. I found myself studying the rasping vents. These past fifty years were by far the longest pause in its eruptive cycle since 1631. I knew enough to realize that it could sleep for decades or centuries more before coughing up even a warning column of smoke—no two volcanoes are the same, and a single volcano rarely maintains a consistent eruptive pattern over the course of its life. I also knew that shallower and more frequent earthquakes often heralded trouble, and that if the shaking started, geologists at the nearby Vesuvius Observatory would quickly close off the area. In other words, I wasn't in any danger at all. Still, I wondered how much molten rock was simmering below my feet, waiting to blow. How far down was it? Could it be rising? And if so, how quickly?

After a while, I saw a man, maybe a soccer player from the look of his legs, striding up the path with a blond baby on his shoulders. As they approached, I noticed that the baby was smiling and cooing—what a great bouncing ride he was having. They reached the rim, and the man gave me a nod and tightened his grip on the baby. He murmured something in French to him. Then he shuffled to the rim, planting his legs wide. He tilted forward and looked in.

The baby burst into tears.

One person's fear is another's fascination.

In 79 A.D., when the great natural history writer Pliny the Elder saw Vesuvius erupting across the Bay of Naples, he moved as quickly as he could *toward* it. At the time, Pliny held command of the western Roman fleet at the port of Misenum, which offered a wonderful view of the mountain. When a ferocious column of ash and lava shot up from somewhere on the volcano and then fire broke out on its slopes, he ordered a small craft to take him close enough to study it in detail. He may have been one of the few people in the region who'd known for some time that Vesuvius was more than an "ordinary" mountain, but he had never seen it erupt explosively. For more than six centuries, nobody had.

The eruption cloud soon swelled into the form of a gigantic pine tree, a miles-high trunk of smoke and shattered rocks and fire pluming out laterally along its length into ashy branches. Pliny had no way to know it, but by the time he positioned himself at the bow of his vessel, his slaves starting to pull at the oars, the volcano was already in the process of killing up to 3,500 people. It was also starting to erase several cities from history.

Sixteen years earlier, an earthquake in the region had almost wiped out the cities first, destroying dozens of buildings and temples in prosperous Pompeii, the seaside resort of Herculaneum, and elsewhere. Apparently, Pompeii, whose renowned vineyards ran far up the slopes of the volcano, had just about recovered from the quake when the summit of Vesuvius, eight miles to the north, exploded. Soon ash and lapilli (hardened but still hot lava pebbles) began to rain over the city. As a boy I had seen a rerun of the old black-and-white movie *The Last Days of Pompeii,* based on the novel by the infamous Edward Bulwer-Lytton. (He was the man who wrote, "It was a dark and stormy night.") Consequently, I had grown up thinking that fast-flowing rivers of lava, of the sort featured in the movie's final scenes, caused many of the deaths around Vesuvius and in the vicinity of most volcanoes. But that wasn't true at all. A little boy or girl can, in fact, run faster than most flows of lava that crunch along over the surface of the ground.

Volcanoes kill primarily in other ways. In Herculaneum, on the western base of Vesuvius, a series of huge, expanding waves of shattered rocks, gases, and hot mud rushed downhill, burying everything in compact layers that totaled eighty feet thick. Until archeologists began digging in earnest in the nineteenth century, Herculaneum had been largely forgotten for 1,800 years. In Pompeii, prevailing winds carried ash and lapilli directly overhead, and the dark rain fell so thickly that people indoors and out suffocated or died from inhaling hot and perhaps poisonous air. Within hours, more than twenty feet of the volcano's fine ejecta had smothered them. After that, a hurricane of expanding gases and flying stones that broke out of Vesuvius slammed down over the city, killing and burying whoever was left or trying to return.

In the days before I'd hiked up to the crater rim of Vesuvius, I'd wandered around the excavated remains of these elegant dead cities. It was heartbreaking to walk through the partially reconstructed ruins, the empty colonnaded avenues, tiled bathhouses, and homes decorated with red-tinted frescoes, and then discover an open-air display of the casts of people and animals who had perished. The amazingly detailed casts had been made by carefully removing some skeletal remains from the holes that disintegrated bodies had left in the dry ash layer, and then pouring in plaster. All were preserved in their final, suffering moments. A man on the ground propped on one elbow labors to take his last breath. A women lies on her stomach with her child curled up against her side. A dog still wearing a collar twists on its back, mouth partly open. I could almost hear it whimper. They were such sad and ghostly figures.

While death was raining down on Pompeii, Pliny's boat drew closer to the volcano. The eruptions were still several miles from his position, but lapilli and gas-engorged burning rocks called pumice clattered down on the vessel's deck. Pumice that splashed into the water remained weirdly floating, sizzling and steaming, knocked about by waves roiling from incessant earthquakes. Red and greenish lightning arced everywhere, in bolts, webs, and starbursts. This scene of the underworld literally overwhelming the world of the living, and on such a massive scale, must have terrified even those who saw it from a great distance. Yet instead of turning back, Pliny ordered his slaves to keep rowing, then tied a pillow onto his head with a napkin as protection against the blizzard of cinders and burning stones.

Pliny's obsessive curiosity about the world was nothing new for him. Over the years, it had driven him to compile a thirty-seven volume encyclopedia, *Natural History*, with books devoted to astronomy, geography, mineralogy, zoology, and so forth. He included a list of all the active volcanoes known to exist—about ten! But he also accurately noted that strong or frequent earthquakes often preceded eruptions. As he proudly pointed out in his preface, his *History* marshaled 20,000 facts from 2,000 books. (He made time for all this research by having himself carried around in a sedan chair, which allowed him to read and write as he moved.) A modern sensibility looking back over twenty centuries will detect in Pliny's volumes impressive scientific observation, but also some entertaining nonsense, including tall tales passed on by travelers who'd returned from distant lands.

For instance, my favorite section—Book VII, "Man"—is as packed with the marvelous and the bizarre (though not the dark violence) as anything García Márquez or Kafka or David Lynch ever dreamed up. There are reports of mountain-dwelling men in Ethiopia who have the heads of dogs; a tribe in India called the Monocoli who have only one leg, hop with amazing speed, and cool off by lying in the shade of their tremendous foot; an Italian tribe, the Marsi, whose saliva makes snakes retreat as though from boiling water; and a man whom Pliny himself claims to have seen turn into a woman on his wedding day.

When I first read this chapter, I felt as if I were opening the doors of a *Wunderkammern*, or cabinet of wonders, one of those old, privately financed European collections, sometimes the size of a large room, which displayed dozens or hundreds of nature's marvels alongside objects of man-made ingenuity. Thus, a dried but fully inflated blowfish and the skeleton of Siamese-twin children

11

might flank an inch-high plum-pit carving that depicted the Last Supper right down to the goblets. I was starting to suspect that volcanoes were becoming my own wonder cabinets.

An erupting Vesuvius so close to home must have struck Pliny as equally entrancing—or more so, considering its size and power. Over the fears of his crew, some of whom had also tied pillows onto their heads, he commanded the boat to land, perhaps to help evacuate some of the afflicted on shore. While broad sheets of fire burned on the mountain, Pliny began to inhale ash and maybe poisonous fumes. He collapsed and died before the boat could retreat. He was reportedly later found looking more like a man asleep than dead. The final marvels of his fifty-six years of life, the last things he saw before he died, were the volcano's impossible fires.

The story of his demise—wrapped inside the first known eyewitness report of a volcanic eruption—is preserved in letters written by his nephew, Pliny the Younger. Eighteen years old at the time of the eruption, he was invited to accompany his famous uncle in his vessel, but declined, saying he would rather study. What he studied was the behavior of the incredible conflagration across the bay, and he eventually recorded it in such copious and accurate detail that he was later called history's first volcanologist. I wonder if anybody also called him Pliny the Prudent.

From Naples, I took an overnight ferry south to the volcanic Aeolean Islands, which over millennia had risen burning from the sea. Some of them still burn. Not far to the south of them lie the shores of Sicily. Close to the east is the toe of the Italian boot: my grandparents' birthplace of Calabria. These small and gauzy islands were once home to Aeolis, Greek god of winds, and Vulcan, Roman god of fire, from whose name comes Vulcano: Volcano. In fact, I'd been reading, the tiny island of Vulcano still bubbles with mud baths and an awful stench of sulfur. Tourists with aching joints often ferried in from the mainland and, wearing tiny bikini suits, settled into the goo, like Chinese Buddhas. Thinking about them reminded me of something that Fran Leibowitz once wrote, which is that you don't have to be in Italy long to realize that Fellini was making documentaries. A sign posted near the baths suggested that a dip will cause the hand of God to "sustain you sweetly, transforming your thoughts into balls of music and color."

Stromboli, the most volcanically active of the islands, had been erupting several times an hour for at least 700 years, which is why navigators used it as a beacon and called it the Lighthouse of the Mediterranean. Its behavior was almost unbelievably consistent. As I lay back in my ferry bunk, I recalled that near the conclusion of *A Journey to the Center of the Earth,* Jules Verne's heroes return to the surface in a wild elevator ride atop one of Stromboli's eruptions.

I was up and out before dawn. As we approached Stromboli, the sky grew lighter, and I watched the sun, a pink egg, lift up from the sea. I had stationed myself on the ferry's bare top deck, high above the water, the steel plates slick with dew and thrumming from engines many levels below—a reminder of the earth's mighty thermal motors. Ahead in the distance, the perfect green triangle of Stromboli was growing. *My God,* I thought, *it's nothing* BUT *volcano!* As we drew closer, I watched it occasionally send up a puff of smoke, but its summit fires had already been grayed over by daylight. The green triangle soon towered over us.

I leaned against the railing as we passed by (we would later dock at the nearby and much larger island of Lipari, where I had reserved a room). The shallow pebbled beach seemed to be covered with coal instead of sand. But a look through my binoculars showed that sand it was, or fine pebbles anyway. It was the blackest, strangest looking beach I'd ever seen. Here and there, looking as forlorn as beached whales, were fishing boats that had been cranked ashore with a winch and cable. Behind the beach climbed small, whitewashed homes with cactus gardens and trellises smothered in bougainvillea. Beyond them abruptly rose the symmetrical green slopes of the volcano, 3,038 feet high.

A couple of days later I returned on a tourist excursion, but like a fool I had not booked a trip that allowed enough time for a hike to the summit. I headed to the beach and was soon wading ankle deep in the pebbles. Up close, against my white calves, the beach looked even blacker than before. Then I heard an odd huffing sound. I looked around but couldn't locate it. About fifteen minutes later I heard it again. I looked at the sky—of course, the volcano! Three thousand feet up, a dragon exhaled, almost politely. They were the first eruptions I'd ever heard.

Shortly after dusk, I saw my first moving lava. From our small boat rocking offshore, I watched a red lava fountain shoot up a little ways and splatter back into the cup of the summit or perhaps into the crevasse named Sciarra del Fuoco, Pit of Fire. The consistently modest size of these fireworks, whose flying rocks and gases apparently never reached the rim of the island, had allowed human habitation for centuries. Even when the flying lava was not showing itself to me, I noticed that a low sky directly over the cauldron occasionally glowed red in reflection. Then it would dull out, then glow again.

The water around our small boat had grown very calm. The sky still held some feeble light, and out of the corner of my eye I saw something break the surface a little way off, a dark smooth thing, rolling. A large eel? A dolphin? Probably. Yet it moved so languorously, like a snake in a dream, that it was easy to imagine it a sea monster. That's what a lot of old-time sailors might have thought. My grandmother might have, too. Yanked from school by age ten to herd goats in the hills of Calabria, she had grown up in a small coastal town just forty miles east of here. At the turn of the last century, during my grandmother's childhood, stories of the fabulous hung in the sea air. Some were cautionary tales, like the warnings my grandmother received as a child about strangers who carried the Evil Eye, *"Malocchio!"* Many more were myths inspired by ordinary people contemplating ferocious or unknown geographies. A few miles south of her town loomed Scylla, the massive coastal rock that Homer said sprouted squid-like tentacles. Just off shore turned the whirlpool Charybdis, ancient eater of ships and men.

Of course I had read the usual Greek and Roman myths when I was a boy, but honestly, I had never paid very close attention to them, not even in graduate school. Too much soap opera for me. Here, however, where surreal and powerful natural forces were an unavoidable part of daily life, even hourly life, some of those stories suddenly seemed vital. Did a giant who worked the bellows of a great forge live inside Stromboli? No, but I could see why generations of people might think so.

More than 2,000 years ago, as myths and legends spoke to the popular imagination, a number of Mediterranean scholars were thinking hard about the mechanics of volcanoes and the subterranean world generally. In the fourth century B.C., Aristotle provided the first written explanation of the source of lava: "Sometimes, when the earth has melted because of fire, and then cooled again, a black-colored stone is formed." He also first used the word "crater" (Greek for "bowl") to describe the pit atop a volcano.

Finally, he suggested an answer to the baffling question of why fire would burst from the earth at all. He believed that tremendous winds stored deep in the planet ripped along through tight, subterranean passageways and sometimes the earth's crust. These hard winds rubbing against tunnel walls caused friction, which in turn created heat powerful enough to melt the rock that flew or broke out of volcanoes. Aristotle did not actually come up with the theory himself. He passed it on from the natural philosopher Anaxagoras, but in so doing he gave it an authority that prevailed into the Middle Ages.

As I watched Stromboli from the rocking boat, its dragon breath huffed once more. Lava flew up into the night. It occurred to me that if certain places in the world really speak to you, this was surely one of them.

A few days later I arrived in Sicily, and I was thrilled to learn that Mount Etna was still pushing out great volumes of lava. But how to see this from the cliff-side city of Taormina, where my *pensione* offered views of only a cobblestone lane and a wall of gift shops? "Try the theater," said the friendly lady at the front desk, meaning the 2,300-year-old Greek amphitheater above town. The upper tiers, she suggested, offered a good view of the volcano.

"Good?" In the late afternoon, with the Ionian Sea curving off in the distance and faraway Etna framed by arches, broken columns, cypress trees, and a few thick palms, Europe's largest volcano looked incredible.

It did not at all resemble Vesuvius or Stromboli. More than two miles high (10,919 feet) and perhaps twenty wide, it dominated everything. Smoke poured like mad from its summit. The prevailing winds must have been strong up there, because the billowing, putty-colored ash column flew almost horizontally away, stretching north for miles like some banner of the underworld.

It was a banner that had flown many times over the centuries and been observed by notable figures that included Aeschylus, Pindar, and Ovid. In the seventeenth century, the German Jesuit scholar Athanasius Kircher, who had somehow convinced the Catholic Church to let him roam the Mediterranean for years, studying whatever he felt like, observed it closely. In homage to Aristotle, he drew a cross-section of the earth full of burning tunnels. A kind of latter-day Pliny the Elder, Kircher in 1665 published a tremendous work of scholarship and engravings, *Mundus Subterraneus*. This study of the earth examined the science and mythology of volcanoes around the world, and it included the earliest map showing their planetary distribution.

The book's main focus, of course, was southern Italy. "And with this one onely spectacle of Nature alone," Kircher wrote, "Sicily is (and ever was) admirable. Seeing you can scarce find an Author either of the Ancients, or the Moderns, whom the violence of its ferocious nature, hath not drawn into admiration and astonishment."

Etna was certainly drawing my admiration. Parking myself on a stony bench of the amphitheater, I must have sat for an hour, just watching. But mine was a tourist's or even a painter's point of view, sedate and quiet, a view from the safety of a good ten miles. I was itching to get up there.

The next morning, over breakfast, I got my first close look at Etna's lava, though secondhand. The *pensione* had a TV in its dining room, and over strong coffee and rolls I watched live images of steaming black rocks oozing and clinking downhill. Taller than a man, the lava flow looked bloody in places where its interior temporarily glowed through. One tongue of it had reached the outskirts of Zafferana, an old town that lay partway up the eastern slope of the mountain. That's where the TV folks were broadcasting from. The army had been called in to save the village.

What would it feel like, I wondered, to stare out your bedroom window, the same one your great-great-grandparents looked out of, and see a wall of glowing rock inching down on you?

I decided to go to Zafferana. I finished off my rolls and took a final gulp of coffee. The coffee was for courage, but not because I was about to confront moving rock. I was about to rent my first car outside of the United States, and this in an ancient fortress-village with narrow, twisting lanes carved into steep rock walls. When I got into the red Fiat, I unfolded my map and squeezed out of town slowly but without incident. Then I realized that I didn't know enough Italian to read the traffic signs. Oh well, I told myself, I'll just follow the other drivers and do what they do. This scheme seemed to work, and soon I was watching the Sicilian countryside whiz by.

This was the flip side of missing SueEllen, I realized. Traveling without her law-abiding and cautious voice in my ear, I had the freedom to make all the foolhardy mistakes I wanted to. I drove past villas with red tile roofs, lichen-encrusted garden walls made from volcanic rock, and clusters of orange, lemon, olive, and fig trees. The lushness was a testament to the Mediterranean climate and the extraordinary fertility of volcanic soils.

All the while, I moved uphill. Not long after I reached the edge of Zafferana, I came upon a couple of soldiers in the road, waving their arms. I stopped. I must say, the guys looked dashing in their black ribbed sweaters, and they seemed thrilled to have something important to do. Not far behind them, a roadblock underscored their body language. I didn't need my phrase book to get the message: Town Closed Due to Combination of Lava and Gravity. I turned around, waved to the soldiers, and immediately tried to slip in from several side roads. But all the streets were roped off and patrolled. So were big chunks of the partially blackened slopes above the village, where other soldiers were driving tractors around and wiring explosives, trying to channel away the lava. I saw only a little of this from a distance and pieced together the rest from news reports afterward. This was all very frustrating.

I was beginning to understand that an odd dichotomy seemed to operate around volcanoes, a kind of geologic passive-aggressiveness. Thanks to past eruptions, many volcanoes attract residents to their vicinity with their natural grandeur and rich soils—and then can sustain them for generations. But new eruptions can abruptly and often without warning throw all of that into jeopardy, at least for a while, and literally push away entire towns and cities. That can also make it tough for curious amateurs like me to get close.

The outcome at Zafferana was still uncertain. Whimsical and hard-to-measure subterranean forces meant that the eruption could flag or stop at any time. Then the lava might slow, cool from the surface inward, and harden in place. With dozens of villages dotting Etna's long flanks and dozens of eruptions to contend with over the years, the locals had gotten lots of practice in the art of diversion, digging wide trenches or piling up old lava—always in abundance!—to channel away the new. In 1669, lava sizzled down on more than a dozen Sicilian towns and eventually broke through the city walls of Catania, a good fifteen miles from the summit. At least one town was damaged by a flow that had been heading elsewhere before some villagers uphill broke out their shovels and dug hard.

Human attempts to control or appease nature seem to take as many forms as nature itself. In 253 A.D., as more lava threatened Catania, some residents stood in front of the advance and held up a veil that covered the sepulcher of the city's martyred saint, Agatha. The flow divided and soon stopped. A miracle!

But what about now? If the tractors and explosives didn't work, would the modern Zafferanians try to face down the lava with relics of their own revered dead? Given the security around the town, my guess was that I would not get to see this for myself. As I said, this was frustrating. I had read that the surface of creeping lava cooled fast, but then, pushed from within, continually cracked and clinked like pottery breaking. Thinking about that scrambled my senses, and I really wanted to hear it for myself. And how close could I stand from the front wall of this amazing stuff and not get fried? My guess was that I wouldn't find out today.

So I decided to switch tactics. I would go directly to the source of the trouble—Etna's summit or somewhere close by.

Driving south around the mountain, I passed fewer and fewer cars. Soon the lush fields and the grapevines that twisted up from black soil gave way to agave and clumps of wild cactus. Now and then the cactus rattled in wind sweeping in from Tunisia and

Libya, which lay only 200 miles to the south across the Strait of Sicily. After a while, houses began to drop away, stone walls, and almost all other signs of civilization. When I slowed at a makeshift flea market in a pebbly field, I saw no buildings anywhere. I pulled in. A bunch of Arab-looking guys were hanging around, smoking, standing over ground tarps that displayed oily engine blocks, steering wheel columns, and radiators. Nearby were three Senegalese jewelry merchants looking as dark and thin as petroglyphs. I had seen their doubles in Rome, Naples, and Taormina, selling the same stuff in plazas and parks. Perhaps they were the advance force of a Senegalese entrepreneurial invasion? I could understand their presence in the towns, where they had a reasonable chance to make a buck. But why anybody this far up on Vesuvius thought they could make a living selling Chinese-made watches (or grease-stained alternators) was way beyond me. As I walked around, nobody acknowledged my presence. It was creepy, actually. Like Calabria and southern Italy generally, this side of the volcano was a different country, too. The road climbed gently and began to swing back and forth through piles of lava that looked fresher than anything I'd seen downhill except near Zafferana. The last trees dropped away, although yellow gorse that had taken hold in the lava livened the scene. The road steepened and finally opened into a parking area. Empty. Once again I found myself alone on a volcano.

As I locked the Fiat and looked upslope, I felt far more uneasy than I had on Vesuvius. Maybe it was the sight of so many jumbled, burned cobbles. Long fields of them ran far uphill, potential ankle-breakers even with good boots. Maybe it was the unceasing North African wind at my back, hot and unbelievably dry. I felt exposed, and this was before I began to wonder what might happen if the wind shifted and the great ash-laden plume, which I still could not see, though I heard it faintly roaring, suddenly swung in my direction. At what distance was it safe to approach a churning summit crater? It was one thing for me to shrug off reading the traffic signs on relatively empty roads. It was another to miss the signs of danger up here. I realized how new I was at this.

This was the point at which SueEllen, who loves mountains and especially the world above tree line, would have refused to go farther. I scanned the sky for clouds and the potential for lightning, which I hate. Three times I had been pinned down on high Rocky Mountain slopes by terrifying bolts, and every time I thought the finger of God would zap me into dust. But I couldn't find a cloud anywhere. I hoisted my daypack and headed uphill.

I thought of Empedocles, who in roughly 430 B.C. disappeared on or near this volcano. Many legends say that he reached the summit, and attempting to prove to his followers that he was a god, took a great leap of faith. As Horace wrote:

> Empedocles to be a Godd desires,
> And casts himself into th' Aetnaen Fires.

In contrast, all I desired was to feel the tremendous power of the living earth. But I also found myself thinking that if a sixty-year-old in a robe and sandals had managed the summit, I could at least try to get close. I gulped water as I climbed. Past the scrape and clatter of the cobbles, past the rasping of the wind and my breath, Etna's faint roar grew.

An hour later, during my third or fourth water break, I still couldn't see or smell the plume. By Colorado standards, I wasn't high at all. Yet I was shaking a little as I listened to Etna. It made a jet-engine roar, an amazing roar.

Suddenly I remembered the first time the natural world shook me to the core. Point Lookout Beach, Long Island. I was fourteen or fifteen, sure-footed and agile, and so I figured it would be no big deal to pick my way out to the end of the long rock jetty. I could watch the deeper-water waves build in the wind, and it would be like standing in the middle of the rolling Atlantic. I jumped from boulder to boulder, pausing to study the foam below me as it seethed between the jetty rocks, washing over and around barnacles and crabs and rocks cushioned in sea moss. I knew enough to keep an eye on the wind, which seemed to be holding steady. The universe, however, was not.

Though I couldn't feel it, the earth was spinning on its axis and waltzing with the moon in a graceful ellipse around the sun. As I clambered farther out on the jetty, the immense and invisible powers of this cosmic dance—the gravity of the sun and moon, the earth's centrifugal force—were colluding to haul a great watery bulge over the surface of the sea.

In other words, the tide was rising.

When I turned around finally and looked back at shore, I discovered what that meant. The rough ocean was gnawing at parts of the jetty that had been dry twenty minutes before. Then, midway between me and dry land, a huge gray wave smashed over the rocks. Had I been there, I'd be gone. It was the most frightening moment of my life . . .

While Etna roared, I looked back downhill. Perhaps ten miles off was the lacy rim of the sea: Sicily's ever-changing coastline. I felt as if I were standing on a bulge in the earth that might keep on bulging and push me into outer space. As Empedocles might have noted, huge volumes of Air and Water were swirling all around me, while mixing beneath my feet and far above me were Earth and Fire. Over the top of the volcano and partway down the other side, the tractors scratching away near Zafferana seemed suddenly absurd—toys for kids playing soldier. The Italian army had no more chance against Etna than I had as a boy against that giant ocean wave. And Etna's phenomenal thermal engines were not even running hard.

With the wind still blowing and my water supply almost gone—sun- or heatstroke lurking as ominously as anything the volcano might throw at me—I realized that I had had it, at least for today. I didn't feel like being a martyr to anything, including my own ignorance.

This was disappointing, sure. But I told myself that I could live with it. I'd fly home shortly. And soon enough, I suspected, I'd be hiking toward more rising fire, edging close to another "miraculous Operation of Nature." In other words, I'd become hooked on volcanoes.

INTO THE
RING OF FIRE:
KILAUEA AND UNZEN

*Normal mountains are really dead mountains
compared to volcanoes.
We've fallen in love with mountains alive.*

—Maurice and Katia Krafft

SueEllen and I flew to Hawaii to take part in an international conference on literature and the environment, a growing specialty for both of us. Deep down, though, I had come to the Islands for much more compelling reasons: to finally feel the heat of lava and to chase a pair of volcano ghosts. In many ways these activities turned out to be much the same thing, but let me tell you first about the lava.

It had been more than a year since I approached the roaring summit of Etna, my last immersion into what I was starting to think of as the borderless, wild country of Volcano Land, and I was hungry for more. In more than a decade of joint travel to places like Bulgaria, Kenya, Zanzibar, a year of teaching in China, and then a week on the Trans-Siberian Railroad to Moscow, SueEllen and I had skipped a number of "easy" destinations. We could save England and the fjords of Scandinavia until we were old—that was the way we tended to think about it, or at least I did. Consequently, this was our first time in Hawaii. But the second I stepped off the plane at Hilo, on the Big Island, I wished I had been coming my entire life. Tremendous bursts of pink and orange bougainvillea spilled over walls of volcanic rock. Slender palms swayed in ocean breezes. Blood-red anthurium flowers and shiny green elephant ears dominated every garden. I was aware that I was being manipulated by the same clichés of tropical paradise, some of them not even native to the place, that show up on every Hawaiian shirt ever made. I was knocked out, anyway.

Beyond the airport, though, we discovered an island very different from anything I was expecting. Hilo, first of all, was a small and funky town with no skyscrapers or surfers, not one second of piped-in Don Ho. In the old business section that fronted the harbor, stucco buildings from the 1920s stood among clusters of wooden stores and warehouses that needed paint jobs. Some of them seemed to lean into each other or sag under the weight of humidity that was already curling our hair and frizzing up my beard. Some areas along the waterfront looked like they'd never quite recovered from the tsunami that smashed through in 1960, flattening parking meters and pulling people out to sea as the debris-laden water retreated. The surge of water, spawned by a tremendous earthquake in Chile, had raced unimpeded across thousands of miles of open ocean until it slammed into this volcano of an island that had risen out of the sea. Hilo happened to be the first place that it hit. As we walked around, SueEllen and

I took turns spotting bright yellow tsunami warning sirens bolted to posts and metal towers.

"Funny," I said, glancing at the glassy harbor with its post-1960 seawall of huge lava rocks, "when I'm on land, I don't usually think about the sea jumping up to get me."

"Me neither," SueEllen said. "But I do now."

The sirens turned out to be a fixture of coastal life on all the islands.

At the Suisan Fish Market not far from downtown, we watched wiry Japanese men with silver goatees haul their night's catch from the ice-filled holds of boats, then drag them on wagons to be weighed for auction. In an open-air warehouse, hundreds of tuna fish lay on their sides, shining as slickly black as seals. Some were so thick and muscular they looked almost round. They were just beautiful. *Protein bombs,* I told myself, thinking about the food chain and human need, reaching for a justification for all this death. SueEllen was already looking bummed. But of course the fish had already turned into commodities, their flanks tagged with slips of pink paper indicating their weight.

On narrow side streets and along Kamehameha Ave., which hugged the harbor front, plate-lunch joints advertised specials. At a raucous farmer's market under an enormous tent, I bought tamales from a Peruvian woman and thought they were the best I'd ever tasted. SueEllen examined orchids and vases crammed with bird-of-paradise, mounds of bananas, taro, tomatoes, and lychees. There were T-shirts with swirling images of Madame Pele, Hawaiian goddess of fire, who legends say unleashes volcanic eruptions with a mere kick of her heels. One of many Pele myths explains that she was born in Tahiti but was chased away by her sister after a vicious argument. She retreated across the Pacific by hopping from island to island, leaving fire at each stop. In Hawaii she bounded from Kaua'i to O'ahu to Moloka'i to Maui to the Big Island, where she now boils beneath a crater of Kilauea volcano. Her movement followed the same sequence by which the Hawaiian Islands rose smoking from the sea.

How could these legends have nailed down the truth of a geologic story that took millions of years to unfold? I had no idea. But since then, while learning about other indigenous tales of landscapes in violent action, I have seen the same spooky knowledge operating time and again.

To get to Kilauea, which I had heard geologists jokingly refer to as "the drive-in volcano," we first cruised roughly mountainward —or *mauka*, as the islanders say. (As opposed to *makai*, or seaward. State buildings, I learned, are painted green on the *mauka* side, ocean-blue on the *makai*.) We drove for about half an hour toward the village of Volcano. Even though we were heading partway around the mountain as well as up, we eventually climbed 4,000 feet. Yet the road seemed hardly to rise at all. Finally I began to see that the highway was ascending one very subtle, lava-formed plateau after another, old basaltic terraces that had crumbled into soil and been greened over for years. The air streaming through the car windows grew cooler, and the palms and the eucalyptus gradually dropped away, replaced by squat, red-tipped *'ohi'a* trees.

Just past Volcano, a village tucked into a thick but low tropical forest, we entered Hawaii Volcanoes National Park. "But where are the volcanoes?" said SueEllen as we drove through more forest—mostly *'ohi'as* draped with bromeliads and mixed among giant ferns. It was a good question.

We passed the sprawling visitor center, then turned into a parking lot at the big hotel called Volcano House. We got out of the car and strolled up to a low stone wall. On the other side of it was nothing at all—nothing but miles and miles of moist Hawaiian air. The entire world, it seemed, dropped away into what was easily the biggest pit either of us had ever seen. It was a black crater perhaps three miles across with sheer vertical walls maybe a thousand feet high in places, though much lower in others, and it was fringed around most of its top by tropical forest. "Drive-in volcano" was no joke.

Beyond the crater, which was tilted slightly downhill and away from us, ran miles and miles of hardened lava—black and gray extrusions, looking like spilled gravy, from this crater and others. Beyond the far edge of the lava shone the light blue of the Pacific. Along one area of the shoreline, a cloud was boiling up, drifting off to the west. That, I assumed, was where lava was emptying into the sea. Later I learned that the cloud was diffusing into volcanic fog, or "vog."

It took me a while to understand the scale of what I was seeing. There was the crater alone, for instance. From dozens of places on its cracked black floor, flimsy columns of steam called fumaroles slipped out and faded into the air. After a few minutes, I spotted a moving red dot, then a yellow one, and another red. Ah, the shirts or windbreakers of tourists who looked like ants, far-off hikers on one of the faintly worn paths that crisscrossed the blackness. Compared to the size of the hikers, some of the fumaroles suddenly didn't look so flimsy. There was a good deal of Yellowstone National Park going on down there—a Yellowstone of the Pacific!

This pit was Kilauea's famous caldera. On and off for decades, it had apparently been an incredible, burbling, steaming sea of red lava. But not, unfortunately, now. Over much of the last thirty years, thanks to other vents bursting open on the volcano and channeling off the pressure from below, the lava here had subsided. As the glowing rock sank down in the crater, the surface had cooled, crusted over, then cracked and buckled in places. In theory, at least, the caldera floor could always heat up again and turn back to liquid.

Volcano House, which had been built on the edge of the caldera when the lava still bubbled and smoked, was the most recent in a series of lodges on the same site. The first had been a grass hut erected in 1846 by a sugar planter, an entrepreneur who charged guests a fairly high-end one dollar a night. In the nineteenth century, Isabella Bird, Theodore Roosevelt, and Mark Twain had visited. In *Letters from Hawaii,* Twain described what he heard from the brink of the caldera: "It is no trick at all to imagine that you are sweeping down a river on a large, low-pressure steamer, and that you hear the hissing of the steam about her boilers, the puffing from her escape pipes, and the churning rush of the water abaft her wheels. The smell of sulphur is strong, but not unpleasant to a sinner."

———

Two days later, I had a chance to compare what Twain had heard in the caldera to the ceramic clatter of hardened lava under my boots. It was an extremely weird sound. But then, everywhere I looked, I saw weirdness. SueEllen and I were hiking across the deadland we'd first spotted from the parking lot. No, not the cracked caldera floor, but the blackened flows that I had seen running all the way down to the ocean. Thanks to my children's book, for which I'd roped in a technical advisor, United States Geological

Survey scientist Robert Tilling, who was widely respected in the volcano world, I had managed to convince scientists at the Hawaiian Volcano Observatory to let us tag along with some graduate students who were conducting a survey of the lava.

But "race along" was more like it. Out over crunchy, dried black lava we flew, up and down, over and around flows that had cooled during the last few years or, for all I knew, the last couple of days. The slope was very gradual. I saw *aa* lava, which dries into a very rough, fragmented surface, like much of what I had noticed on the slopes of Etna and Vesuvius. (A Hawaiian word, it's pronounced ah-ah, like the sound you'd make if you had to walk over it barefoot.) Mixed in with the *aa* were patches of *pahoehoe*, which is a smooth and billowy lava. Mark Twain had wandered over it, too, and he wrote that much of the terrain was rumpled into "great shining rolls . . . like boa constrictors in a state of repletion."

It was only midmorning, but this was August, there were no trees in sight, and already the sunblock on my forehead had reliquified and began streaming into my eyes. I figured SueEllen was suffering, too, since she hates to hike fast. As a teen-aged camp counselor in Colorado, she had learned to amble in the mountains at a pace appropriate for ten-year-olds, a pace that also let her identify dozens of wildflowers and compose haiku in her head, a pace that she had preferred to follow ever since. Well, there sure as hell wasn't time for that this morning. She was behind me somewhere now, and I had enough to think about—I was absurdly trying to take notes as we moved.

My borrowed hard hat, which I'd hastily adjusted a notch too large, clanked and slipped with every step I took. *What's the rush?* I wanted to ask the students. But they were half my age and also probably hurrying to beat the afternoon sun. We were just miles from the southernmost point of the United States, and sun-baked lava, I'd been warned, could radiate like a stove top. It could turn into Death Valley out here. Death Valley in the middle of the ocean—that was another Hawaiian surprise. Thank God there was an occasional breeze.

After a while, somebody called out, "Skylight coming." Though he said this casually, everybody instantly slowed down. Twenty yards ahead, heat waves shimmered above what looked like a jagged hole in the lava. We edged up to it. I looked in.

What I saw was impossible.

If the sun had poured itself into a river and then run off beneath the surface of the earth, it would have looked like this: a rushing, red-orange current of glowing lava. That is, liquid, luminous *rock*. Yes, an impossible river of melted stone surged by just ten or fifteen feet down. I wiped sweat from my eyes and despite my better judgment shuffled closer to the hole, which was about as wide as a dining room table. Waves of heat pushed back at me, making me grimace, making even my teeth hurt, until finally I had to retreat a step. Except for a barely audible *shh-h-h, shh-h-h*, the flow made no sound. "Skylight" meant a place where the roof of an active lava tube, or underground channel, had caved in. But "earthlight" might be a better term, I thought as I stood there, because this opening offered a look *into* the living planet. Besides, more heat and light seemed to be pouring out of it than in.

Continuously since 1983, this tube or ones like it had been seething with lava from the Pu'u O'o vent of Kiluaea, which gushed out of the volcano five or six miles uphill from where we stood. Precise lava routes were impossible to know, one of the graduate students explained to me. Sometimes a tube branched apart, then rejoined itself or another tube. Sometimes it tunneled new paths through underground cracks and channels in the old lava, changing direction by the hour. Thus the constant need for surveys like this one. Along the way, a flow or a part of one could spill onto the surface and spread overland for a while. When that happened, the fast-moving and syrupy lava—so unlike anything I had seen or read about in Italy—tended to spread out and cool, blacken over, slow to a crawl.

Back home, as preparation for this trip, I had watched a few National Geographic and other videos of Hawaiian eruptions, but even scenes of other skylight flows had not prepared me for standing here. SueEllen had shuffled up beside me. She didn't look the slightest bit put out by our forced march, but maybe that was because she had become transfixed, too, by the glowing skylight.

"Unbelievable," she murmured, making me think about some other unbelievable things we had seen together, such as 100,000 pink flamingoes bustling on the shores of a soda lake in Kenya. Whenever we managed to pull our gaze from the skylight, we just grinned at each other.

"Yeah," I replied finally, "you can't make up anything better than this." I felt immensely privileged and grateful to see this. I mean, God, just below my feet the newest earth on Earth was glowing like the sun and rivering down to the sea!

One of the students unfolded a long rod tipped with a thermometer and stuck it a little way into the hole. Well over a thousand degrees Fahrenheit. And that was just the air above the lava, if you could call it air. At one point the wind shifted just slightly and I got a whiff of the most foul-smelling stuff that ever hit my nose and throat. I twisted away, squeezing out tears, and whipped out a kerchief. After a while, somebody said he was sorry that he'd forgotten to bring the marshmallows. Somebody else said that he and a buddy had once cooked up some steaks over a skylight, grilling them the natural way.

Another wave of heat and sulfur rolled over me, and I had to turn away. It was shocking how even a small, contained, and nonexplosive flow like this one could threaten danger so quickly and hint at the astounding amount of heat farther down, in the planet's interior. I thought back to my uneasy climb up Mount Etna. Even though I had turned around on the volcano before I actually felt the heat of its roaring inferno, I had acted foolishly there, even recklessly, I realized now. I had approached the smoking summit too closely, especially since my field knowledge of eruptions amounted to zip and I wore no helmet to protect me from randomly flung rocks. Not to mention what gases might have done. Plus, I hadn't told a soul where I was going or carried a cell phone or a walkie-talkie.

After a while, we moved off downhill from the skylight. We walked slowly now, like tai chi masters, trying to avoid breaking through thin crust or an unstable roof that might cave in to form a new skylight, which would surely be the last one I'd ever see. But I wasn't sure how to evade what I didn't know how to recognize. If lava was a book, SueEllen and I were illiterate. We decided to stay in the rear of the file.

After fifteen minutes, our party had approached a cliff that overlooked the ocean, though we stopped much sooner than I would have on my own. I wasn't sure why we were keeping our distance. Nevertheless, down below I could still see a tongue of lava oozing across a black beach. I figured it had come from the tube we'd all just looked into, though I knew another flow might have fed it. With one or two other guys, I edged a bit closer, and

I could feel SueEllen hanging back. Later on she mentioned that one of the students told her, "Those guys are crazy. Newly formed ocean ledges are notoriously unstable." In retrospect, I suppose that was another foolish move on my part, although, really, I didn't creep nearly as close to the brink as I wanted to.

Meanwhile, air and damp sand had slowed the lava and turned its surface to dark sludge, but here and there a breakout blob glowed dull red. Then a wave crashed in, blasting apart the blob in a fury of steam. Black chunks of rock flew up and out, and I thought of Madame Pele.

Another legend I had heard described her marriage to Kamapua'a, the god of water. Theirs was a steamy and brief relationship, an explosion of temperaments: fire and water. Well, yes. And I understood now why we'd stopped so far back from the cliff edge. None of the fragments were landing anywhere close by, but one always could, and for the first time I felt grateful for my hard hat.

I turned and looked back uphill, past Volcano House looking tiny above the old caldera, to the higher slopes of the volcano stretching up and away for miles. "The Big Island" was no misnomer, that was for sure. In fact, the island as a whole was by far the most massive mountain on the planet. Formed by almost nothing but syrupy lava slipping up through the earth's crust, then spilling across the seafloor and piling up over millions of years, this wide, wide mountain had come boiling up through 20,000 feet of ocean and then risen another 13,800 feet into the air, making it taller from summit to base than Mount Everest. Its twin summits, Mauna Loa and Mauna Kea, were the highest points in the Pacific Ocean. Mauna Kea means "white mountain" because it is sometimes covered in snow—while orchids bloom in patches of jungle at its base! Atop Mauna Kea sits the highest observatory in the world.

Below me on the beach, the surf washed over hot lava, blasting it apart. The boom was the sound of the Big Island growing still larger.

———

What on earth—or *in* the earth—makes all of this happen?

The simplest and shortest possible answer was the heat under my feet, both nearby and deep, deep down. Or heat moving on a planetary scale. To understand how this movement creates volcanoes, mountains, and so much of the world that we call landscape or even "scenery," consider the structure of the "solid earth," which is built, very roughly speaking, in layers.

As the students who were standing with me on the lava had already learned, at the center of our planet lies a very hot and very dense nickel and iron core. More precisely, though, the center consists of a hard core sheathed inside a softer one. The inner core, roughly 1,800 miles in diameter, is a nuclear powerhouse that, like much of the rest of the earth's interior, has been radioactive for the 4.3 billion years of the earth's existence. The inner core cooks along at a temperature as high as 6,600 degrees Fahrenheit, but it is squeezed by so much pressure from the tremendous bulk of the planet that its nickel and iron don't melt. The outer core, which is about 3,200 miles in diameter, is cooler (though still plenty hot) and molten, meaning fused or liquified by heat.

Wrapped around these cores is the even less hot, less dense, and more pliable mantle, composed of silica and many other elements. This zone makes up the remainder of the earth's interior. Though much of the mantle is solid, certain regions of it are not.

Its temperatures range from 4,500 degrees nearest the core to about 2,500 degrees just beneath the crust.

Finally comes the cool and brittle crust of the earth, which runs about twenty miles thick, though this can vary. This can seem like a lot if you're standing in your backyard trying to dig a hole for a fence post, but compared to the roughly 4,000-mile depth of the planet—the distance from where I was standing in Hawaii to the center of the core—the crust wraps the planet about as thinly as a shell does its egg.

Scratching the surface of their world, some thinkers in Aristotle's time, about the fourth century B.C., knew that the farther you go underground—say, down into the shaft of a mine—the hotter it gets. Deep tunnels seared by fiery subterranean winds made a good deal of sense (as did the bowels of Hades). But the ancients lacked the technology that would have helped them understand the full planetary scale of a heated earth, not to mention its implications. Because of the profoundly uneven distribution of its interior temperatures (outrageously hot core, cooler mantle, cold crust) our planet operates as a gigantic heat transfer system. In short, the earth leaks heat, and that leakage takes place through geothermal and finally volcanic action.

Heat inside the planet moves by extreme slow-motion convection currents. It works something like this: in the lower, hotter regions of the mantle, material slowly rises and expands. Over the course of hundreds of thousands or millions of years, it keeps "floating" upward because, continually expanding, it remains less dense than what's around it. Under less and less pressure, relatively hard material begins to soften and melt. After a while it forms (or joins) a plume, a steady stream of upward-moving magma, which is molten rock mixed with dissolved gases. As the

37

now plastic or even molasses-like material approaches the crust or begins to work its way in, it keeps expanding and often pools up inside of what geologists call a magma chamber. Sometimes many cubic miles in volume, the chamber acts as a holding tank for the magma's final rush to the surface, after which—*Boom!* an eruption of Vesuvius, or *Poof!* a small spurt from Stromboli—the magma becomes known as lava. In other words, a magma chamber is the anteroom of a volcano.

But volcanoes don't pop up just anywhere. Magma has that relatively hard crust to get through, and so, heat-driven, it pushes up and out against thin or weak spots, or it slips up into preexisting cracks, probing for places of least resistance. The cracks in the earth's crust are widespread and tend to follow a pattern. Another way of putting this is to say that the crust is actually composed of many rigid, but restless, fragments—or tectonic plates.

Big as they are, continental and seafloor plates are nevertheless the earth's perpetual pilgrims. They wander over the face of the planet at a rate of an inch or so per year, or about as fast as your fingernail grows. They tear apart, grind over and under one another, or rub alongside each other. On one of the largest of these, the 3,000-mile-wide North American plate, ride Canada, Mexico, and all of the United States except for that thin slice of California west of the San Andreas fault. The North American plate, with a velocity of an inch per year, is ferrying most of the United States toward Japan at a rate of eight or so feet per century. Talk about westward expansion. Another giant raft, the India plate, has carried the once-separate landmass of India into the Asian mainland with such speed and force that the collision has pushed crustal rock five miles into the sky. Thus the Himalayas. They aren't volcanoes themselves, but they have been raised by tectonic action.

About 220 million years ago, all of today's continents were joined in a super-landform called Pangaea (Greek for "all lands"). We know about Pangaea not just from plotting in reverse the present course and speed of plate movements. We know, among other reasons, because fossils roughly 220 million years old, as well as the chemical signatures of rock, closely parallel one another on the facing Atlantic coasts of Africa and South America. This strongly suggests that the two landforms were once one, confirming the hunches of many observers who over the years, studying maps, thought the two continents looked like matched jigsaw puzzle pieces.

But why do all these plates move? The answer seems to be seafloor spreading, which is caused by huge volumes of magma rising between two oceanic plates that are being pulled apart. The most prominent example of this submarine scar, or rift, runs in slightly zigzag fashion down the middle of the entire Atlantic Ocean. As hot magma wells up along thousands of miles of the crack, it turns into lava as it meets frigid, ocean-bottom water. The lava quickly cools and hardens onto the edges of both plates, wedging them a tiny bit farther apart. Over eons, this process causes the two halves of the seafloor to move away from each other.

Therefore, seafloor spreading appears to be the engine that powers continental drift, pulling, for example, South America and Africa away from each other and into other plates and so on and so forth. I didn't hear about any of this until I got to college because the idea of mobile continents was widely accepted only in the 1960s, after underwater military technology developed during World War II had been turned to civilian use, finally helping to confirm the theory. Most of the world's ocean bottom has been formed by magma sizzling up from the mantle and adding to the planet's crust.

The majority of the world's visible volcanoes form along or near the ragged borders where plates grind past or over or under one another. If you want to see a fiery volcano, therefore, you should visit these boundaries. As I climbed Mount Etna and Vesuvius, for instance, I was also trudging over part of the roughly north-south convergence of the Eurasia and Africa plates. More large plates converge along the edges of the greater Pacific Ocean than anywhere else on the planet, forming tremendous chains or arcs of volcanoes. These include the Aleutians, the Cascades, the Andes, and volcanoes in New Zealand, the Philippines, Japan, and Russia's Kamchatka peninsula. Together they form a glowing necklace of heat leaking from the planet. This is the Pacific Ring of Fire.

But the Big Island of Hawaii, like Yellowstone National Park, smolders nowhere near the border between plates. In fact, it sits smack in the middle of the gigantic Pacific plate. The Big Island also drifts with the plate over a persistent heat source from deep in the mantle that has "burned through" the crust—what volcanologists call a hot spot. Layer after layer after layer of lava erupting through the hot spot has built up one Hawaiian island after another from the bottom of the ocean. First Kaua'i, then O'ahu, Moloka'i and Maui have been formed this way, and it's only a matter of time—a hundred thousand years? a million?—before the Big Island rides its crustal conveyer belt far enough to the northwest to sever its connection to the earth's rising heat. To the southeast, a volcano called Lo'ihi is already rising from the Pacific floor. Madame Pele churning her way through another relationship. In perhaps 12,000 years, this volcano will break the surface of the ocean.

The shapes and behaviors of volcanoes vary widely from place to place, often due to the nature of the material that passes through them, though with volcanoes there seem to be big exceptions to everything. The lava that has poured out of the Hawaiian hot spot happens to be not very rich in silica, so it tends to run smoothly, like syrup. This is why the Big Island, still too young to be deeply scoured by erosion (unlike Kaua'i), is so wide. Mauna Loa, "Long Mountain," is called a shield volcano because it resembles a warrior's shield lying on the ground.

Some other volcanic material, on the other hand, tends to break loose sporadically and explosively because of the pressure building on it from below. A relatively thin channel of rising magma can produce contained and even regular burps like the ones at Stromboli. But in thicker channels, this process can also blow ash and rock chunks miles into the sky. A temporarily closed volcanic system, such as the one inside bulging Mount St. Helens in 1980 or in Vesuvius in 79 A.D., can also produce pyroclastic flows, probably the most dangerous of volcanic eruptions. "Pyroclastic" means "fire" and "broken," but broken-out-fire might be a better description of these glowing avalanches that can burst from a mountain flank with no warning at all, then roll downhill at 100 miles per hour in a chaos of burning rock fragments mixed with searing, rapidly expanding gases. Depending on the terrain, they can fry everything in their paths for five, ten, even twenty miles.

In general, explosive eruptions eject, often helter-skelter, the widest variety of hot matter—ash, cinders, pumice, lava "bombs" (flying clumps of soft lava), sizzling boulders cracked loose from the preexisting summit of a volcano, steam, you name it. Eruptions thick with cinders often build a steep triangle—a child's drawing of a volcano—like Stromboli and the top part of Vesuvius where I stood and watched that baby burst into tears. Volcanoes that over time erupt in a combination of ways, explosively and with great extrusions of flowing lava, are called composite or stratovolcanoes. Japan's Fuji is a classic example, having coughed up large amounts of ash and lava more than a dozen times in the last twelve centuries.

But a volcanic eruption can change its behavior in seconds. Thus the "impetuousness" of Madame Pele and so many volcanic gods and goddesses. Here in Hawaii, where lava slips so quietly down to the sea (until a wave hits it, that is), there is a trail where the preserved footprints of ancient, sandal-clad men testifies to an eruption that probably killed them in seconds. And new vents that have broken open on Kilauea in the last few decades have sent sheets of bright red lava fountaining hundreds of feet into the air.

Around volcanoes, you never really know.

Nobody had seen more of that wild uncertainty, at unbelievably close range, than the pair of ghosts I'd been tracking. I don't mean Pele and her consort Kamapua'a. The ghosts I was after had also been married, but much more happily, since their volcanic passions complemented each other rather than clashed. Their names were Maurice and Katia Krafft, ordinary mortals but the world's most famous—or notorious—volcano watchers and photographers.

Ever since I'd started to hear stories of them a few years earlier, I'd been intrigued by their passion for volcanoes, by their desire and willingness to hike to the edge of a blowing crater while shattered, glowing rocks thudded down around them. Although their behavior sounded as if it bordered on insanity, they weren't nut cases at all, volcanologists I'd talked to had assured me. But they were scientists who really believed in *hands-on experience*.

And they loved the Big Island. Entirely by coincidence, I had booked SueEllen and myself into a lovely old country house called My Volcano, a B&B in Volcano village that turned out to be where the Kraffts had frequently stayed—one unit had been wired especially for their fax machine and other equipment. One morning, over a breakfast of pancakes and macadamia nuts, I leafed through a few of their signed photography books. The B&B owner, white-haired and rugged-looking Gordon Morse, was a lifetime Hawaiian and volcano fan himself. Once, about thirty years before, while eating a cucumber sandwich one afternoon on a slope of Kilauea, he had heard a rumble and seen great red sheets of lava spurt without warning from the earth. He understood what the Kraffts were about. Now that I had stood on the lip of a skylight and seen lava rivering right under my feet, I think I did, too. I was beginning to understand that edgy state of mind in which deep interest or fascination can pitch over into obsession.

Apparently, in Italy, I had been following in the footsteps of the Kraffts for some time without realizing it. After I had flown home from Rome, I watched a video in which Maurice and Katia took turns talking to the camera. Their marriage was fate, they implied, and the fate first struck at Stromboli volcano, years before they knew each other. In the 1960s, they had met at the

University of Strasbourg, on the French-German border, where Maurice was studying geology and Katia geochemistry. But quite independently, each had fallen in love with the third party in their relationship—erupting volcanoes—while on childhood family trips to Stromboli. They had seen the lava fly in the night, and became instantly inspired by "mountains *alive*," as Maurice liked to call volcanoes, and that was that.

As graduate students, they taught themselves to shoot pictures and videos, mainly as a way to finance their more and more ambitious expeditions. Maurice, who was gifted at public relations, liked to explain that they had needed to eat, and after all, "to eat stone is quite difficult. We have tried it!" Often working for days without sleep while cinders bounced off their hard hats, they filmed and took field notes and measurements: at Etna, Réunion Island in the Indian Ocean, Mount Augustine in Alaska, and dozens of other eruption sites. Their skills as scientists and artists improved fast, and soon they were completely self-supporting. They had no children, no teaching or research obligations. After seventeen books, five exuberant films, and increasingly popular European lecture tours, they'd turned into Emmy winners and the world's most swashbuckling volcano photographers.

They knew almost everyone who crawled on or near simmering craters, or so it seemed, and the telephone and the fax machine in their Rhine Valley home took in messages day and night. "Hurry!" a colleague in some remote jungle might say. "It's going to blow!" Within hours, their gas masks, light meters, and cameras clanking around their necks, they would jet off to Mount Agung on Java, El Chichón in Mexico, or anywhere the heat of the restless earth broke out in photogenic fire. Toward the end of the

1980s, their major goal in life had crystallized: to document the great eruptions of our time. *All* of them. In 1988 alone, they circled the globe eight times.

In the words of their friend and fellow volcanologist Bob Tilling, of the United States Geological Survey, Maurice and Katia had become "the Jacques Cousteaus of volcanology." Or as a lot of their friends affectionately called them, "The Volcano Devils." But some people who saw them in action called them crazy. They were certainly eruption addicts, apocalypse junkies, with probably much more desire than true scientific need to creep as close as they could to rising fire, and they had climbed more than 200 active volcanoes, the places they called "earth giving birth."

You've probably seen their work on television and in magazines. They built a photo archive of 300,000 volcano images and compiled a wonderful collection of volcano art and rare books and films. By 1991, the last year of their lives, they had become scientists with the souls of artists, souls of fire. They were both still in their forties.

Like many geologists, they were also physically tough. Ninety-five-pound Katia sometimes strapped on a backpack that looked like it weighed as much as she did. In their graduate student days, she and Maurice would load their gas-measuring equipment and camping gear onto bicycles, and up through muddy jungle paths they'd go. Or they'd crunch along for miles over just-hardened, jumbled-up, black glass lava, then spend the night huddled in a pup tent in howling winds at eighteen or twenty thousand feet.

They'd trudge right up to a lava geyser spurting a quarter-mile high, uncap their lenses, and get to work. Clunking along in heat-resistant Tin Man suits they'd designed themselves, or wearing pointed aluminum helmets that sloped over their shoulders to deflect lava-spatter, they'd approach a crater gloved hand in gloved hand. Curly-haired, bearish Maurice would scan the sulfurous sky for whistling lava bombs while slender Katia studied the ground for orange cracks or rivulets of 2,000-degree Fahrenheit rock flows. Filmed by an assistant from a much safer distance, they appeared to be dancing before a curtain of flames.

Lava sometimes melted the soles of their boots. Heat warped their camera lenses. If they weren't careful, gases that smelled as bad or worse than the stuff I'd gotten a whiff of could "process" the film in their cameras long before they got it back to the lab. Their cameras grew so hot they sometimes had to wear tinfoil masks to keep their cheekbones from getting singed.

Once, in a crater in Java, they launched a rubber raft on a 600-foot-deep volcanic lake full of diluted sulfuric and hydrochloric acid. While local sulfur miners squatted on shore, looking on in silence, Maurice paddled happily around, now and then fighting a breeze that tried to push him to the middle of the lake. He took bottom samples until the acids ate through the steel cable hooked to his collecting bottle. Of course, the Kraffts arranged to catch most of this on film, and soon their fame, or maybe their notoriety, expanded.

"A volcano is like a wild animal," Maurice explained in the interview I saw. "He's blind, he doesn't see you, and you are sort of a crazy witch doctor who wants to understand his stomach problems. So you have to stay a long time and observe his habits."

Then Katia, smiling behind her outsized glasses, said, "You have all these noises all around you, like you're in the bowels of the earth. And compared to this giant volcano, you are just *nothing*. This is very nice to feel." I found myself nodding as I heard her say this, and I remembered the way that my early travels through the immensity of geologic time had helped to put my mortality in perspective.

And finally Maurice, with a twinkle in his eye, said how fantastic it would be to build a titanium boat and one day *put in* on a bright orange lava flow that had risen from the secret heart of the world. It would be the kind of flow they had so often seen gushing out of Pu'u O'o on Kilauea, one of their favorite volcanoes. They had bought retirement land just outside Hawaii Volcanoes National Park, so that even in decrepit old age they could edge their wheelchairs to the wall at the old Kilauea caldera and peek in. Maybe, as it had in Mark Twain's time, it would be boiling again.

Maurice loved to talk about that lava boat, and maybe not just because it made for good press. Off they'd ride down the long slope of a volcano, he and Katia. They'd fly the French flag and wave to all their friends as they navigated an incandescent river down to the sea!

In late May of 1991, the Kraffts talked by telephone with Harry Glicken, a volcanologist friend who was doing research in Japan, on the far western edge of the Pacific Ring of Fire. They talked about how Mount Unzen, on the island of Kyushu, not far from Nagasaki, was really starting to pop. A great number of small pyroclastic flows had been racing down the mountain's slopes in relatively contained routes.

Glicken had devoted his career to researching the behavior of pyroclastic flows. His story was well known in the world of volcanology. As a young man in 1980, during the weeks leading up to the final, dramatic eruption of Mount St. Helens, he had been living in a trailer on a forested ridge about six miles directly across from the trembling flank of the snow-covered volcano. With a pair of binoculars, he had watched the flank bulge outward at a rate of up to five feet per day. His job was to look for evidence of mudflows or avalanches and report his findings via radio to the USGS. St. Helens's last dangerous eruption had occurred more than a century earlier. No one knew when or how or to what degree its ongoing eruptions would increase. As a precaution, however, Forest Service workers had flushed hunters and fishermen from the woods near the volcano.

On the day before the eruption, Glicken left his post to drive to the University of California at Santa Barbara for a long-scheduled appointment with his geology professor to discuss his graduate work. As arranged, his place was taken by his USGS supervisor, Dave Johnston. The next morning at 8:32 A.M., the swollen flank of the volcano suddenly rippled, churned, and slid away in gigantic blocks. It was the start of the best documented landslide in history. Within seconds, the slide released the fantastic pressure that had been building inside the volcano. Out burst a pyroclastic flow with temperatures of 500 degrees Fahrenheit. The expanding cloud atomized or flattened almost every Douglas fir in its path, peeled the paint off a car and flung it across a road.

"Vancouver! Vancouver! This is it!" Johnston famously shouted into his walkie-talkie. Those were his last words.

Harry Glicken, of course, was spared, and ever since he's been studying pyroclastic flows. When he met up with Maurice and Katia at Mount Unzen, their passions for volcanoes and disaster prevention would merge.

According to a Japanese legend, the shake and rumble in volcanoes like Mount Unzen is caused by a giant catfish. Normally the gods keep the fish under control by pinning it beneath a large rock. But sometimes, when the gods are sleeping or away, the fish wriggles free. One day in 1792, the catfish beneath Unzen thrashed so hard that a landslide roared down over Shimabara City, at the foot of the volcano, and into Shimabara Bay. The tumbling mass of rocks, shattered trees, and soil, plus perhaps the shock waves of the quake, generated a tsunami, which took off across the bay in a great watery bulge. When the bulge rolled onto distant shores, it pulverized wooden homes and villages. The eruption killed 15,000 people in one great blow.

Then Unzen fell back asleep. A graceful, tiled-roof temple was built at the base of the volcano to commemorate the dead, and over the next two centuries a population once more grew out around the mountain. Tea and tobacco farmers planted brilliant green fields across the ash-rich slopes. Despite the temple and the presence of numerous hot springs, people began to forget or ignore the fact that they were living on an active volcano. Up until the last few decades, none of them could have known that some volcanoes can slumber 700,000 years or more between major eruptions. Volcanologist Robert Decker has written that a human contemplating a volcano is like a butterfly that lives only a few weeks contemplating a thousand-year-old redwood it has landed on. How could it know that the tree was ever a sapling, that it hasn't stood there like a pillar forever?

Now the fish under Unzen was thrashing again. The 5,000-foot-tall summit puffed out fire and ash, grew a grainy millimeter or two. Its tea fields turned black and gray. Magma creeping up through the throat of the volcano had formed a lava dome, a bulge near Unzen's bare summit, which began to crumble away in up to thirty pyroclastic flows per day. That was an extraordinarily high number.

Maurice and Katia hopped onto a plane. Over the years, their volcano travels had made them more and more aware of the potentially fatal effects of volcanoes on large, nearby populations. That was an awareness that they could help spread, and so they'd been working on a safety video for civil defense officials. Unzen's pyroclastic flows would probably give them some of the last shots they needed. On Réunion Island, Maurice and Katia had once filmed such a flow at night. Their slow-motion sequence showed lit-from-within rock chunks tumbling and bouncing downhill like giant rubies and sapphires, an eerie avalanche of the planet's riches. The eruption looked far more beautiful than deadly.

The Kraffts' fame and the drama of the eruptions had preceded them to Unzen. On June 3, a couple of dozen TV and newspaper photographers and reporters who had gathered near the foot of the volcano followed Maurice, Katia, and Harry Glicken to a makeshift observation post partway up a slope. Two miles from the source of the eruptions, the Kraffts unpacked their equipment and started filming. The site allowed them to view the summit as well as look down into the curving Mizunashi River valley—a ravine, really—where the flows had been rumbling harmlessly by for days.

"I hope to see bigger ones than these," Maurice had said almost impatiently, but with a smile, on camera. Then he and Katia settled in to wait. A Tokyo TV correspondent wearing a yellow slicker stood with his back to the summit, positioning himself for

his cameraman. Others fussed with shooting angles and light meters. They adjusted their lenses, tripods, and microphones.

The continents were adjusting, too. The Pacific plate was
grinding itself beneath the Eurasian plate. Molten rock that had
been edging up from deep inside the planet rose through harder
and cooler rock, slipped up between the subducting plates,
climbed toward Unzen's summit. More rock soup shoved from
below, squeezing some of the magma to one side, making the
lava dome bulge.

Finally the dome broke.

Squinting through his lens, Maurice probably saw right away
how uncommonly large this eruption was. Katia, peering through
binoculars, might have noted how fast the debris seemed to be
coming. Down the valley along the path of the other eruptions
roared the expanding ink-dark cloud shot through with rocks
and searing gases and the swordplay of lightning.

"Civilization exists by geological consent, subject to change
without notice," writes historian Will Durant. And without any
notice at all, the searing avalanche—which turned out to be ten
times larger than any of the flows that preceded it—split in two.
One fork, dense and heavy, curved downslope as expected. But
the other, lighter fork veered hard right and surged uphill. It took
dead aim at the ridge where everyone stood.

At the nature and literature conference that was my nominal
excuse for flying to Hawaii, I met a teacher from Japan who told
me she had seen a live broadcast of this event. The correspondent in the yellow slicker, talking excitedly, stood in such close-
up on the TV screen that it was difficult to see what was closing
in on him. And because he was so intent on the camera, he had
little idea what was about to happen, either. Suddenly there was

a roar. He started to turn, his handsome profile swinging around, his mouth flying open. Then everything went black. The footage was never shown again.

As the pyroclastic flow swept toward him, Harry Glicken would have known that there was nothing to do. Deep time was about to collide with the present moment, just as it had for Dave Johnston.

The Kraffts would also have known that there was nothing to do. Perhaps, though, Maurice and Katia had time to catch each other's eye. Perhaps they managed to reach out and hold hands. Perhaps they saw a titanium boat coming for them from the secret heart of the world.

FROM EARTH
TO THE STARS:
PARÍCUTIN, MEXICO

To begin with
I never go out to look for a landscape:
I let the landscape find me, throw itself violently
over my sensibility.

—Dr. Atl, painter and Mexican revolutionary,
Dr. Atl: El Pasaje como Pasion

February 20, 1943, Michoacán

Demetrio Toral, deaf and mute, had not gone out to look for a landscape. Not at all. The one that he already knew so well, the flat cornfield he was busy plowing for his boss, took all of his time and energy. But by the middle of this sun-drenched afternoon, a new kind of landscape had literally crept into position to find *him*, to come rumbling up out of the field and fling itself over his sensibility. Toral was seconds away from becoming one of the few persons in history to see, if not hear, the birth of a roaring volcano.

53

The windless, sky-blue afternoon must have doubled his shock, for who can imagine cataclysm on such a gorgeous day? Images from centuries of folklore, sermons, scripture, church paintings—and, in recent decades, Hollywood—have conditioned us to expect a dark fist of clouds or a howling wind to herald most good-sized natural disasters. But a volcano-in-waiting responds to forces of internal weather only: minutely shifting temperatures in the earth's mantle; contending "pressure systems" in rocks of varying density, stresses that over millennia have caused a billion tons of magma to plume up from realms unimaginably deep in the planet. Rising fire.

All that Demetrio Toral had for warning were some white vapors. They were floating up from the furrows he had just cut and from the deeper hoofprints of his ox team. How odd these must have looked to him, these thin and ghostly emanations. Given the heaven and hell nature of his faith, he may have thought that his blade had somehow nicked the roof of an immense underground furnace.

And in a sense it had. Eight or ten miles below his feet, a magma chamber had been sending upward a slender column of gas-engorged molten rock. For weeks or months or years, the broiling rock had been wriggling up through the planet's cracked and brittle crust. Its leading edge was now simmering just feet or inches below Toral's plow.

Dionisio Pulido was at first fooled by the weather, too. He was Toral's boss and the owner of the cornfield. Working nearby, he thought he heard the grumble of thunder and paused to look around for clouds. Pulido was worldly enough to know that small earthquakes had been shaking the area recently, even if he wasn't sure why. On this sunny afternoon, though, everything looked so peaceful, a fertile oasis in a planet that had gone crazy with war. Tremendous armies were clashing in Europe and Russia, in the Pacific, in North Africa. And yet here the landscape looked as tranquil as ever, quilted with neatly tended cornfields and avocado and apple groves, dotted with symmetrical hills covered with oak and pine.

If Pulido had gazed to the north in his search for storm clouds, he would have seen the sunlight bouncing off the creamy, mismatched bell towers of the pretty church he attended every week in San Juan Parangaricutiro. The church sat three miles distant and slightly downhill from where he stood. Because construction funds had run out, one of the bright, blocky towers rose to only about half the height of the other. Money was a chronic problem in this isolated and very wide valley 300 miles west of Mexico City. Electricity was only a dream, and few of Toral's neighbors and friends wore shoes. Most spoke a Tarascan Indian language that had nothing in common with Spanish.

But soon Pulido heard a much louder and closer rumble. By the time he realized it was *underground* thunder, the cornfield was shaking hard enough to almost knock him down. The sound seemed to come from a small hole in the field that he'd been trying to fill for years. As he turned his attention to the hole, he saw the impossible happen. A crack ran out from both sides of it, and then a part of the field near the rupture puffed up into what Pulido's wife Paula, who was working beside him, later described as a confused cake. The cake swelled to Paula's eye level, collapsed, then sent dust and a choking wave of sulfur over her and Pulido. Soon, black smoke shot whistling from the rupture, followed by burning stones.

Demetrio Toral, who had gotten the closest look of all at this impossibility, unhooked himself from the plow and ran in a panic for San Juan. Paula did, too. Pulido stayed to unyoke the braying oxen. Later on, he'd recall how in those first terrible moments he prayed to the crucifix of El Señor de los Milagros, Lord of Miracles, which stood upon the altar in the unfinished church. Pilgrims had been coming for years to visit the church and pay homage to El Señor, who Pulido believed protected the village and had helped his thirteen children enter the world in good health.

Now the roaring was growing worse by the second. Glowing stones clattered into a pile around the smoke and fire geyser. When a nearby tree caught some cinders and burst into flames, Pulido fled, too.

The blast furnace in his cornfield roared all night. You could see and hear it from the village, from miles beyond the village, the sounds of explosions rising and falling like the booming of surf, or cannon fire, or the confused hoofbeats of tremendous horses. Residents described it in all those ways. Soon the rupture they were calling El Monstro was flinging rocks and boulders into adjoining fields. By morning, the closest falling stones had formed a cone thirty feet tall, and high-flung ash and cinders were drizzling down for miles around, blackening much of the valley.

Every few seconds, lightning ripped through the eruption column. The bolts were sparked by pressurized molten rock bursting into air, expanding so rapidly that it fractured down to the level of tiny, charged fragments of glass that interacted violently. The result was an electric supercharge, a frequent and sometimes deadly accompaniment of volcanic eruptions.

By the next afternoon, El Monstro had taken the shape of what volcanologists call a cinder cone, a steep conical hill built up by the cinders and glowing rocks flying out of the earth. To Dionisio Pulido and his neighbors, it may also have looked like a steaming pyramid taller than any church tower. In fact, it was already the height of an eight-story building. Two days later, the pyramid stood twenty stories high. With a tube now open to the surface, the boiling magma chamber a few miles below the cornfield had found a vent for its internal pressures and was sending up everything it had.

Within days, crowds of sightseers, reporters, and volcanologists arrived. Sometimes the volcano's fireworks and the lava fountains that burst out of its sides turned the night sky lurid, and the visitors broke into applause. But the Tarascans, who had nowhere else to go, wandered around coughing and crying. They rubbed their eyes, pressing wet scarves and crumpled shirts to their faces. An erupting volcano is a filthy thing, and the villagers began to resemble hunched-over creatures made from dirt or mud. Over the next few weeks they watched their horses and cattle suffocate from the powdery ash, or starve because grazing on cinder-choked grass ground animal teeth into stubs.

The fear of divine retribution never lies far below the surface of Catholic culture. In the cluster of hamlets around Parícutin, people began to talk about signs and wonders. Perhaps, they whispered, they were being punished for the recent desecration of a large cross that had been erected by priests as a peace symbol after a community land dispute turned bloody. Local legend held that the conflict had left a man dead very near the spot where the volcano had cracked open the earth. A council of town elders had been predicting dire consequences ever since. Another omen, or so it seemed now, had preceded the volcano by almost exactly a year. A plague of locusts had swept into the valley, darkening the skies and settling in the trees in such masses that branches and limbs sagged, then snapped under their weight. Dionisio Pulido and some of his neighbors soon enough recognized the volcano for the geological insurrection that it was. But for many others, science continued to contend vigorously with religion, magic, and myth. Despite the poverty that had plagued them forever, people began to refer to the years before the volcano as a Golden Age, a time of songbirds and flowers and prodigiously fertile soils.

Parícutin roared on, and one day, dozens of women appeared in the plaza of San Juan. Tightening their shawls, they formed a line, knelt down, and shuffled toward the church, begging El Señor de los Milagros to push the fire and glowing rocks back underground. The volcano kept growing.

Within a month, it stood five hundred feet high. After a year, it was a thousand feet tall, almost half a mile wide, and it resembled—in size and shape, though not color—many of the symmetrical green hills in the valley. Only the food reserves from previous strong harvests, plus the efforts of the International Red Cross, were keeping the villagers alive.

An erupting volcano can overwhelm a landscape and a community in many ways. While ash, cinders, and rocks flung a black cloak over the Tarascan villages up and down the valley, lava broke out through the side of the crater. Much of it was dark, craggy, slow *aa*. And from the second day of the volcano's life, almost without stop for nine years, the lava chugged out of the earth in massive volumes.

Sometimes these rock rivers crunched forward just inches a day, making what U.S. volcanologist Ray Wilcox would long remember as a strangely pleasant music. Sometimes the gooey interior of the lava broke through its cooling, ceramiclike surface, and then a red-hot tongue would surge ahead, covering a hundred yards in a few hours. It was like one country invading another. Not the army of a country but the country itself, landscape truly on the move, clinking and crackling with the sound of pottery breaking, re-forming, breaking again. Sometimes it moved along in a wall up to thirty feet high, bulldozing tons of soil ahead of itself.

Always, the lava moved downhill. One year and two months after Dionisio Pulido's cornfield cracked open, lava reached the outskirts of San Juan. Then it clinked through the church grave-yard. Meanwhile, the relatives of the dead, working their rosaries or wailing, backed away.

Since this was a slow-motion invasion, the village had had some time to adapt. The church's oak doors had been carted off in sections on mules, pews and confessionals had been unscrewed from the floor, stained-glass windows packed and trucked away. Some villagers hoped that an earthquake measuring station set up by the volcanologists would somehow stop the lava. Others went straight back to their religion, hammering into the ground a file of shoulder-high wooden crosses between the church and the ad-vancing force. The lava inched up to the first cross, nudged it back, set it on fire. One by one, burning crosses tilted backward and then disappeared under the great push of stone.

Near the end, the bishop arrived. He conducted a final Mass in the church, which stood empty now except for the Lord of Miracles and the villagers who hadn't already fled (or as anthro-pologist Mary Lee Nolan later noted, who had simply lost the will to live). After the last amen, worshippers surged forward and kissed El Señor on the face and feet. They kissed the stripped-down altar.

An argument arose about whether to leave El Señor in the church as a last-ditch effort to stop the lava. The bishop settled it two days later by carrying the crucifix outside. A procession fell in behind him, and with whatever belongings they could pack onto mule carts or their backs, the villagers walked nine miles to San Juan Nuevo, a new townsite that the government had picked out for them.

Within days the lava touched the side wall of the church. The wall stood several feet thick, a mixture of concrete and old volcanic rock. As the lava piled up, cracks spidered out in the wall, there was a series of groans, and then the whole thing gave way. The lava burst into the church, crunched over the rubble of the fallen roof, and knocked down the opposite wall. Somehow, the square foundations of both bell towers held, splitting the sluggish flow of rock into two rivers. The rivers rejoined themselves and moved on.

Eventually, just about everything in the region was overwhelmed: almost all of San Juan as well as four smaller hamlets (including Parícutin, after which the volcano had been named); the farmland, which had been the only permanent prosperity anybody had; and just about every plant and tree within five miles of the crater—an area botanists came to call the "Total-Kill Zone."

There was a ripple-out effect, too. Ash that piled up miles from the crater eventually clogged and diverted streams, generating slurry-like floods that destroyed downstream dams and irrigation systems well beyond the Kill Zone. An insect that was a natural predator of a sugarcane borer was wiped out by the ash, and so the borers soon multiplied, ruining distant cane fields that had survived the eruption itself.

Soon after Parícutin burst into his life, Dionisio Pulido realized that he'd lost his cornfield. On the other hand, he'd acquired a volcano. It was one of only three "brand new" continental volcanoes to have been observed anywhere. Ironically, one of the other two, Jorullo, had broken out of a ravine just fifty miles southeast of Pulido's valley in 1759. It erupted for fifteen years, then fizzled out. The other came roaring up out of the earth in 1538, in Italy's Phlegraean Fields a few miles west of Naples. Monte Nuovo vomited smoke, fire, and stones bigger than an ox, according to Pietro Giacomo de Toledo, an eyewitness. In just seven days, "New Mountain" built itself up to a height of 450 feet, then dropped into silence. Nothing has been heard from it since.

But Parícutin, Pulido had been told, was the most closely observed of these from the instant of its birth. And thanks to newspapers, radio, and newsreels, the whole world knew about it. On the chance that his land had risen in value—for it had certainly risen in other ways—he erected a sign at the edge of his property:

VOLCANO FOR SALE

DIONISIO PULIDO, PROPRIETOR

A buyer showed up within a week.

Watching him approach from a distance, Pulido would have seen a skinny, white-bearded figure shuffling along with odd, almost mincing steps that set off tiny explosions in the still-warm ash. Short and pale, smoking a skinny and ridiculously long cigar, this man must have looked ancient, must have looked as light-boned as a bird, someone whom a gust of wind might lift and blow back to the cafés and plazas of the capital, where his gentleman's vest and jacket would suit him better than they ever could in this rugged poor-man's country. He also wore a pocket watch and a floppy Panama hat.

Dionisio Pulido could see, beneath the hat, a pair of unblinking raven eyes. The eyes stared past him to the volcano.

It didn't take long for the man to arrive at a price. Seventy-eight dollars. Seventy-eight dollars to buy a volcano.

Nor did it take him much time to hire a mule and pack it with saddlebags. Then, with surprising strength, he pulled it toward the burning crater and its awful fumes and noise, closer than any of the villagers and most of the scientists and journalists dared to go. He stopped the mule on a hill of steaming cinders, set up an easel that looked every bit as rickety as he did, then pulled out pencils, paints, and brushes. As lightning from the eruption column boomed overhead, he began to work.

He passed his sixty-ninth birthday painting and drawing on the ash piles around the volcano. At age seventy, he was still there, working every day, trudging across a world that looked like desert sand dunes, a blackened Sahara. Now and then he moved around the valley, closer in or farther out, trying different perspectives. But he rarely strayed from sight of the volcano. Despite his indoor pallor and citified airs, the old man turned out to be physically tougher than most men a third his age. In fact, he spent virtually every night breathing the volcano's poisonous fumes in a dilapidated, ash-clogged hut that he'd turned into a home and studio of sorts. By the time he finally packed up and returned to Mexico City, he'd completed thousands of drawings, paintings, and studies of Parícutin, this newest revolution of the Mexican earth.

His name was Dr. Atl, and he was a revolutionary himself, many times over. In fact, he was one of the weirdest and most remarkable figures in all of Mexican history.

In Nahuatl, the old language of the Aztecs, *atl* means "water," and it was not always his name. In 1875, in Guadalajara, he was born Gerardo Murillo. This may have been one of the last ordinary things to happen to him.

As a little boy, he became obsessed with Jules Verne, who was probably the world's first great writer of realistic, genuinely vertical literature. (The first, that is, unless you happen to think that Dante is a realist, too.) Young Gerardo read and reread books like *Journey to the Center of the Earth, 20,000 Leagues Under the Sea,* and *From the Earth to the Moon*—well-named narratives of fantastic journeys that literally reach far down into the earth or the sea, or far up into space. He published a school newspaper that serialized his own Verne-inspired undersea adventure novel, *Shipwrecks of the Pacific.*

He also rode on expeditions into the Sierra Madre with his Uncle Francisco, a gold prospector. During the first of these trips, Gerardo was so slight that he traveled curled up in a fruit basket hanging from one of his uncle's mules. According to one of Atl's biographers, Beatriz Espejo, the rugged, Zorba-like Francisco eventually "put a gun in his hand, made him drunk with his friends, taught him to be generous" and "introduced him, in a primitive way, to the art of becoming a man."

By design or osmosis, Francisco also introduced him firsthand to towering mountains, to the soul-stirring majesty of the Mexican landscape and the lost civilizations whose architects and high priests, Gerardo came to believe, had tried to imitate those peaks, especially the volcanoes, by building pyramids toward the sun. For instance, the fabulous Aztec capitol of Tenochtitlán, today's Mexico City, was a carefully laid-out cluster of luminous temples that rose tapering out of a lake. The lake sat in a valley walled on three sides by gigantic, snow-covered volcanoes.

By his mid-twenties, Gerardo Murillo was painting and writing like mad. One of his early short stories apparently inspired John Steinbeck's novella, *The Pearl.* He traveled frequently to Paris, rubbing shoulders with more famous turn-of-the-century rebels, including Picasso. He studied philosophy for a while in Rome. But unlike his compatriots, he occasionally fled the comforts of the city for wild nature, traveling to Sicily, for instance, to live alone on the slopes of Mount Etna.

And in 1906 he visited Naples. There he met another multi-talented obsessive, the American inventor Frank Perret. A former assistant to Thomas Edison, Perret had sailed to Italy under doctor's orders to build back his health after years of overwork. As it had many times over the centuries, Vesuvius happened to be rumbling. After Perret got his first good look at its pyrotechnics, he apparently felt something go off in himself. Soon his plans for R & R were a memory; he'd decided to study the volcano full-time. Because he lacked the proper equipment (for his background was not in geology but elevator motors), he sometimes improvised in ways that Gerardo Murillo would have admired. For instance, to create a homespun seismograph, he set a brass bed in cement. After the cement dried, he'd clamp his teeth over one of the railings to feel for subtle earthquake vibrations. I like to think that Gerardo joined him occasionally in this task, the two of them kneeling side by side at the altar of the bed, their eyes closed, their gold fillings and bicuspids pressed to brass, waiting for the twitching of Vesuvius, the faint rising of its stone.

Gerardo's European travels occurred during the heyday of Atlantic steamship crossings, and one day in 1911, after rough weather on a homebound voyage had soaked him to shivering, he began to jokingly refer to himself as Atl, or water. Later on he added Dr., apparently on a whim.

But his choice of an Aztec word for his new identity had been carefully thought out. Tossing his surname overboard while steaming home from the Old World to the New helped him separate himself from another Murillo who had long irritated and embarrassed him. Bartolomé Murillo was a seventeenth-century Spanish portraitist whose academic style and subject matter—mainly, royalty and the very rich—was still in vogue in Mexico City when Atl was learning to paint.

More important, Atl's new/ancient name let him embrace the Indian lines in his ancestry and in all of Mexico's. He'd had enough of the art of conquest and its colonial aftermath. His country deserved something new and daring. Mexican artists, he began to write and teach, should portray the struggles and dignity of everyday people and their breathtakingly beautiful, everyday land. And he, Dr. Atl, should help lead this pictorial revolution.

Which he soon did. During the first three decades of the century, he was all over fast-changing Mexico, the leading voice for artistic nationalism and the mural painting renaissance. He helped launch the careers of David Siqueiros and his own students Jose Orozco and Diego Rivera, and he apparently did not mind that their careers in art, especially mural painting, soon eclipsed his own. (Years later, as a joke, Frida Kahlo would paint a tiny dog on some of her canvases and call it "Dr. Atl.")

But Atl, being Atl, could never engage himself in politics alone; his curiosities kept shooting out everywhere. He wrote a six-volume work on the churches of Mexico with photographs by Kahlo. Passing through the United States, he visited Woodrow

Wilson in the White House. He collected butterflies with the passion of Nabokov. He took tremendous solo hikes into the mountains and celebrated his return with long, cold baths. For his paintings he invented *atl-colors:* crayons made of wax, resin, and pigments, which didn't fade and created gritty textures that you couldn't get with oil paints—textures especially effective for portraying falling volcanic ash.

Not long before he died at eighty-nine in 1964, he persuaded architect Jacobo Konigsberg to draw up plans for a futurist city populated by artists of many disciplines, nationalities, and beliefs— a city that he hoped would become the intellectual center of the planet. Olinka, Atl called this utopia, after a Nahuatl word meaning "where the movement begins." Olinka would feature helicopters for personal transport and a thirty-story space needle made of aluminum and crystals. It would rise from the shiny, black, basaltic floor of a place Atl had visited and painted many times over the years: the crater of a dead volcano in the Valley of Mexico.

Again and again he returned to volcanoes and the roots of Mexican culture, which he believed were inseparable. Once as a young man, after being spurned by a woman, he retreated for half a year to the high snows of El Popocatépetl, "Smoking Mountain," the ancient and immense 17,800-foot volcano that shadows Mexico City and Puebla, hundreds of miles to the east of where Parícutin would later burst from the ground.

Why seek solace on a volcano? Perhaps Atl sought to console himself with clear, cold air and gigantic views while hiking in a landscape that reminded him of childhood adventures. Maybe the immensity of El Popo and its buried fires helped lend perspective to his own incendiary feelings. For whatever reasons he went, Atl brought along all of his energies and eccentricities.

In a hut he built inside El Popo's crater rim (the huge volcano had been dormant, though far from dead, for about seventy years), he slept barefoot under only a serape. In the morning, according to friends who visited him there, he'd pull back a canvas tarp he used as a door, wave out the frigid alpine mist with his hat, then tear down the canvas and start painting on it. In 1921, when he was forty-six, he published a book inspired by these experiences, *The Symphonies of Popocatépetl.*

A few years ago, in a cozy reading room in the Library of Congress, I had the chance to examine one of the few remaining copies of this volume. Back then, I knew almost nothing about Dr. Atl. I had heard of him for the first time only a few months before, when I ran across a few pages about his life in the wonderful *Parícutin: The Volcano Born in a Mexican Cornfield,* by Smithsonian Institution volcanologists James F. Luhr and Tom Simkin.

Now, as I held the heavy and oversized copy of *Symphonies of Popocatépetl,* I admired how elegant it was, its thick cover faded like an Italian tapestry and yet also somehow aglow in antique light. It looked like it hadn't been pulled from its shelf in decades. If I opened the cover too quickly, I worried, would I crack the spine? Or maybe worse, would the book's contents prove the obviously strange and mysterious "Doctor," whatever that part of his name meant, to be mainly a crank? I had enough writer friends to know that talent is no hedge against looniness. I had also learned enough about volcanoes to know that their powerful, stand-alone magnetism draws a lot more to their slopes than just crazy weather.

But Atl's book held up in every way. It revealed bold, red and black woodblock prints of El Popo spurting fire—volcano images that seemed to tremble on the page and amply convey the passion that years later would drive Atl to actually buy a volcano. And while it soon became clear that Atl's prose could lurch toward the superheated (borrowing, perhaps, from Renaissance volcano-witnesses like Pietro Giacomo de Toledo, whose reports he'd no doubt read), his words definitely carried a punch. In the volcano's "venerable old age," he wrote, "its entrails stirred, and from the decayed lip of the Colossus, fire shot forth again. Oh marvelous teaching of nature!"

Oh marvelous allure of Mexican volcanoes and geology gone wild. That's what I thought as I slowly turned the pages. But more than that, I suddenly realized, I wanted to travel south—far south. It was time to see Atl's paintings for myself, and his volcanoes.

January 1999, Mexico City

The National Museum of Art turned out to be a cavernous place with marble staircases and extravagant grillwork, but surprisingly dim lighting. At first, SueEllen and I wandered through some gloomy, high-ceilinged portrait galleries. We passed wall after wall of ten-foot-tall, blue-veiled Madonnas, saints, kings, and satin-robed dignitaries. We strolled in near-silence through two or three hundred years of this stuff, almost of all it, I was beginning to understand, examples of the reverence for power and wealth that Dr. Atl and his modernist friends were rebelling against.

Then we hit the twentieth century. Brilliantly plumed gods and birds swept across the skies! Luminous tomatoes, mangoes, calla flowers burst from the wicker baskets of market vendors! Rituals of daily work filled up frames or whole walls: Indians pounded maize and rolled out tortillas, bargained in crowded stalls, bent their thick, earthenware bodies over bean fields, assembly lines, wood-fired stoves.

I knew that many of these cultural eruptions had been stirred up by Dr. Atl. But where was *he?* SueEllen and I had strolled through the entire first half of the twentieth century and hadn't found one of his paintings. A frustrating pattern seemed to be forming. We'd been in town for two days, but I'd come up with no Atl footprints at all. I'd checked out half a dozen impressive-looking bookstores near the old city center. Zilch. I'd dialed up scholars and geologists at two or three universities, but nobody picked up the phone. I began to wonder if Atl had been entirely forgotten.

And then SueEllen saved the day. Overcoming her natural shyness, she used her Spanish, which was much better than mine, to ask at the front desk of the museum. There were some locked-up galleries, it turned out, a result of budget cuts and the cost of keeping the lights on. Such a shame, said the dark suit behind the desk, shaking his head, *lo siento.* I tried to look even more crestfallen than I was, and SueEllen patiently explained to him how seeing Atl's work would mean a lot to me, how long our journey had taken, from the high mountains of Colorado, et cetera.

Soon we were following a guard back upstairs. He jangled some absurdly large dungeon keys, pushed open a wooden door three times his height, and shooed us in.

We stepped into cool night. A light clicked on, then some others, and suddenly a tremendous wall of lava loomed right in front of me—a steaming wreckage of piled-up, oncoming rock. The canvas was maybe fifteen feet wide, meaning that Atl must have finished it in a studio after sketching it on site. But, my God, the lava wall looked as wide as the whole world, the sizzling rock advancing in a stuttering avalanche. My throat began to feel a little dry, as though I were somehow stuck in the Total-Kill Zone around Parícutin that Dionisio Pulido and his neighbors knew too well. Off in the distance, in the painting's elevated background, smoked the source of the lava, the furiously erupting Parícutin itself. High above it, wind-driven ash dropped in curtains of chain mail. The ash, too, seemed to be moving closer. I got the feeling that it would soon drift over me and fill up my lungs. I could practically smell it coming. No painting had ever affected me like this.

The guard looked on, nodding and smiling, gesturing for us to take our time, for this was truly his gift to us, and the museum's, a private showing. I studied *Lava and Cornfield* a while longer. Atl's scientist's eye for detail was clearly at work in the way he suggested with red splotches the briefly emerging interior heat of this *aa* lava. And Atl the visionary as well: the size of the onslaught conveying the overwhelming strength of the unruly earth. SueEllen and I looked at each other, a bit stunned. Neither of us had expected this kind of power.

But then, when it comes to volcanoes, nobody ever does.

It wasn't always this way. Pre-Columbian people may not have known much about the inner workings of the planet, but millions of them lived along or in sight of the great wall of volcanoes and other mountains that runs south from the Valley of Mexico down to the Patagonian tip of Argentina. That's a stretch of almost 5,000 miles, and many of the cultures that lived there respected, feared, and worshipped the powers of snow-capped, fiery peaks.

In September 1519, two months before Hernando Cortés, already on the mainland, marched into the Aztec capital of Tenochtitlán with horses, cannons, and 500 soldiers, El Popocatépetl began to erupt. Several times a day, it blew out ash clouds and tongues of fire. A smoking El Popo was nothing new to the Aztecs. Their codices noted a volcanic explosion as early as 1345—the first documented New World eruption. But no one in the Valley of Mexico had seen anything this large or violent in decades. *El Popo's* dark plume of ash stretched for miles and earthquake tremors raced across the valley. Soon, the Emperor Moctezuma's high priests were gathering daily at the Great Teocalli to watch the spectacle.

As they conferred on the steps of the pyramid-temple where thousands of human sacrifices had been performed over the years to appease sky and mountain gods, they may have begun to tremble themselves. It was their job to interpret the signs and wonders of the universe, and a cluster of recent events had put them on edge. A comet had flared for weeks across the heavens, terrifying the populace. Night after night came reports of a woman or a ghost of a woman gliding through the city, weeping without pause. Nobody ever saw her, but her incessant crying put everyone on edge.

And now, huge and ancient *El Popo* was raging. As the highest point in the Valley of Mexico, its brilliant white summit was the first place in the Aztec world to capture the life-giving light of the sun, and at night it was the last to let it go. And so the priests nervously squinted into the distance. They had also begun to hear increasingly ominous rumors of a fierce, blond-haired, ironclad warrior marching west from Veracruz on the Gulf of Mexico. Nearer and nearer he marched, his army of soldiers riding huge animals that nobody had ever seen before. The seers began to worry that their empire, maybe even the universe itself, was wobbling out of control.

In fact, it was about to explode. By the time El Popo stopped erupting three years later, in 1522, Moctezuma was dead, murdered by Cortés, and his empire no longer existed. Tenochtitlán's royal archives and gardens had been destroyed, its aviary of vermilion flycatchers, copper-tailed trogons, blue-throated hummingbirds, and other tropical birds burned to cinders. The Aztecs had been thrown into chains, then forced to dismantle their temples, stone block by stone block. Large parts of the Great Teocalli would soon become the foundation and walls of what is today the largest cathedral in Latin America.

And fiery El Popo had predicted and then witnessed it all.

Many of the most spectacular volcanoes on the planet have squeezed up through the convergences of crustal plates that run down the Pacific coasts of Mexico, Central, and South America—the Latin American portion of the Ring of Fire. A world map that shows both volcanoes and plate boundaries might give you the impression that just about every volcano from Mexico City's El Popo down to southern Chile qualifies as beachfront property, so rigorously do the plate edges and coastlines seem to overlap. But that's only an approximation, a mistake of scale. The places where plates collide or tear past each other are gigantic, ragged, sometimes anomalous things. And some volcanoes, like El Popo and nearby, equally huge Iztaccíhuatl (White Woman), stand more than one hundred miles inland. The volcanoes of Mexico have been formed thanks to the Pacific Ocean-bottom Cocos plate smashing into and grinding below the North American plate.

Farther south, the sub-Pacific Nazca plate converges similarly with the South American plate, pushing up the Andes and allowing magma to slip through to form more than 200 volcanoes. Here, still growing, stand the highest fire-and-ice peaks on earth, including more than a dozen that soar above 20,000 feet. Straddling the border of Argentina and Chile, the volcano of Nevados Ojos del Salado, 22,589 feet high, tops them all.

It should be no surprise, then, that in various cultures south of the Valley of Mexico, these stunning peaks were frequently worshipped as gods or treated as altars to fierce natural forces. The rituals of appeasement could be fierce, in turn. For instance, to ensure peace from Coseguina volcano, ancient Nicaraguans threw a young girl into its crater every twenty-five years. In El Salvador, girls were sometimes bound and thrown into lakes to keep volcanoes from exploding or to ensure rain for crops. One report suggests this occurred at Lake Ilopango as recently as 1880.

In Peru, Chile, and Argentina, Incan shamans eyed distant white peaks during festivals held four or seven years apart, or during times of war or political stress. As offerings, they searched for the purest, most beautiful children in each quadrant of the 2,500-mile-long empire. Eventually, a boy or girl of ten, eleven, or twelve was chosen. She was dressed in a fine alpaca shawl and adorned with silver pins and pink spondylus shells that teams of runners brought inland from the Pacific beaches. Wearing a macaw feather headdress and leather slippers, she was paraded around a town square or perhaps a rain forest clearing. She was often brought to the capital of Cuzco, a high-altitude city bathed in the silvery light of so many stars that names were given not to constellations but to the shapes of the relatively few black splotches among them. Turtle. Condor. Jaguar. The child's parents were given gifts or privileged positions in the community. She herself was most likely promised immortality.

On a journey that could last for weeks, she was then led over Andean passes on a llama-trek to the top of a mountain or volcano. At the three-and-a-half or four-mile-high summit of a peak like Llullaillaco in Argentina, El Plomo in Chile, or Sara Sara in Peru, air turns pitifully thin and colossally cold. One of my CSU teaching colleagues, Robert White, once camped above 19,000 feet on Aconcagua (Quechuan for Stone Sentinel) in preparation for a summit ascent. Each morning, his thermometer hovered around ten degrees Fahrenheit, and that was *inside* his high-tech tent during the height of the Argentinian summer. To bend down and pick up just a few stones to add to a windbreak exhausted and confused him. "I felt one degree separated from my own consciousness," he told me. He eventually made the summit. A week later, a team of seven climbers got trapped in a storm and died of exposure and altitude sickness.

Imagine these conditions operating on a child in the year 1450 or 1510. If she managed to reach the summit alive, she didn't last long. A corn-alcohol potion was often forced on her. She may have been ritualistically clubbed, as well. Then she was lowered into a womb-like grave strewn with sacred red earth, drinking cups, and gold or silver statuettes of llamas or people or spirits. In other words, she was given to the mountain and sky gods to help maintain the traditional order of the universe. After the sacrifice teams sealed her up, they quickly started back home. This was a profoundly vertical world, in metaphor and fact, and proof of the wide extent of these sacrifices has been discovered in only the last ten years or so. The highest tombs on the planet are now being located and sometimes excavated on one Andean volcano after another. A museum at Catholic University in Arequipa, Peru, displays the remains of one of these poor children of the air. In 1995, a very fit team of archeologists found "the Ice Maiden of Ampado" on a volcanic summit 20,700 feet above sea level. The scientists packed her thin body in snow and plastic, then hefted her downhill on their shoulders before she could thaw.

I once stood for a long time in front of her present resting place. She was not the mummy I expected her to be. She was a frozen-solid little girl pried from a crater rim four miles into the sky. In the central room of the museum, she sat in a thick glass freezer, her hair tightly braided, her ropy arms reaching for her knees, which were partly drawn up to her chest, as though she died before she could hug herself warm.

Some glitch in the refrigeration system made the glass frost over every hour or two. As I stood inches from the freezer, watching her slowly fade from sight, I told myself that the high snows were reclaiming her. I found it comforting to think that the cold fog was offering her respite from a world that never let her grow up and that even 500 years later wouldn't leave her alone. She looked about ten years old.

In the far less disturbing museum that SueEllen and I were visiting in Mexico City, I noticed that Dr. Atl's gigantic lava canvas hung next to a much smaller painting, one called Clouds over the Valley of Mexico. What struck me right away about this image is how Atl made the mountainous horizon and the clouds closing over it bulge up to suggest an exaggerated curve of the earth. This was a Mexico so full of energy it could hardly sit still for its portrait.

Atl himself couldn't sit still, either, at least to judge by the next canvas that caught my eye. Shadow of Popo looked *away* from the volcano and must have been painted as Atl stood close to the summit or as he imagined himself floating a little above it, like some modern-day *santo*. The canvas invited me to gaze down and out over the mountain's blue penumbra as it stretched for miles across twilit farmland, the shadow-tip of El Popo's summit reaching out to touch the far-off horizon.

This image of a prodigious, growing pyramid also suggested landscape on the move. And not just a growing volcano, but mountains in general, the planet's crumpled-up ranges building and then eroding away over the immensity of time—the liquid nature of everything. Shadow of Popo also looked like it was meant to evoke Mexico's ancient, pyramid-building glories, the power, imagination, and ferocity of its volcano-worshipping civilizations.

After SueEllen and I thanked the guard for his kindness, we visited the museum bookshop. That's when I found a heavy, wider-than-high retrospective of Atl's work, published in 1994. So he hadn't been forgotten, after all. *Dr. Atl: The Landscape as Passion* offered a rich sampling of his charcoal sketches and luminous atl-color-on-wood paintings of Parícutin, plus images of volcanoes from all over Mexico. As I leafed through the pages, I saw how much Atl himself really did roam over the landscape during his long life. What a restless soul he must have been, this pale, skinny, world-class mountaineer who climbed to the vertical ends of the earth.

And sometimes beyond. When single-engine planes began to putter over the Valley of Mexico, this new book told me, Atl often hitched a ride, becoming the first painter anywhere to take to the skies. Soon he'd invented "aero-portraiture," bird's-eye views of landscapes that deepened the bulging-earth effects he'd been using on his mountainscapes.

Two paintings I was struck by in the book, works he completed in his mid-seventies, at first made me wonder if he'd hitched rides with the Mercury astronauts. These images placed me higher above the earth than any plane Atl could have flown in—except, of course, the plane of his imagination. For instance, *Mouth of Volcano* tilted forward from a miles-high viewpoint, forcing me to stare thousands of feet down into the moonlit maw of El Popo, whose summit sailed among bunched-up clouds. And *Crater and Milky Way* seemed to have been painted by somebody hovering on the edge of space itself, gazing far down over El Popo's lonely blue snows while its gigantic sister volcano, glacier-clad Iztaccíhuatl, arced away over the rim of the wheeling planet.

As I leafed back through the retrospective during the next few days, I wondered if these last two images were suggesting that Atl had made some sort of turn toward religion in his last years. I'd seen old age do stranger things to people, and perhaps the aging firebrand had tried to compensate for the dark pull of mortality and physical decay by positioning himself up among the stars. But then I reminded myself of what may have been the most remarkable fact of his life. It turned out that Atl paid dearly for working and sleeping so close to roaring Parícutin, for having breathed all those noxious fumes day and night for more than a year. The subterranean poisons eventually made his teeth fall out. Worse, the chemicals aggravated circulatory problems that turned into phlebitis in one leg, then gangrene. In 1949, he had the limb amputated. Thus, at age seventy-four, he was forced to clump around on heavy wooden crutches. Yet even then he wasn't done with volcanoes. Within a year of losing the leg, he grew restless again and somehow fought his way to the top of El Popo. It's more than three miles high! This was a man who simply wanted to climb.

Today, El Popocatépetl looms over the lives of one in five Mexicans. Given that Mexico City may be more populous than any city on earth (though who really knows?), more than twenty million people live within its potential eruption range. Many live in the vast and dry lake bed from which the pyramids of Tenochtitlán once rose. After I emerged blinking from the National Museum and stood on the sidewalk for a moment, I got the feeling that I could hear and feel the beehive hum of all those souls, although maybe it was only the traffic. I could also sense El Popo, invisible behind Mexico City's famous smog, dominating the skyline to the south.

SueEllen and I had idled so much in the galleries and gift shop that we'd picked up a case of "Museum Back." The only cure, we knew, was fast walking. Forgetting her wariness of large cities, SueEllen took off with me down Avenida Tacuba. It was a good thing the sidewalks were wide, though, because they were brimming with the out-of-work young, thousands of quick-eyed young men and women in clean white shirts and blouses, jostling around, looking for something, anything. It was heartbreaking, the same street movie I'd seen in other places teeming with crowds of the unreasonably hopeful: Bangkok, Nairobi, Santo Domingo.

And, I knew, we were walking among the lucky, the ones who'd escaped or so far avoided the endless slums rimming the city. I thought about our nice downtown hotel, the Best Western Ritz, which was affordable to us only because of the severely depressed *peso*. Then I realized that I was paying a surcharge in guilt.

But the energy humming everywhere around us soon distracted me. Along the prairie-wide Paseo de la Reforma, pop-up stalls jammed the sidewalks. Twelve-year-olds hawked mountains of sweaters, soap bars, shampoo bottles, magic elixirs,

Swatches, piles of Indian blankets and knock-off Gap jeans. Every couple of minutes, somebody called out, "Hey, Mister!" and held up a lurid, Aztec-warrior-and-maiden poster that commemorated a local volcano legend.

For two days I'd been trying to piece together this myth. It seemed that a princess pining for her warrior lover, who was from a different tribe, heard that he had been killed in battle. Grief-stricken, she poisoned herself. But too soon! For he wasn't dead, after all. When he returned and discovered her body, he built two gigantic mountains. On the summit of one of them he laid her to rest. This was Iztaccíhuatl volcano, whose snow-topped series of peaks (really several volcanoes in one) resembles a woman lying on her back under a white sheet. On the other mountain, El Popo, he retreated to die, but not before holding aloft her funeral torch, which you can see smoldering even today. Or something like that. There are many versions.

Since the collapse of the Aztec empire, El Popo had erupted about two dozen times, growing quiet in 1947. But in the mid-1990s it had started up again. Since then it had forced an occasional closing of the airport, dusting the Valley of Mexico in ash and low-level anxiety. Judging by the grin on the boy trying to sell me the poster, I wondered if the rising fire didn't also stir up dreams.

We'd come to a fancier part of town now and had to slow down and thread our way through mounds of clothes and Chinese-made toys arrayed at the curb in front of elegant boutiques. Most of the sellers worked with headsets on, dancing and singing, while men in three-piece suits frowned out at them through plate-glass windows. I felt sorry for those older guys.

But again, the energy zinging everywhere tempered the feeling. At the big intersections, a juggler, or a fire-breather, or a couple of unicyclists wobbled through waiting traffic, working for tips. A circus of survivors!

Over the last few days, SueEllen and I had watched a club-footed flutist and several teen-age mariachi bands commandeer subway cars or buses, smash out a song or two, then hustle back off. We'd ridden in a cab with a plastic vampire-bat model of former president Carlos Salinas de Gortari swinging from the rearview mirror. The driver kept flicking it with his finger: payback for yet another politico who promised reform while stashing away millions in Europe.

SueEllen and I came to a side street called the Avenue of Lost Limbs, and mostly because of its name, we turned in. There were some musicians plugging in speakers and guitars. In minutes, they began to crank out high-octane rock. Only then did I realize that the whole band was blind.

Swaying to the music, I thought back to the previous week, to the "pre-research" part of my trip. Because we both teach and write, SueEllen and I sometimes front-load a vacation onto our fact-finding travels, although really it's often hard to tell where one ends and the other begins. This time we started in Oaxaca. We found big crowds swirling there, too, and high spirits bouncing off the streets. Plus this: Christmas week meant that folk art was in full flower.

Two days before Christmas, I was sipping coffee at a sidewalk cafe on the *zócalo* when some trucks rolled in stacked with lumber. Out jumped men with hammers and saws, and soon dozens of tables had sprung up under the gigantic trees of the plaza. By late afternoon the tables were packed with nativity figures and *santos,* some of them three or four feet tall. Every one of them was carved from radishes.

Yes, radishes . . . some as big as my forearm but much more gnarled. They'd been washed, sculpted, and pinned together with toothpicks into contorted magi, camels, elephants, giraffes, and cathedrals. On almost every table, as well, Mexico's homegrown Madonna, the Virgin of Guadalupe, ascended from grottoes of radish rocks or mountain springs carved out of radishes.

This turned out to be the Night of the Radishes: a religious festival and competition among teams from the Oaxacan countryside, the grand prize a new pickup truck, which was a genuine fortune. Most of the teams looked like families to me. While the crowds swelled and old men wearing sashes marched around the plaza blowing dented horns and pounding drums in geriatric Knights of Columbus-type units, a pair of grandparents at almost every table whittled away at the scarlet skin and moist white meat of the radishes. They handed finished pieces to adult sons and daughters, who expertly stuck them together with toothpicks, sometimes lashing the larger figures to pre-built frames. All the while a youngster or two pitched in by spraying the finished parts with a water bottle, since corruption of the flesh came fast to the freshly peeled radishes.

And I thought, How appropriate in a country that seems to celebrate the Day of the Dead *every day*. That devotes fantastically ornate altars to the dried body parts of saints, that displays the mummies of nuns in upright coffins, that has manufactured a million cut-outs, paintings, and papier-mâché figures of grinning skeletons. Everywhere, the bony dead had popped back out of the ground to drive cabs, ride bikes and motorcycles, sit down to feasts, dance, play fiddle and guitar . . .

The blind rock band rocked on as I stood with SueEllen on the Avenue of Lost Limbs, in the shadow of El Popo. What a country! And the more I thought about it, the more I sensed that the old revolutionary energies that powered Dr. Atl and Rivera and Siqueros were once again rising from below.

Culture has so often been imposed on Mexican people from outside or above—by Cortés and his army, by the Church and its European-trained artists, by one corrupt government after another. But maybe just as often, these forces have been countered from below. Counting Oaxaca, I had walked through probably a dozen churches, and in each one I saw traditional statues and paintings shoved to the side or overwhelmed by gaudy mangers and Bethlehem towns. Squat nativity figures in serapes mobbed the altars. They'd been fashioned from dried marigolds, straw, clay, hammered tin, and shiny obsidian.

In a tiny chapel one afternoon in Oaxaca, I discovered a Virgin of Guadalupe rising out of a pile of rocks that seemed to have burst with her Parícutin-fashion, right through the altar. They were real rocks, too—gas-pocked volcanic cobbles as big as watermelons. A few had even tumbled into the main aisle, as though the unruly countryside was about to reclaim the church. The Virgin, who'd probably been cast in Madrid or Rome, looked nothing like the short women who bustled outside. But she'd been draped with ribbons and blinking Christmas lights and adorned with flowers. She'd been transformed into Our Lady of Everyday People. And like any good revolutionary or crowd of the oppressed, she was *rising*.

A week later, we found ourselves 200 miles to the west of Mexico City. Finally, Parícutin!

Moments after we climbed out of the car where the dusty road petered out, a boy popped out of nowhere and offered to guide us out through the huge lava field. His name was Joaquín, he was nine, and he promised me that he *knew* this place. I smiled and shrugged, then pointed to the guide we already had— Juan, a computer science student who spoke passable English and who'd borrowed his mother's car to drive us out here from Uruapan, the nearest city and the capital of Michoacán.

But Joaquín just laughed and fell in with us anyway. We were clearly his amusement for the day and maybe a good tip besides. He took off ahead of us, skipping along the up and down trail that somehow would take us to the mismatched white bell towers in the distance. Growing larger and brighter against the black lava, they made a bizarre and thrilling sight. Joaquín seemed thrilled to just be himself. He kept looking back and chattering at us, whipping a yo-yo around, setting off ash explosions with every step.

The lava was thick and very rough, *aa* all around. A few miles beyond the church loomed the gray form of Parícutin. Though it wasn't putting out even a wisp of smoke, it looked much more intimidating than I was expecting—like the barrel tip of a gigantic buried cannon.

In late February 1952, nine years after it burst out of Dionisio Pulido's cornfield and created a Total-Kill Zone of ash and lava, the volcano began to die. In a single day its artillery fire dropped off to popgun level. The lava stopped flowing. For another week or so the crater wheezed and gave off some noiseless puffs, and then that was that.

This might be the first volcano I've heard of that shut down so emphatically. It's true that some others have been known to drop into silence or *relative* quiescence for thousands or hundreds of thousands of years after a major eruption. But then they've started up again. Other volcanoes run hot and cold much more frequently. The smoke that I saw churning out of Mount Etna signaled at least the hundredth time in twenty-five centuries that the volcano has erupted.

But scientists think that Parícutin is really, most sincerely dead, as are all the other cinder cones that dot this valley where Dionesio Pulido once tended his cornfield. At a high point on our trail to the church, I scrambled atop a rough scallop of dried lava, turned a careful 360, and tried to read the valley's book of deep time. I counted more than a dozen Parícutin-like hills within five or six miles. Most were cloaked by oak and pine forests or a green fuzz of bushes. Some retained almost entirely their classic cinder-cone or pyramid shapes. Older ones had been badly dismantled by wind and rain and slow settling. But they were volcanoes, all right, or once were, and some looked only hundreds or a few thousand years older than Parícutin. "Morphologically youthful," as the rock doctors say.

Yet still dead. Like Alexander the Great, John Keats, and late-'60s rock stars, they flamed out gloriously, which is apparently the tendency of the thousand or so small craters (compared to El Popo, that is) in this dense, middle section of the Mexican Volcano Belt. This volcano cluster runs roughly east-west across seven hundred miles of southern Mexico, a part of the Pacific Ring of Fire. All of this means that this former land of the Aztecs, the Toltecs, the Olmecs, and whoever lived here before them has suffered invasions from below for a good ten million years. Truly Olinka, as Dr. Atl might say: "Where the movement begins."

This also means that while Dionisio Pulido and his neighbors couldn't have known it, Parícutin's abrupt arrival in their midst was only a matter of time. Also a matter of time will be the birth of the next Parícutin and its dose of the newest earth on Earth. The next eruption, however—a year from now, or a thousand— will most likely be foretold by the high priests of contemporary science, the wizards of satellite telemetry, computer simulations, deformation and seismicity studies, and whatever other techniques and gizmos help them to read the omens of the inner cosmos. You might call this "deep mapping."

After we had hiked for a sun-blasted hour, SueEllen, Juan, little Joaquín, and I found ourselves in the shadows of the bell towers, which turned out to be much bigger than I had imagined. I became aware of another party poking around nearby. Hoots of laughter, voices, then nothing as the lava swallowed the sounds. The rock was ridiculously thick and pocked with caves and pits; it was much more jumbled up than anything I'd scrambled over in Hawaii. I felt a rush of affection for my high-topped boots, which had been broken in so nicely by our Colorado mountains.

Now and then I stepped or leaped over black crevasses ten and twenty feet deep that made my stomach turn when I thought about falling. A stumble could shred me beyond recognition. I fretted for a while about the way Joaquín was scrambling around, singing and whistling, though he did look at home: Lava Boy. Still, I was relieved when he finally sat in the shade of an up-turned formation to work on his yo-yo tricks.

All around, mosses, lichens, and ferns seemed to be enjoying the shade, too. From moist niches above and below me, small pines twisted up toward the sun. Not bad for a Total-Kill Zone.

But then, for more than half a century, winds and storms had been blowing in seeds, soil particles, and other sources of the nitrogen crucial to revegetation. Seeds also migrated in by passing through the bodies of deer mice, towhees, grosbeaks, and tanagers—predators that had come to dine on spiders, beetles, wasps, and other insects. The bugs had crawled, flown, or been wafted onto the lava field from its less sterile surroundings. The world is indeed a movable feast.

In less sun-baked spots, especially, the tiny roots of new plants were drilling through ash and crumbly lava, prying it apart, breaking it down into pebbles and dust and then moisture-holding soil. Rain was also aiding the manufacture of new soil by "weathering" the lava rocks—that is, by helping to crumble them and tease out, in time-release fashion, nutrients in soluble form accessible to plants. As it has many times before, this impossible geography will eventually turn into some of the most fertile earth anywhere, another Golden Age of agriculture for little Joaquín or his great-great-grandkids.

The growing Parícutin soil was some of the newer earth on the planet, its organic starter pots nurturing a variety of pioneer species. This was good to remember, a suggestion that not everything in the natural world diminishes all the time, at least not over the long haul. I made a note to tell myself this the next time I felt overwhelmed by loss.

I saw something move: a tiny, dust-caked old man picking his way over the burnt rocks. Behind him clambered a chunky couple about my age and three hearty teenagers in rugby shirts, pressed jeans, and Nikes. Upper-crust Mexico City types, I figured. The old guy, no doubt their local guide (and maybe Joaquín's grandfather, for all I knew), wore a faded Goodyear cap, beat-up jeans, and a ripped shirt. Plus cracked leather boots wired to rubber-tire soles. Footwear by Goodyear, too?

All of us were exploring the interior of what used to be the church. Courtesy of the lava, we were scrambling over it, actually, probably fifteen or twenty feet above where the pews were once bolted to the floor.

But what was this? The old guy was waving over his clients. They gathered close, and he pulled himself up to his full height, which was about level with one of the teens' armpits. None too subtly, SueEllen and I and our guides edged our way over.

He started softly, in a Spanish, if that's what it was, that I couldn't make out at all. Now and then as he spoke, he swept an arm over the wild pavement of lava. Or he pointed up-valley toward the gunmetal crater of Parícutin, to the cinder slopes where Dr. Atl first set up his easel. But then his arm dropped to his side and he stood very still, reciting from memory, it seemed, speaking in almost formal cadences.

SueEllen and I exchanged one of those looks that come to us on only the best trips, a look that says, *Can you believe how lucky we are to be seeing this?* And then it hit me: the old guy was *chanting*. He was singing the Homeric tale of this place—his place, a place he could probably remember from the time before the volcano. He was passing down an epic poem of earth wars and omens, broken walls, the forced retreat of the villagers. This was a kind of deep mapping, too, this stylized story of his people and their land, and, for all I knew, it was a divination of their future, and he was giving it every ounce of dignity it deserved.

Our guide Juan was struggling with the translation, whispering to me in spurts of jumbled English. I nodded at him but didn't really care. The old guy's body language and timing were story enough for me. That plus the natural and human histories evident in everything we'd been climbing over and through. After a while I looked past the old guy's Goodyear cap to a fragment of church wall that poked up through the lava near where the altar must have been. Except for the bell towers, it was the only part of the church still standing or at least visible.

About a ladder's height above the lava—although there was no ladder to be seen—I noticed a square recess in the wall, a shelf once fashioned for a *santo* or a plaque. Now it held a vase of freshly cut, sky-blue flowers. In front of the vase, in a clear glass cup, a tiny candle burned.

An offering to the volcano? Or a more traditionally Catholic reminder of El Señor de los Milagros? Maybe it was both those things or neither. But whatever the candle meant, it was clear that somebody had gone to a tremendous amount of trouble to keep it going.

I looked at Joaquín, who had stopped fiddling with the yo-yo out of respect for the old guy, and I thought: he's a pioneer species, too.

Later that afternoon, the old guy's party had disappeared back into the lava, their voices fading quickly, and SueEllen and our guides seemed to have wandered off somewhere. Suddenly I was pleasantly alone. I leaned back against one of the bell towers and stared at the cone. After a while I began to imagine it as Dr. Atl might have seen it on his first day here in 1943, in its full-tilt volcanic rage. I closed my eyes and watched him, his thin figure yanking the panicky mule, pulling it toward the awful heat and lightning. I watched him set up his easel, then work until the dusk made him quit.

But even then Dr. Atl didn't leave. In the picture I had of him, he stood perfectly still in the hellish glow of the cauldron, and as night dropped he watched flying cinders and lava chunks turn brilliant red. He stood for hours and watched the fires roar, the flames snapping off into a thousand sparks. The sparks floated up through the night sky, wobbling and twinkling, rising higher and higher until they mingled, finally, with the stars . . .

I opened my eyes. I realized suddenly that I was imagining a lot more than Parícutin erupting. I was imposing over its dead crater yet another Dr. Atl image, a painting that I had seen for the first time in person at the National Museum. It was called *Volcano and Starry Night*. Impressionistic, almost primitive in style, the small canvas conveyed what may be Atl's most sweeping vision of all: planetary fire turning into star fire, the earth-trapped heat and light from the Big Bang radiating back out from the planet's core and up through the mantle and then the crust, escaping through volcanoes into the black reaches of space.

I'd learned enough about Mexican art by then to realize something else, too. Atl probably modeled *Volcano and Starry Night* after a famous sixteenth-century codex that portrayed a stylized El Popo flinging its burning cinders into the firmament. The codex depicted the infamous 1519 blast of smoke and fire that prophesized and then witnessed the coming of the conquistadors and the destruction of the Aztec world. Though the codex illustration and Atl's painting were created four centuries apart and represent different volcanoes, both connect deep earth to deep sky, the mundane to the transcendent. Both evoke a geothermal version of a Tree of Heaven. The tree illuminates how transformation occurs everywhere, all the time.

On the day before we were to fly back home, SueEllen and I received our own doses of earthly transformation, and they rocked us to the core. We were back in Mexico City, being mostly tourists again, wandering through the second floor of a small but elegant art museum not far from the former site of the Great Teocalli. The place had once been an old colonial house. Cool and high-ceilinged, it was full of stone arches that surrounded a square courtyard. A magnolia tree stood in each corner of the square. This quiet and shady place offered a nice break, I thought, from the dynamo hum of the streets, the crowds, the poverty, the whole country. In other words, I was ready to go home.

I was standing in front of a case of gold jewelry, my eye drawn to a fantastically ornate crucifix that hung from a chain against a backdrop of black velvet, when suddenly SueEllen, standing nearby, made a small cry. She grabbed my shoulder.

"I feel sick," she said.

"Sick? What kind of sick?"

"Dizzy . . . the flu . . . I don't know . . ."

This surprised me, but she did look pale. So I slipped my arm under hers, and then I began to feel light-headed myself. I noticed the crucifix. Very, very slowly, it was swaying in its case.

It took me an absurdly long time to realize that the building was swaying, too. I turned and looked down through one of the arches into the courtyard. All four magnolias were doing a kind of hula dance. I'd never seen trees move like this.

"Earthquake!" I blurted out at last, as Spanish and English erupted in the gallery, everybody coming to the same conclusion at once.

But there was no screaming or running like you see in the movies. The energy seething up through the earth and into our building seemed to be rolling a lot more than jerking or staggering, and I didn't hear any underground thunder or loud cracks, thank God. I reminded myself that the people of Mexico City had felt the earth lurch many times, usually without disaster. On the other hand, in 1985 an earthquake split open buildings all over the city, killing thousands of people. Only blocks from our hotel, faceless, three- and four-story ruins still stood empty, their cracked stone walls trussed up with giant wood beams and steel cables. Even the homeless seemed to avoid them.

I glanced straight up. Hmmm. The ceiling was made from fitted stone blocks, each one heavy enough to make a tortilla out of me. And then the world rolled again, mildly, and I rolled with it, strangely serene in my light-headedness, although, really, I had no idea what we should do. Sprint downstairs and stand in the courtyard? Flee the building altogether? Curl up in a corner?

SueEllen was squeezing my hand, hard, when a well-dressed woman standing in an arched doorway motioned us over.

"A good place to wait it out," she said calmly, like the veteran she was, as others drifted over. A few people whipped out cell phones and started talking fast. The woman smiled at us and nodded upward. *No problem,* she seemed to be saying. *This massive arch was built to last forever.*

But that's forever from a *human* point of view, I thought. Forever as in six, eight, maybe ten centuries, a span of time, it was true, which lasts longer than the reign of most cultures. But not nearly as long as the reign of plate tectonics, the endless revolution inside the planet.

Finally the rolling stopped, or seemed to, though you could never tell about aftershocks. As we learned on the TV news back at our hotel, this quake—my first—was good-sized, 7.1 on the Richter. But it caused little damage in Mexico City because of its swaying nature. That and the fact that it was centered a few hundred miles to the west of us, out past the Parícutin country that we'd just come back from.

Our hotel room was on the fifth or sixth floor, and SueEllen didn't like that at all. That evening, as she studied the little wall chart that showed the escape routes to the stairwells, she said, "How do we know that the Big One won't come in the middle of the night?" Not likely, I thought, though I suspected that nobody knew how to do the kind of deep mapping that could predict that.

Then I got an idea. I fetched an empty Coke bottle from the trash, rinsed and dried it, then balanced it upside down on the night table. Even a small tremor might knock it over and give us time to run. I thought Frank Perret would have been proud of me. And SueEllen always got a kick out of my jerry-rigged inventions, like the time on a car trip when I figured out how to heat up bagels and tortillas on the engine block.

"Ta-dah!" I said, pointing to my earthquake warning system. SueEllen laughed. We got into bed and turned out the lights. For a long time we lay on our backs, first chatting and joking, then fading into silence, staring at the ceiling. Or maybe it was the earth we were really peering into.

At least that's what I was doing. Somewhere today, I realized, the next Parícutin had edged closer to being born. And halfway across town, in that locked, dark gallery of the National Museum, Dr. Atl's volcanoes had once again jumped back to life. I could see them trembling in their frames, their brilliant fires squeezing up from below, breaking into sparks that stuttered toward heaven.

TIME OF
THE VOLCANO
SOUFRIERE HILLS, MONTSERRAT

Another explosion in the night,
Everyone tremble with fright.
Keep the faith, don't lose your mind.
Let's go on one day at a time.

—Arrow, reggae artist
"One Day at a Time"

I went to the Caribbean island of Montserrat to discover just how people go on one day at a time. I also wanted to see what happens to a once-stable community when a volcano lays serious siege to it. I wondered how powerfully and in what ways the sense of home tugs at people who have been displaced from their land not by human menace but by nature itself. How does anyone find hope in such an impossible situation? It's one thing to have a fire-spitting monster like Paricutín pop out of your backyard. It's another to have a long-dormant volcano—say, the jungled-over mountain you have admired through your kitchen window for decades—abruptly roar back to life. That's like watching your kindly old grandfather, dozing in his recliner, suddenly jump up, demonically possessed. And that's exactly what happened in 1995 to the 12,000 residents of Montserrat, the "Emerald Isle," a green dot of a place only six miles wide by eleven long, in the volcanic island arc of the Lesser Antilles.

A quick history. During July 1995, for the first time in four centuries, a slender column of smoke and steam began issuing from Soufriere Hills, the cluster of 3,000-foot-tall peaks that form the highest point on Montserrat. By early August, a few more vents opened on one of the summits. Earthquakes shook the flanks of the volcano and the southern, more lush and fertile part of the island. On a map, Montserrat is roughly the shape of a pear, and the mountain that islanders were just beginning to realize was a volcano smoldered in the middle of the fat part. Just three miles to the west lay the coastal city of Plymouth, the capital and only town of any size.

On August 21, accompanied by a series of artillery booms, the first large eruption from Soufriere Hills blanketed Plymouth in an ash cloud and caused darkness for fifteen minutes. The ash muffled the shape of Plymouth's high-peaked and gingerbread-trimmed colonial buildings. It piled up in bedroom corners and kitchen cabinets and seeped into the carburetors of motorbikes and rattletrap Toyotas, into the computers in the banks and Commonwealth offices.

By September, scientists who had flown in from the West Indies Volcano Observatory in Trinidad had determined that a crater had formed atop Chances Peak and that a dome was swelling up inside it—a potentially dangerous development. Sailing by on his second voyage in 1493, Columbus had been so struck by the craggy terrain of the island that he named it after the serrated mountains that loomed over the Monastery of Montserrat in Spain. The steepness of those mountain flanks, plus the island's size, only thirty-nine square miles, made the situation doubly dangerous. So far, Soufriere Hills had erupted with just a tiny fraction of the power of Mount St. Helens, but even if the violence increased only slightly, where were people supposed to run?

In October, boiling mudflows raced down the southwest side of the mountain, exacerbated by heavy rains. A month later, incandescent lava was visible on the peak. Volcanologists urged the government to evacuate Plymouth, and a medical school that catered to U.S. students, the island's largest employer, relocated to Saint Martin. The volcano grew wilder and wilder, letting loose pyroclastic flows that roared downhill in this direction and that, frying everything in their paths.

Finally those paths went through Plymouth. Avalanches of searing gas and fractured rocks swept over the downtown and the cruise ship pier and out to sea, hissing and losing momentum in the blue-green water. From the air, scientists could see how the flows had pushed out the shoreline by ten, twenty, thirty feet, building the island incrementally while at the same time destroying it. Had Plymouth not been evacuated, just about everyone crowding up into the northern third of the island, who knows how many might have died?

Many Montserratans wondered if they weren't dying anyway as their spirits shriveled month by month in the drier, far less beautiful Safe Zone that was protected from all but the most catastrophic of eruptions by a wall of steep hills, which were themselves once formed by volcanoes.

Two years later, more than half the island's residents had become refugees. Some families coped by moving in with relatives in the north. Others crammed themselves into hastily arranged church shelters stuffed with cots, the pews piled up in corners. Sometimes squalling babies and confused old men and women were separated only by bedsheets hung from wires. Others set up house or business inside giant steel ship containers that reeked of motor oil and turned into sun-baked ovens by 10 A.M.

Thousands more had fled to nearby Antigua, Guadeloupe, or Martinique, or jetted off to the United States or their motherland, England, where they could only dream of sunshine and papayas and mangoes.

There are easier places to travel to than an active volcano; the closer you get, the more things tend to fall apart. I came to understand this intimately when I set out for Montserrat a few years after the eruptions had started. On the Friday before the start of our CSU Thanksgiving week vacation, I got up well before dawn and peeled back the bedcovers to say good-bye to our miniature dachshunds, Marmot and Weasel. The guys had spent the night smushed against us, as usual, and they felt as warm to my touch as fresh-baked loaves of bread. They sighed as I rubbed their stomachs. In the kitchen, while coffee brewed, I hugged SueEllen and assured her for about the tenth time that I wouldn't be sneaking into any volcano danger zones. To this she quickly replied, "You mean other than the island itself?"

"You're more awake than you look," I said.

"I sure am."

None of that cowboy stuff for me, I promised. But of course she knew better. I read pretty widely, but SueEllen inhales books, and merely by looking over my shoulder, so to speak, she had absorbed almost as much knowledge about volcanoes as I had. Plus, she had been watching me pack and repack, my excitement obvious. She also knew I took more risks when I traveled alone. Nevertheless, she told me she trusted my judgment. It was the right lie at the right time.

Marmot and Weasel appeared at our feet, stretching and yawning, so I let them out. Coffee in hand, breathing the last cold air I'd get for ten days, I followed them into the backyard and looked at the dark hills to the west. Our beautiful and quiet valley lies tucked between some of the first foothills that rise up from the Great Plains. More and more often, this crumpled geography had been prompting me to roam through realms of deep time.

Right now, for instance. While SueEllen joined me with her tea and the guys trotted around, sniffing at everything as though it were the first day of their lives, I looked down at the sandstone slabs under our picnic table. They had probably once lain inside one of the Sahara-like dunes that covered parts of Colorado when Pangaea was breaking up more than 200 million years ago. That was at least 100 million years before dinosaurs called iguanodons may have lumbered across our yard.

Suddenly I had a vision of SueEllen and the doggies and myself on a global road trip. We were standing close together on the raft of the North American tectonic plate as it tore off from Pangaea, heading west. I imagined us cruising over the surface of the earth in fast-forward (the way you can simulate that on computers in natural history museums), and SueEllen's hair and Marmot's and Weasel's absurdly long ears were blowing back in the breeze. We were like Maurice and Katia Krafft in their titanium boat, minus the broiling lava.

It was true that SueEllen and I had become fellow travelers on both intellectual and physical journeys, reading and writing about places we visited, their ecology and history and quirky characters. But, God, what I dreamer I had turned into over the years. It was good that I didn't stay long at Rensselaer Polytechnic Institute, the engineering college I went to out of high school, back in my math nerd days. I saw now that I'd been destined all along to dream and write.

When I finally kissed SueEllen good-bye, she said, "Have fun and be sure to keep those planes up in the air!" I drove through the still-dark valley, my headlights sweeping over a mule deer standing frozen by the side of the road. I told myself that it probably posed more danger to me than closely watched Soufriere Hills. In truth, though, despite my habit of logging on to the weekly e-reports from Montserrat's volcano observatory, I didn't know what to expect. I'd been to the Caribbean once, but I'd barely heard of Montserrat before the eruptions started. Besides, photographs of some of the volcanic landscapes I'd hiked over so far—Kilauea, Etna, Parícutin—had not come close to conveying the feeling of actually being there. Even a National Geographic video hadn't prepare me for the overwhelming experience of getting out of the car on Johnston Ridge at Mount St. Helens and getting my first view of the blast zone. I stood almost six miles from the summit of the great broken mountain and took in the sight of a million flattened trees lying in the same direction—an entire forest that in seconds had been made to resemble the fur of a gigantic animal. I felt the power of that eruption as never before.

So I didn't know what I would find on Montserrat, this faraway speck in the sea that could change by the hour or the minute. For me, however, uncertainty usually equaled excitement. When I rolled onto I-25 south, I stomped on the gas.

Changing planes all the way, I flew DIA to Miami, to Puerto Rico, to Antigua's VC Bird International Airport. Under ordinary circumstances, I would then board one of the island-hopping specials that Antigua-based LIAT Airlines had operated over the years throughout the Lesser Antilles. Antigua to Montserrat, my guidebook told me, was a puddle jump of only fifteen minutes. But that was only provided you had a place to land. Montserrat could no longer offer that. Soufriere Hills had wiped out its only airport.

I didn't understand exactly how that could happen, but I had plenty of time to think about it. The ferry service to Montserrat that the British Government had recently funded would not leave Antigua's capital of St. John's until late Saturday afternoon. Planning for this, I had booked myself into one of the cheaper nearby beach hotels.

A bit too cheap, I soon discovered. My room was full of mosquitoes and greasy air that an overhead fan did nothing to relieve. The only solution for the bugs was to slather myself with DEET, but then when I sank back on the sheets, I stuck. Soon I was sweating, too. Lying in the dark, already missing SueEllen and the dogs and the crisp Colorado air, I wondered if this trip was going to be worth it. The mosquitoes hovered inches over my skin, afraid to land but furiously discussing the situation among themselves. They whined deep into the night.

I woke, mashed into the bed, to the pounding of the housekeeper. When I told her I wasn't ready, she just laughed, then sauntered away, her sandals slapping concrete. After showering, I opened the door to daylight and a mild sea breeze. The world had gotten ten times better.

Over breakfast in the patio restaurant-bar that overlooked the beach, I struck up a conversation with a slim, tired-looking man with a British accent. Great luck! He was an insurance adjuster who said he'd been going back and forth to Montserrat for weeks. Dozens and dozens of cinder-block houses, corrugated tin-roofed huts, and shops had been bashed to pieces by the volcano's pyroclastic flows or been flattened or buried under ash. Many others sat unharmed but abandoned on parts of the island too dangerous to visit even briefly. Thus, he explained, home owners and business people had to fish around for videotapes or old photographs to help prove the value of their property. It was slow going. He was much more accustomed to the quick knock-out punch of hurricanes.

"Never seen anything like it," he said about the selective devastation of Soufriere Hills. He shrugged over his tea. "And the volcano looks like it will be in business for a long time."

Nearby, a smiling woman in a sundress had laid out a gift shop of sorts on a stone wall. She caught my eye and called out, "Hey, there. Now don't you be afraid to come look!" I wandered over in the already-hot sun, bought a T-shirt full of bright fish for my niece Léa, then asked if she'd ever seen the volcano smoking across the water. My map told me it was about thirty miles away. No, she said, but when the wind was right, or wrong, Antigua sometimes caught the faint rain of its ashes. I asked what she thought of the Montserratans who had refused to leave. She gave a kind of shiver. When I told her I was about to ferry over there myself, she just shook her head.

We puttered away from Antigua on the *Admiral Bay*. There were about thirty passengers, and I may have been the only one who was not a returning Montserratan, at least to judge by the conversations around me. The ferry was small, and it seemed even smaller when I looked back into the receding harbor of St. John's, where a blazing white cruise ship the size of an apartment building was docked. No, make that the size of a city, with a floating population to match. At lunchtime, over a plate of shrimp rotis at a rooftop restaurant in the old downtown, I had watched the cruise-hordes pour down the gangplank and beeline for the dockside casino and cluster of nearby restaurants serving tourist specials. Almost nobody from the ship ventured more than two blocks into town.

It was clear that the development rimming the harbor, unimaginatively called Heritage Quay, was designed so that you'd never have to wander through an actual neighborhood or talk to a West Indian who didn't have a tray in his hand. That could turn tricky. In light of the colonial history of the island, the usual New World story of sugarcane and slaves, I thought the Disney-inspired name of the development evoked a darker "heritage" than was ever intended. Still, a lot of money was obviously pouring in, and at least some of it was going to locals via jobs. This made me wonder what the Montserratans were doing to get by now that their tourist business had collapsed.

In glorious sunshine and a mild headwind, the ferry ploughed through aquamarine water. But soon the sun fuzzed over, then blinked out behind clouds boiling up from the west. The wind rose, the sea darkened and heaved. Flecks of foam shot by the windows, and in no time we were burbling through leaden waves that swelled to twice the height of the boat. The engine seemed to be straining. Visibility dropped to a few hundred yards.

Babies and toddlers began to cry, and their mothers didn't look too happy, either. I wasn't thrilled myself. I knew that this squall had nothing to do with Soufriere Hills—it was simply fast-changing sea weather—but it nevertheless evoked a vague sense of dread. And I remembered something that a ranger at New Mexico's Capulin Volcano National Monument had told me back when I was researching my kids' book. Sometimes, when winds gusted in from the Sangre de Cristo Mountains or dark clouds began to clot above the extinct cinder cone, a worried-looking boy or girl might approach and ask, "Does this mean the volcano's about to explode?"

The sea-wind picked up. Several times we wobbled up a long swell, then shot off into thin air. Once we whomped so hard into the bottom of a trough that I thought the keel might crack. The ride was supposed to take an hour. More than two hours passed before I got my first glimpse of Montserrat through needles of rain. A distant gray rock rose out of a gray sea and disappeared into a gray cap of clouds. We were going to dock *there?*

But then the rain stopped as quickly as it had started, and we slipped into a steep-walled cove I had not seen coming. It was almost dark now; I had forgotten how quickly evening falls in the Caribbean, and the clouds made it happen even faster. I had no idea what part of the island we were on. We eased up to a concrete pier that looked brand new but big enough to accommodate at most two *Admiral Bays* at a time. As the crew tied up, I looked around the cabin. Ten or twelve passengers were hunched over seasickness bags.

I'm happy to say that I wasn't one of them, but I did totter uphill from the dock, trying to find my legs and silently thanking the boat builders and crew and whatever sea gods had spared us. Soon I caught up with an elderly couple who were dragging between them a hard-sided suitcase. It was like one of those behemoths my dad had in the '50s. The man wore a suit and tie and the woman a church dress and wide hat. I offered to take over for her, but she shook her head. She was friendly, though, and told me that they'd fled to England about a year ago. She'd had it with standing in her ash-laden Montserattan backyard, the bougainvilleas shrouded gray until rain washed them green again, and worrying about the columns of new ash that surged miles into the sky.

She looked at me over her glasses and said, "And that was just the smokin' stage, you understand. Only the Lord knew if it would really blow, and He wasn't tellin'."

Now they were back with food and clothes for her sister's grandkids. Plus, she admitted, she missed this place, even with its misbehaving mountain. England was gray, too, although for different reasons. Gray and too cold for her tropical bones.

Finally, she let me take her side of the suitcase. The thing practically yanked my arm from its socket. What did these grandkids eat, I wondered—rocks? Or maybe she'd stuffed it with armor and steel helmets for the whole family.

Customs was a hammered-together hut that looked like it had been finished ten minutes ago. Somewhere a generator thrummed, pushing out anemic yellow light. I had read that vacationers once accounted for about a quarter of the island's GNP, and I hoped the tourist "infrastructure" had not been whittled down to just this.

The lines moved slowly. When I finally reached the front, a sullen young woman in a blue uniform took my passport. She turned it this way and that, lingering over every entry: Thailand, Kenya, Mexico. This of course was recreational reading on her part since she couldn't possibly care where any of us had come from. Montserrat had peaceable relations with every place on earth except maybe its own volcano. Finally, in classic border-cop fashion, she stamped the passport hard and jerked a thumb over her shoulder. The island had its newest official visitor.

Outside, a pack of waiting relatives swept up the elderly couple and helped them into the cab of a pickup. The younger ones hopped into the bed, and then the truck took off. I was milling around with some of the other arrivals when the generator shut down. In the suddenly quiet darkness, there were no other lights, and thanks to the clouds, no stars. The bustle of Antigua felt a thousand miles away.

Three weeks earlier, searching the Web, I had found a place to stay: Erindell Guest House. Then I confirmed the reservation on the phone with a live wire named Shirley Spycalla, who spoke in a crisp British accent tinged with island rhythms and who promised to have a ride waiting for me at the dock. But now, none of the cars or trucks seemed to be labeled with Erindell or anything else. A moment later, a tall, burly guy was standing in front of me, jingling keys.

"You the guy from Colorado?" He had the courtesy to make this sound like a question. "Joe-Philippe," he said, shaking my hand. He led me to a minibus. When we got going, I looked at his dashboard clock and calculated I'd been traveling for more than thirty-six hours.

I had also been thinking about how stories seem to ripple out from living volcanos. Like seismic waves, they tremble away from the source to meet you sometimes long before you arrive. They alter your expectations, piling on one point of view after another, each new perspective throwing light on one or several or all of the ones that had come before. The insurance guy I met over breakfast, the T-shirt lady, the nice old couple, the customs agent who moved with the speed of continental drift—spending time with them was like riffling through a book of Hokusai's Fuji prints.

And that remained a pattern during my next few days on the island, as I dropped in on people pretty much at random or as circumstances allowed, which was close to the same thing. Everybody I talked to, every patch of island I stood on or hiked through, offered a different take on Soufriere Hills. Everybody had a View, or Views, on the subject. And eventually I developed a few surprising ones of my own.

When the minibus crunched into Erindell's driveway, a woman in a flower-print smock strolled out and said, "You must be John. Welcome!" This was Shirley Spycalla.

"But I must tell you," she quickly added, "we are overbooked for your first two nights—all three rooms. It happens, especially when you are the only game in town. Actually, the only game in the country."

"Oh," was all I could think to say. I flashed back to the small tent and summer-weight sleeping bag I had planned to bring and then rejected. "Go light" was one of my travel mantras, sometimes to a fault.

But there was no problem, Shirley went on. She explained that later tonight she would walk me over to their neighbors' place, and they'd put me in a spare bedroom set up for these occasions. It was quite nice, plus a way to spread around the visitor money.

She smiled broadly. "But first things first. You must be starving. How about some goatwater stew?"

Inside, a sturdy-looking guy in shorts and a T-shirt got up from watching football. "Lou," he said warmly. "The husband." He was clearly from the U.S., to judge by the way he talked. He led me to a swivel stool in the kitchen part of a big, airy room with cinder-block walls broken up by sliding glass panels. Obviously their home.

Lou handed me an Amstel and tilted an open bag of chips my way. He had the easy manner of a veteran bartender. He also had an old-time football player's nose and a knobby pair of knees with some zipper-like scars. It turned out he'd played a bit for the Green Bay Packers, just before the Lombardi glory years. We talked awhile, then he wandered back to the TV, which was hooked to a satellite dish. I looked around. Everything seemed so comfortable, so normal. It was hard to believe that we were sitting on a living volcano.

Shirley chopped and stirred, sipped tea, and chattered away. Goatwater stew was an island specialty, she told me: goat meat simmered with cloves and rum. Another was mountain chicken, which meant the really big frogs that hopped around out in the jungle. Provided they had not already been cooked by the volcano, ha-ha.

She had lived here—"on island" is the way she said it—for twenty-seven years, and was born in Trinidad, at the bottom of the island arc. She'd lived in Grenada during her first marriage and had relatives scattered in the Caribbean, the United States, and Asia, including a brother who designed skyscrapers in Indonesia.

In my notebook I wrote, "Sharp woman—mass of black curls, olive skin, looks/talks likes she's from everywhere, a *masala* of cultures."

How long had she and Lou run Erindell? She sighed. "Only since the volcano kicked us out of the bar business."

We were in the Safe Zone here. But only a few miles south of us stood the ruins of Shirley and Lou's beach-front bar, the

Last Call. Nowadays, Shirley said, it looked onto a beach piled helter-skelter with blasted palm tree trunks and burned rafters that the sea had pushed north from the ruins of Plymouth.

"Oh, that place used to be *so* much fun," she exclaimed, looking suddenly over at Lou as though she wanted to dance. "Plants hanging all over. Everybody dropping by for sandwiches and a beer, tourists and islanders both, the steel drums going. Many times at sunset we'd just kick back and stare out over the water, waiting for the green flash."

Most mornings, Lou reported for work at the nearby golf course. "I managed the place," he said, appearing at my side with a fresh Amstel. "Every day the same thing. Twenty minutes of paperwork, cruise around on the cart to see if the golfers were happy, which *of course* they were, then eat and play golf." He shook his head and grinned. "Jeez, it was the best job I ever had!"

Those with the best jobs now, Shirley added with an edge in her voice, were the engineer and aide worker disaster junkies who'd been helicoptering in and out from Antigua for two years. (The copter was a mode of transport that I'd rejected as too expensive for my budget.) The workers included bridge builders, surveyors, heavy-equipment operators, and a recent guest whose specialty was designing concrete plants in countries plagued by the world's various kinds of revolutions: political coups, floods, typhoons, volcanoes. But Shirley admitted that these soldiers of misfortune did help Erindell stay in business.

The stew was ready. She plunked a bowl in front of me and poured herself more tea. She took a sip and sat down across the breakfast bar. After eyeing me for a while, she leaned my way.

"Here it comes," Lou said wearily. He got up and went back to the TV.

Shirley ignored him. "Geologists can talk," she started softly. "And I'm sure they're right about their science. But would you like to know why our beautiful island has really been suffering so much?"

I nodded, my mouth full of goat meat.

"The volcano is *getting even.*"

She had a theory, which she claimed was shared by many an islander. A couple years before Soufriere Hills woke up, visiting anthropologists digging near the airport unearthed thousand-year-old Arawak remains. They'd been buried in ancient ashfall and were therefore very well preserved. "An interesting discovery," Shirley said. "All well and good."

Pause.

"But then they took the remains off-island to the States somewhere, to analyze them. And they didn't ask permission of a *damn soul!*"

Really big pause as she ran her hand through her hair.

"Let me tell you, *God is not asleep!* And wouldn't you know, it wasn't long before our volcano rumbled to life. I suspect that it may not calm down until those remains are returned." She slapped the counter. "When you spit up in the air, it's gonna come back down!"

And so the earth struck back. The volcano spewed out ash and rocks to refill the holes that had been torn in the island and in the culture. This struck me as a modern version of an old story that went back at least to the Greeks. It was also what scholar Dorothy Vitaliano called geomythology, in this case, perhaps, Antigone with a volcanological twist: the dead as refugees, making more refugees.

Shirley turned out to be right: this would be the story I most frequently heard during my island stay. Some Montserratans told me their version of it with a twinkle in their eye, others by angrily shaking a finger at my nose, as though daring me to doubt them. But the message was always the same. A deal had been struck to tear the dead from their homeland, and nobody who mattered, including the dead themselves, had been consulted. The eruptions were cosmic payback.

On Sunday morning, my first full day "on-island," I went for a drive with the couple who had put me up in their spare bedroom, Rob and Beryl Chadwick. Up and down we zoomed in their little Toyota, zigzag crazy everywhere on thin, ribbony roads. We passed simple cinder-block homes that you might see in south Florida, and huts on stilts with rusty tin roofs. Rob drove with Beryl beside him while I sat in back. For a couple of minutes, I tried to write in my notebook. Ha! It was kindergarten scrawl. Trees and bushes whizzed by, unbelievably green, the island all curves and sunshine, and the only clouds anywhere formed the thick wool cap of the volcano, which seemed to be hiding its true nature, or the violent part of its nature, anyway. So far, Soufriere Hills looked like an ordinary fireless mountain with a permanent rainstorm on top.

Rob and Beryl told me they had retired from jobs in England and come to Montserrat, they hoped permanently, not long before the eruptions started. Though their plans to buy were, of course, on hold, they had so far managed to stay by house-sitting. In fact, the home they occupied now was owned by friends who'd fled. Rob and Beryl's family back home thought they were insane to stay.

Not that Rob cared. With his pipe and safari shirt and polite reserve, he had struck me last night as very proper and British, not exactly a major candidate for Margaritaville. But then he'd cranked up some reggae on the tape player and leaned back in a wicker chair with a massive Scotch. Now, as he honked or waved at friends and neighbors, he and Beryl couldn't quit talking about how spectacular the island was, at least before the summer of 1995.

The volcano could be spectacular, too. During one afternoon's ashfall, Beryl told me, she couldn't even see her own outstretched hand. And if you jumped in your car and tried to race your way out of the sudden darkness, you'd better be careful. Seasonal rains turned ash-covered roads to goo and could slingshot you into a ravine.

Rob turned to her and sighed, "You know, our island is now just a pile of rubble."

"Yes, dear. But such beautiful rubble."

They were quiet for a while, then Rob said, "Let's take a look at the airport, shall we?" Pretty soon we'd driven most of the way up a long hill. Suddenly a chain-link fence appeared, bent and pried open in places, but still in good enough shape to stop a car. Rob cut the engine and turned to me. "Exclusion Zone. You go on ahead and check out the view. But don't drop down to the valley floor, eh? I don't want to have to ship your ashes to your wife. Beryl and I will have our lunch up top—it's one of our favorite places to picnic." I'd noticed that he usually walked arm in arm with Beryl, who had a bad hip.

I reached the top of the promontory, and the world dropped away. The road went on, S-curving down into a relatively flat valley several miles long and maybe one wide. It was bordered to my left by the sea with its lacy rim of surf, and to the right by the volcano, its 30- and 45-degree slopes scored with ravines that the locals called *ghauts*. The top was still hidden in clouds.

I peered through my binoculars. The squat stone buildings of an old sugar mill stood in the middle of the valley. Next to these, a rubble-strewn runway stretched into the distance: the infamous airport, defunct. I noticed to my surprise that it wasn't buried under any thick, Parícutin-like rivers of jagged rock. In fact, I didn't see lava anywhere. I wondered why the islanders couldn't just bulldoze the thing back into operation.

Then I put down the binoculars and took in the whole scene. Everything in front of me was like a black-and-white movie that Ted Turner hadn't quite finished colorizing. In fact, though, I suddenly realized, just the opposite had occurred: the pyroclastic avalanches and mudflows that had raced downslope had brush-stroked out miles of greenery, especially down the ghauts.

I had read about a volcano in Japan, Sakurajima, I think, that generated so many mud and debris flows that disaster officials had constructed vast concrete chutes on its lower slopes to contain and channel off the potential destruction. In this way, people still managed to live near the volcano. Apparently its eruptions were relatively small releases of internal pressure. Authorities were confident they'd have time to evacuate everyone if Sakurajima's behavior radically changed.

But Soufriere Hills was evidently much too strong-willed and wild for such polite and orderly accommodations, especially on an island that let you retreat only so far before you were standing in the sea. I looked again at the angle of the slopes and the lengthy death-trails of the pyroclastic flows, a couple of which had swept over the runway. Clearing it for landings and takeoffs would be easy. But how could you convince pilots and passengers that just walking to the plane on the tarmac wouldn't get them killed?

After a while, I noticed that somebody was standing a little ways off to my side. Not Rob, but a big chunky guy with a neatly trimmed beard, late thirties maybe, wearing a T-shirt, jeans, and sandals—standard island gear. He nodded, then gestured downhill, where a hundred yards or so below us an old, red fire truck sat abandoned in the grass.

"Oh, that so slop, Man," he said, shaking his head and coming closer. "They never move that truck, and now the volcano got it."

I checked it out through the binoculars, and suddenly it didn't look so old. But the finish was badly pocked, sandblasted with pebbles and ash. I didn't want to think what the engine looked like.

It reminded me of the gigantic 1991 eruption of Pinatubo volcano in the Philippines, which I had followed at the time, vaguely, through the newspapers and read about since then. The U.S. Air Force's Clark Air Base sat in the shadow of that un-volcanic-looking mountain (which had not erupted in 500 years) on terrain made flat enough for runways by ancient *lahars,* or mudflows. Only five days before Pinatubo spouted pyroclastic flows and enough ash to bury miles and miles of its surroundings up to a depth of 600 feet, scientists from the Philippine Institute of Volcanology and the USGS convinced 60,000 people living within a radius of twenty miles to evacuate. This included 14,500 U.S. military personnel. Literally flying the coop, as well, was a fortune in military jets, C-130 cargo planes, and other high-tech aircraft that even small amounts of ash would have destroyed, just as ash had wrecked the Allied planes near Vesuvius in 1944.

"Yeah," said my new Montserratan friend, looking with great disapproval at the fire truck, "so slop and all that kinda shit."

I asked what he was doing out here on a gorgeous Sunday. Waiting for a friend who'd hiked down past the airport to check on a bull, he said. Like a lot of residents who'd had to abandon subsistence farms on the southern half of the island, his friend had also had to leave animals behind. There was little room or grass for them in the much drier north. Cattle and goats had therefore become nomads, roaming the Exclusion Zone, sipping from scum-covered swimming pools, pushing into living rooms carpeted with ash.

I wondered about the risks of going after them. I knew from listening to KBZT-Montserrat, the island's only radio station, that the volcano had settled into a relatively quiet phase. But who could know when that would end? If the bulging dome or one of the big upper walls were suddenly to give way, how much time— and room to run—would you have? What if a glowing cloud came searing down at you out of the other clouds?

"What if that happened?" I asked.

He cut me a look that said he knew I was a fool but he'd let it slide. "The volcano come down, everybody dead." In fact, it had come down one day this past summer, he said. By late June, in an off-limits area on the western slope of the volcano, a number of dispossessed farmers had taken to sneaking back home for several hours at a stretch to work their fields. This gave them a semblance of normalcy. It also beat playing dominoes and eating government-rationed tinned vegetables in a stifling community hall shelter. But suddenly there came an explosion, then a long rumble. A pyroclastic flow had burst out of Chances Peak, the highest point on Soufriere Hills. A surge of hot gases and flying rocks swept down. Nineteen people were killed.

He spoke so gently, this island man, even about nature's violence. He unwrapped his sentences a syllable at a time. For a while we simply stood together in silence. Then he began to tell me about himself, his wife and kids and their home in Plymouth with its sloped rows of banana stalks, sweet potatoes, dasheen, and cassava. They had a backyard bush they loved, called the Pride of Barbados, whose yellow flowers attracted butterflies that his youngest boy liked to chase in wobbly circles, as though he were a butterfly himself. Soufriere, the most common species was called sulfur butterfly.

"House, job, the whole damn town, all gone now . . ." Gone also a lively sense of community, calypso bands pounding away under the big twisted tree on Plymouth's town square, the musicians playing as much for the locals as for the cruise ship crowds.

"You were born here?"

"Yeah. And got some Red in me. My forefather's fathers fathers fathers and somethin' like that." Except the way he said it was: *faddahs.*

"Red" meant the Irish indentured servants who in 1632 escaped the British on nearby St. Kitts. Soon they were clearing Montserrat's jungle and planting cane, then shipping in West African slaves to do the dirty work. The island's original inhabitants, the Arawak Indians, had pretty much died out by the early eighteenth century. This meant that my new acquaintance went about as far back on the island as anybody.

I told him he seemed amazingly even-tempered, considering how much he'd lost and whatever it was the future held.

He shrugged and scratched his beard. "Got my health. Got my wife and kids."

We spotted his friend in the distance now, moving with one of those slow-motion, loose-limbed gaits you tend to see in equatorial places. I had once concocted a name for this, the Tropical Crawl, and had worked on perfecting my own version of it when I'd lived in Florida after college. But the only volcanoes in Florida had been dead for tens of millions of years, then worn down by erosion and paved over by a thickening plate of coral.

Mr. Tropical Crawl looked so laid back, you'd think the volcano didn't even exist. Or maybe he realized that Chances Peak was much too real, that it loomed far too high and dangerously over everything in his life, so he was turning every casual swing of his arm into a message:

You hold off now.

And keep your CHANCES to yourself.

It wasn't quite noon, but the sun was already sledgehammering my brain. I'd left my hat in the Toyota. A breeze crackled through an acacia tree behind me and sent some yellow butterflies tumbling past. The man from Plymouth folded his arms and said, "You know, the volcano be all over one day. Lots of tourists again." I wanted badly to believe this. I'd heard from Shirley that after months of waffling, the government had agreed to pay airfares for whoever wanted to resettle in England, and that thousands of refugees had taken them up on it. The more we talked, though, the more I suspected that the man from Plymouth would never be one of them.

Besides, he explained, turning to me, some good had come out of all this, something few people ever get to see. He smiled sweetly. Whenever he felt like it, he could walk his three boys up here or to some other places and show them the island's expanding shoreline, the ever-growing mountain. It was proof of God's power, the Old Testament come back to life.

"You know, the Lord He made this world in seven days. On this mountain He makin' it again."

When I squeezed back through the chain-link fence to rejoin Rob and Beryl, I realized that I'd already broken my promise to SueEllen. And gee, it took me only a day. But then, standing way the hell up on a hill hardly seemed like a risk.

Rob announced that a beach visit was now in order. Beryl needed to collect more driftwood for the tropical fish mobiles that she sanded and painted at home, then gave to kids in the shelters. At breakfast I had been delighted to discover her sunroom clattering faintly with schools of fish hanging from invisible monofilament: goofy eels and smiling rock beauties, triggerfish with blood-red lips and flirting eyes and outrageous slashes of color. They seesawed and turned in the morning breeze, making me feel as if I were lounging at the bottom of the sea.

The driftwood beach lay a few miles into the Exclusion Zone on the southwest part of the island, a few miles south of Lou and Shirley's place. As we approached the Zone, we came to a shady bend in the road and coasted to a stop. Just ahead, a policewoman leaned against a zebra barrier.

She approached us smiling, clipboard in hand, her giant black leather belt creaking with equipment: mace, baton, walkie-talkie. She had great cornrows. Rob leaned out the window and gave her his name and phone number. She scribbled and nodded, checked our plates, looked at Rob hard. "One hour," she said, and walked off to drag back the barrier.

"Called ahead this morning," he told me as we edged through. "They'll let you in for a while. At your own risk of course." Meaning: if you get incinerated, don't blame us.

But I noticed the barrier didn't seem to exist at all for pedestrians. They sauntered in and out on paths worn through the undergrowth beside the road. Or they moved past the guard with a grin and a nod. Women lugging babies. Guys with six-packs or bunches of bananas slung over their shoulders. Kids dribbling a soccer ball.

A hundred yards in, we approached Ram's grocery store. "Biggest and best on the island," Beryl said with a bit of pride. But that was not saying much. The open-air shops I'd seen so far had carried only a few brands of canned goods stacked into sad little pyramids. When I had popped into one for a bottled water, I noticed that even the geckos eyeing me from the countertop looked dispirited, half dead from heatstroke or boredom.

Last night, Shirley had hinted that the scientist or bureaucrat who determined where the Exclusion Zone started had apparently held some longtime grudge against the owner of Ram's. That's why the store now sat on the *wrong side* of the line. A brilliant pettiness. The customers didn't seem to care. Clumps of women lounged on the market's front steps, sipping Cokes and fanning themselves, shifting babies from arm to arm. They were laughing and yakking away as though it were just another day in paradise. And in a way I suppose it was—a Sunday, too.

I think I was starting to understand their nonchalance. Do any of us know precisely where life's major danger zones begin and end? *Oh, I see, I'm safe right here. But over THERE?!! That's where earthquakes and cancers grow, that's where God reaches down to flick your car into a ravine.*

I recalled the fast walk I'd taken early in the morning on a jungle path near Rob and Beryl's place. It felt great to stretch my legs in the green shadows, and soon I'd plunged off-trail. Crashing and hauling myself up a slope, I grabbed for vines and roots while my boots slid in red mud, caught, slid again. I stopped finally to catch my breath.

Something made me turn my head to the right, very slowly. Maybe three feet from my shoulder, sticking straight out from the slope, was a snake. It hung unmoving in the air, intent as a dagger. Its slender black and yellow head and its spooky yellow eyes shone in the speckled light. I couldn't ID it, but thank God I knew that Montserrat had no poisonous snakes. Still, it riveted my attention. So I edged away, the better, also, to admire its handsome markings from my own zone of safety.

Risk waits for you everywhere, all the time, I figure. So why stay home or in your hotel room? Over the years I've taken endless mild chances in the tropics: waded hip-deep in south Florida swamps, hiked rain forest trails in Thailand and Ecuador, wandered off from my brother-in-law's Land Cruiser into shoulder-high, lion-colored grass in Kenya's Masai Mara. Water moccasins, king cobras, and green mambas don't kid around, so I guess I've often put myself within biting range of real trouble, ground lightning.

And of course I loved it. I'd have flown off again anytime to Ecuador's Oriente, where a few years earlier, my friend and Colorado neighbor Steve Shulman and I hoisted packs over our heads and waded chest-deep into a muddy river behind our Indian guide, David. At midstream in a tangle of reeds, David stopped and called back, "Watch your step. Many bad snakes here."

Oh. Since I couldn't see a thing in the coffee-colored water, I just kept putting one foot in front of the other—*squish, squish*—more feeling than sound. I moved forward not so much in dread as in hyperawareness that danger can be the twin fang of the beautiful, a great way to make the nerve endings zing, which is beautiful in itself. Isn't this one reason why so many of us privileged First-Worlders jet off to wild and remote lands?

But what if you already live in one of these places and make your livelihood from the earth itself? Or what if genuine peril erupted in your backyard, as Soufriere Hills had? What do you do then, and not in just the first few days, when disrupting your daily rhythms costs little in time and energy and money, but six months later, two years later? I suppose if you haven't bailed out you adapt. You keep the ash masks handy and pray more often. Maybe you work on your Tropical Crawl. You throw the kid onto your back and have a Coke with your friends on the front steps of Ram's grocery store.

A few hundred yards past Ram's we left most of the people behind. We cruised through the husk of Salem, a few blocks of faded huts on stilts. Rob pointed out bare spots where houses had sat before they were trucked off to the Safe Zone after this little community, considered to be safe itself for the first year or so of the eruptions, became more threatened as the volcano grew unstable. Bougainvillea bloomed like mad, and here and there a door hung open, giving the place an eerie, what's-wrong-with-this-picture air.

We passed Arrow's first recording studio, then the Air Martin building where Sting and George Harrison used to cut their CDs. We got out to inspect the Vue Pointe Hotel, once the island's finest. Shortly after Plymouth had been evacuated and then destroyed, the hotel turned into a kind of capital-in-exile, full of makeshift shops—a travel agency, a bank, and so forth. No longer. Dusty, red-roofed hexagonal suites surrounded a swimming pool; six inches of gray muck dried in the deep end.

"Cows stay here now," Rob said.

The same went for the golf course that Lou used to manage. We bumped past slowly. The fairways were streaked with mudflows. Cows, which had sunk to their ankles on one of the putting greens, cropped unruly grass. It was ironic, really, to see wild nature reclaiming land that had itself once been "reclaimed," as the engineers and developers loved to say. Serves us right, I thought, for the impudence of our bulldozers. But the golf course also saddened me, it looked so forlorn, and I decided not to mention the cows to Lou.

The road soon swung out to the beach, then broke off where a little bridge once stood. The Belham River had washed it away, Rob said. *"This?"* I practically shouted, looking down at a mud-clogged trickle. Rob said that with little or no warning the stream could turn into a chute full of scalding muck from the mountain-top, a tsunami of geothermally heated mud. That's what took out the bridge. Rob turned the car around and cut the engine. He left the keys in the ignition. There was certainly nobody around to steal them.

We crunched around on the beach, which was bumpy with shells and dark volcanic sand. Chunks of airy pumice, rock that floats, lay everywhere. Beryl poked around for driftwood. She had many hobbies. One of the most impressive of these I'd seen late last night, when she showed me the scrapbooks she'd been compiling since 1995: a superb history of Montserrat during its time of the volcano. A series of aerial photos was especially striking.

First came a shot of Chances Peak with a small glowing dome. Another taken weeks later showed a bigger dome. The next caught the dome sprouting a pair of "plugs" of stiff lava, powered from pressure below, that looked remarkably like devil's horns. When Beryl mentioned that the horns were the height of five-story buildings, she threw the entire mountaintop into a new perspective for me. Several photos later the horns had disappeared, having crumbled like the dying lava coals they really were. Bit by bit, they had disintegrated into pyroclastic flows that seethed down long, twisting valleys. They were valleys similar to the one we stood in now, except that the Belham River Valley still shone bright green.

While Beryl stuck close to the car, Rob and I crossed a plank half sunk in the warm river muck. I followed the streambed up-valley with my eye and saw that it wriggled for a mile or two before disappearing into high, lush jungle. The jungle in turn disappeared into a wreath of clouds.

If we heard an eruption, I figured, we'd have two minutes to get back to the car and floor it. Rob's U-turn and the keys in the ignition made new sense. So did the hard hats I noticed in the Toyota's back window.

But all the same, I had to admit something to myself. I didn't feel any danger at all. The nearby beach, the valley, and the buttery Caribbean light were all so gorgeous that I *still* couldn't grasp the impossible fact of the volcano, its unreal power, the reach and speed of its potential strikes.

Rob pointed to a glass and concrete house sticking out of the high jungle. "Damn shame," he mumbled. It turned out that an elderly couple from the States had it built as their dream home. Sank all they had into it, then much more after it came in at twice the price they'd planned. They couldn't sell it these days, of course. And since they had nowhere else to go, they were up there even now, rattling around without electricity, with no hope of their utilities working anytime soon, if ever again.

Oh, those sad prisoners of paradise, growing old in candle-light and fear, despite all their years of careful planning.

I stared for a while at the glass wall that poked out of the jungle, and I willed myself to imagine a better life for them, in which they could revel in their view down one of the most beautiful valleys I'd ever seen. I imagined dusk settling around them, the shadows deepening in their living room as they decided to enjoy a sunset drink on their balcony. Then I saw the man uncorking some wine. I saw them settling into patio chairs, toasting their shared life, laughing. And maybe laughing at the mountain, too, daring it to burst open and let loose its deadly froth, daring it to overwhelm them with its immense freight of fire and darkness.

<hr>

"Come on in," called a voice from the open door of a tin-roofed shack as Rob and Beryl and I walked through sunny rows of cassava. We were on the final leg of our Sunday tour, a social call on their friend James Lee. If you used that name around the island, you'd probably get a blank look. But then somebody might say, "Oh, Mountain Man! Why didn't you *say* so?"

I stepped tentatively into the shack. Total darkness, and humidity that suggested hanging bats, dripping water, and stalactites. Soon, though, two large shadows began to materialize, a man and a woman pulling themselves into sitting positions on a bed. The bed filled half the shack. Just past it stood a wall of furniture, a couch piled onto another couch with two armchairs on top. Nice stuff, it seemed like, but beginning to molder. Near the foot of the bed a two-flame gas burner sat on a box. Above it hung a pink wind-up cuckoo clock, the only decoration in the place.

Introductions. A regal nod from the woman, James's wife, Annette. James leaned forward and shook my hand quite softly, but his grip was iron. I could see him well enough now to notice veins and muscles popping under his T-shirt. His manner and dusty leather face suggested somebody close to sixty. His body suggested somebody else.

When the volcano struck them, he had needed that body. He and Annette were living up on the south slope of Soufriere Hills, not far from a spectacular jungle waterfall, in what was probably the largest and most exquisitely located house on Montserrat. James had had it built out of volcanic rock, and its six-bedroom opulence was a testament to how far he'd come on the island.

"Born here dirt-poor like lotsa other folks," he told me now, speaking slowly. "Was a young man laying stone, when one day the boss man, an elderly white man, a contractor, he pulled me aside and said he liked the way I worked, the way my mind worked, too. He showed me things, took me around. After a while I was runnin' crews, then my own contractin' business. He was a good man."

And James was on his way to prosperity. The house he had built was perched on seventeen acres and offered a stunning view of other island mountains rising out of the water far away. Life was good, and nobody in the household worried very much when suddenly one day they noticed a bit of smoke spiraling up from the mountaintop. The smoke was followed by occasional earthquake tremors that made the tea in James's cup turn momentarily into a choppy little ocean. That was troubling, but nothing they couldn't live with.

But then in the middle of one night James was awakened by a world-deep rumble. It sounded like 500 jet planes zooming in. Zooming in but not leaving—that was the shake and roar of the thing.

"You can't imagine the sound," he whispered to me, his shoulders grazing Annette's on the bed. "You just can't."

And then the world went crazy. It began to rain ash and steaming cinders and stones, then rocks as big as suitcases. A car-sized boulder whumped nearby. The electricity snapped off. Down crashed parts of the roof. James sprinted through the dark house to the splintered wreckage of his eighty-year-old mother's room. He waded in, shoving aside beams and clawing through rocks and roof tiles until he got to her. From there he raced off to his grown daughter's room. He worked so furiously, he didn't realize until he'd gotten everyone out that nails had run right through his feet.

Everyone eventually recovered.

But not the waterfall. It doesn't even exist anymore, a large mutation in the geologic evolution of the island. The house doesn't really exist, either. They've had to leave it. It's too close to the volcano, and James wasn't crazy enough to risk going back to rebuild it. He prided himself on being a reasonable and adaptable man. In fact, he got by now by moving houses instead of constructing them, and he told me that no matter where he "drops one," a family or maybe two is living in it within an hour. They may or may not be the owners. In more ways than one, the island keeps moving.

For now, he and Annette were staying put. The walls of their old place still stood, James explained, his hands suddenly moving fast as he and Rob, a skilled plumber, began to talk about how to make it livable again, if the volcano ever let them.

Annette crossed her arms and looked as though she'd heard this conversation many times. She turned to Beryl and me. "All I know is, I'm not moving anywhere new until he puts in at least one room, and that's the bathroom."

I gathered there was no rush. The tin roof of the shack kept out rain; Annette made bread from the cassava she grew, just as the original Arawaks had; and their two boys were studying at universities in England. James looked at me and said, "Had nothin', then was King of the Mountain. Had lotsa nice things, and can have 'em again if I think that's important." He leaned forward in the gloom, the bed creaking, and tapped my shoulder. "I think you know what I mean."

After we left, Rob told me people thought James was a natural for political office. Mountain Man, M.P.! And I could see it, his common touch, that calm self-assurance and strength. Me, I was ready to follow him anytime through a night of burning cinders.

Over the next few days, I kept running into him. He would drive by smiling, calling out one of the island's odd, one-word greetings: "Okaaay." Or he'd wave me over with a pony beer and insist on giving me a ride. The more we talked, the more reflective he turned. He explained how he and his neighbors could live with the somber fact of the volcano because there's no way we can control nature, which after all has created us. It's not like you've lost your house through carelessness or gambling and then have to walk by it every day and see somebody else living there. That would just kill you. Nope, nature gives and nature takes, and that's how it is. And maybe Montserrat could be a model for people around the world, an example of accepting with grace whatever trouble life dishes out.

One afternoon I was reading in the abandoned home that served as the Montserrat library when James strolled in to meet Annette, who was grazing the shelves for fat novels. "Gettin' your volcano story?" he asked as I hunched over a book about the sacred mountains of the world. I said I was.

"You look worried, though. Don't you know you shouldn't let things get to you?" He put a hand on my shoulder. "Somebody's botherin' you, somebody at work or somethin', here's a trick. Write their name down on a slip of paper, then put it in your shoe. All day long, every step you take, you're steppin' on *them*. This works. It puts you back on top. Remember, no matter what, you gotta stay on top."

That night, over dinner once again at Erindell, I heard from Shirley and Lou about another, earlier trial sent by nature. In 1989, Hurricane Hugo scored a direct hit on all of their lives. As the tremendous winds approached, Shirley remembered, the tide began to surge and palm trees started to whip around. And then a songwriter and musician, a local half-crazy guy everybody called Swordfish, went down to the shore and tried to *drum* the storm off course. It was a well-meaning if very unscientific idea, but when the winds began to tear palm fronds from their trunks, Swordfish picked up his bongos and ran. On his way home his entire house flew past him on the road.

Shirley and Lou, meanwhile, had hunkered down in a basement apartment. The last thing Shirley saw before the TV went dead was a radar image of Hugo's monster eye bearing down on a speck in the sea. *That speck is us!* she thought. Then Hugo landed. Sodden, 150-mph-winds ripped turf from hillsides, flung rooftops far out to sea, and left most Montserratans temporarily homeless.

As the insurance adjuster in Antigua had pointed out to me, even the worst hurricane passes quickly, letting victims focus their energies on rebuilding. But a simmering volcano can bear down all the time. And so Soufriere Hills, which began to erupt at just about the time when Montserrat felt it had fully recovered from Hugo, created very different kinds of tensions.

"Have you noticed"—Shirley stopped in the middle of chopping some vegetables—"when somebody in the government leaves or is let go these days, it's usually a Montserratan. And then *two* Brits take his place. They're in every corner of the government now, watching."

She took a deep breath, as though she could sniff conspiracy on the trade winds. "The old Empire is shrinking—look at Hong Kong—and they've got to put their people somewhere, so they put them here, pushing islanders out of jobs. But God knows where they get some of them."

Then she told me about the new police commissioner. In the middle of the night recently, he woke up to an ominous rumbling. He sprinted outside in his pajamas, yelling about the volcano, the Big One coming at last. When he stopped yelling, he heard only the electric pinging of tree frogs, the incessant and beautiful chorus of the Montserrat dark. It turned out the rumble had come from the ice maker in his refrigerator.

Shirley sighed. "Whatever backwater they'd shipped him in from had obviously never seen such comforts."

Shirley brimmed with what islanders called "Montserrat smarts." She seemed to know at least a little bit about an astonishing variety of people: housewives, Samosa vendors, bank clerks who gave her the real deal on the island's now-chaotic finances, a man named Rock who had somehow managed to keep hoeing his field up on the volcano without getting killed. She told me about the looters who had motorboated over from Guadaloupe— three fools who sneaked into the ruins of Plymouth only to have their getaway boat run out of gas as they pulled away with their booty. Drifting helplessly toward wave-smashed cliffs, they had to radio the police for help. Crime solved!

On this evening, though, she seemed to be working her way deep into conspiracy theory. Of course I was egging her on, even if Lou seemed to want nothing to do with it. How many times had he heard this before?

With their threat of physical destruction, erupting volcanoes obviously raised everyone's anxiety. But I was beginning to see how they might also exacerbate preexisting cultural tensions. In the Valley of Mexico, some of Moctezuma's high priests, who had heard rumors of metal-clad warriors marching their way, probably suspected that terrible things would soon follow. Perhaps they then projected their fears onto a coincidentally erupting El Popo.

Here on formerly laid-back Montserrat, the volcano had stirred up resentments of a government that had not yet shed all of its colonial trappings, a government that was now forced by the volcano to act with totalitarian abruptness, closing banks and gas stations and pushing people from their homes. Some of these feelings were given voice in a scrappy weekly newpaper, the *Montserrat Reporter*. A typical entry in a column called "Jus wonderin" read: "Jus wonderin whether the calm of this week was a result of Gov. Abbot's call for law and order or just plain despair." I later looked up that call and a few other proclamations from "the Gov." He invariably sounded like a parent scolding the kids.

Shirley segued smoothly into her next theory. There was a land grab afoot. With real estate prices down to zilch, the Brits and others were gluing up the bureaucracy, blocking access to insurance monies, and waiting for home owners to give up and sell cheap. While Shirley talked, Lou came over nodding fast, saying that some of the engineers who'd stayed with them had the gall to ask what they'd take for their place.

Even if it was their home-in-exile, Lou and Shirley's place looked pretty wonderful to me. The yard was rimmed by ginkgo trees and frangipani and speckled with red and yellow butterflies that bumbled around like flowers on the loose. From the breakfast deck I could look over their small swimming pool far down to the sea and make out the distant, faint tracery of St. Kitts and Nevis, old broken volcanoes. As in Hawaii, the silver-blue horizon offered the illusion of an exaggerated curving earth, or some immense force bulging up from below.

By Monday, I'd had it with conspiracy theories and was badly in the mood for some Scientific Smarts, so I made a visit to the Montserrat Volcano Observatory. The MVO sat atop a green rise called Mongo Hill, in the northern Safe Zone, and looked like it once was somebody's almost-finished dream home. The first thing I noticed inside was that I couldn't see out at all, which seemed odd for an "observatory." In the Seismicity Room, as I came to call it, windows once designed to catch ocean breezes were jammed shut behind opaque jalousie slats and layers of drum-tight plastic. These let in only dim smudges of light.

Fluorescent bulbs provided the rest, fizzing over the hum of air conditioners. I was told that the windows sealed out not just great-looking scenery, but volcanic ash. Ash and computers don't mix, and the computers and other machines crowded into this sterile, white room were the real eyes of the place.

Blinking, beeping, hooked up to satellites or decoding messages from tiltmeters, seismometers, and gas-measuring devices arrayed on Soufriere Hills, the computers peered into the volcano and Earth itself. They offered in-sight. They plotted stress lines and cracks, measured dome growth and the island-shaking big stuff. They also recorded the microshocks that were evidence of rising or shifting magma below and up through Soufriere Hills. More than 10,000 tremors had been measured since 1995, most of them too slight for a brain surgeon to feel.

But they were big enough to indirectly suggest the tremendous crustal plate collisions that had formed the island arc of the Lesser Antilles over millions of years. Ocean crust grinding westward from the Mid-Atlantic Ridge was being subducted under the Caribbean plate, allowing magma to slip up along the raggedly curving line of their convergence. And the process continues: a new volcanic island is growing from the seafloor just north of Granada. Kick 'em Jenny boils just 500 feet below the surface of the Caribbean, its turbulence sometimes visible to ships sailing overhead.

Montserrat itself has been created over several million years in roughly three stages. The northern part came first (which is why it is the most stable part of the island, accommodating the Safe Zone), then the aptly named Center Hills region, and now the dangerous south. "Now" is a relative term, of course, since scientists say that Soufriere Hills has been erupting for 100,000 years, on and off.

Another thing I noticed about the Volcano Observatory was that it was a young person's world, not a graying hair in sight. There weren't even any of the scruffy guys in faded L. L. Bean shirts I usually identified with, the guys I'd seen squinting at computer screens at the Hawaii or Cascades Observatories, or in the rabbit warren of the Smithsonian. In fact, a slender graduate student with dreadlocks and rimless glasses was doing the squinting now. In T-shirt, shorts, and sandals, he moved from screen to screen, tapped keys, and stared at waterfalls of green numbers.

About twenty minutes after I arrived, in strolled a tall, broad-shouldered woman in a blue MVO T-shirt and Lycra pants. She couldn't have been much over thirty. "Gill Norton," she said with a British accent and a strong handshake. Though her dark hair was pulled back neatly in a ponytail and a pen was clipped to her shirt, she had a wind-blown triathlete look, as though she'd just whooshed in by Jet Ski™ from Antigua.

In fact, after getting interested in geology as a teenager by cracking open ancient volcanic rocks in the hills near her home in Sheffield, England, she had studied and worked all over the place: Wales, Kenya, China, the former Soviet Union. Gill's PhD fieldwork included analyzing soil samples from Ol Doinyo Lengai volcano near the Kenya-Tanzania border. Its ash layers from long-ago eruptions have been used to date the evolution of early man in nearby Olduvai Gorge.

Officially, she was the Deputy Chief Scientist at the MVO. That's second in command, she told me with a smile. Second in command over the life and death of thousands of Montserratans, because the deep-earth data the machines collected would help her tell the island's evacuation director how quickly and radically to act.

Gill's tour of duty was six months on-island, six off. When I asked her how much tension came with that responsibility, she looked me in the eye and said, "Let's put it this way. It's really, *really* important to take a day off now and then." Then she excused herself, sat down at a computer screen, and squinted at a screen full of numbers.

Back home, half of the graduate students in my creative writing classes looked older than Gill. They worried over their essays and stories, or fretted about the ratty jobs that too often await them when they finish their MFA or Lit degrees, such smart, outstanding men and women. None of them, though, was responsible for the safety of whole towns, entire island-countries.

Still, what they and I spent so much time working on, which was to tease out the buried dramatic vectors of a story, an essay, or a book, wasn't really that much different from what Gill and her crew did here in the Seismicity Room. Gill studied the epic earth-novel called Soufriere Hills. She tried to plot its rising action, its climax, denouement, possible sequels. Especially, these days, the sequels.

Geography, I reminded myself, means "earth script," terrestrial writing, the planet's story. While I worked over this thought, a seismograph canister along a wall revolved slowly beneath a jiggling needle, which imprinted it with a record of the volcano's twitches and tics. The endless ink squiggles looked like complex-compound sentences written by hand. Or really one gigantic sentence. It was the edgy planet's timeless plot of tension and release: war and peace, war and peace, war and peace.

Gill came back and showed me around. Soufriere Hills had actually been more active in recent decades than most people realized, she noted. Earthquake swarms, which suggested big magma movement even without eruptions, had rippled through the mountain during the 1930s, the '60s, the '80s. This month, during this small lull in the eruptive mid-'90s, magma was pushing up into the dome at a rate of eight cubic meters per second. This was the equivalent of a truckload of gas-packed, pressurized rock arriving from miles below the surface every two or three seconds, twenty-four hours a day. This was what kept the dome growing and why parts of the upper mountain often blew out in unpredictable but usually relatively small ways.

Sometimes, though, the pressure inside a volcano just builds and builds. If that happened here, Gill said, you'd actually hear a difference in this room. Some of the machines would rise in pitch; they'd sound like chittering birds. If the pressure kept building, they'd start squawking like parrots, and then like parrots gone mad. Which meant that the volcano would probably have reached the brink of climax—a time for some sort of enormous, inevitable conclusion. Time, in other words, for everyone to get the hell out.

If the machines at the MVO ever did scream like mad parrots, it would be Richard Aspin's job to get the populace moving. Evacuating the island would mean more than just getting five thousand people ready to roll while, say, noon turned to midnight and fist-sized burning stones pounded down on tin roofs. The Montserratans would have to be hustled safely off-island without benefit of an airport and with only one real dock, the little concrete wharf where I had landed.

Nevertheless, Aspin looked relaxed enough in his prefab office not far from the MVO. He leaned back in his chair, but not too far back, because the place was crammed with cell phones, two-way radios, computers, fax machines, printouts of emergency codes, and Red Cross volunteer lists.

Somewhere in the mess lay the phone numbers of some of the larger cruise ships that frequented the region, maybe including the floating city I'd seen in Antigua. In case of emergency, Aspin told me, their crews had agreed to edge the ships close to Montserrat to take evacuees from shuttling ferries and helicopters. (At least the refugees would eat like kings, I told myself.) A Royal Navy cutter would orchestrate this escape flotilla. HMS *Newcastle* ordinarily roamed the Caribbean full-time, keeping an eye on British territories from the Virgin Islands south to Trinidad; these days, though, it rarely strayed more than half a day from Montserrat.

There were so many logistics to juggle, and Aspin seemed good at it. But like natural disaster officials the world over, he also had to deal with other, sometimes gnarlier problems. For instance, what I called the Harry Truman Effect—referring not to the ex-president, but the irascible eighty-three-year-old man who once owned Spirit Lake Lodge at the foot of Mount St. Helens. In the weeks leading up to the 1980 eruption, magma crowding up inside the mountain began to visibly push out the slope above Harry's lodge. Near the end, just about everyone for miles around the lake had cleared out, a few of them perhaps cursing disaster officials as they drove off, but leaving nevertheless.

Not Harry. Fortified by Jack Daniels, sixteen cats, and a deep affection for a place he'd shared for decades with his third wife, who'd recently died, he kept rocking away in his porch chair. He told increasingly edgy reporters, who finally cleared out themselves, that he was staying put, no matter what.

And he's still there—under about two hundred feet of mud, rocks, and shattered trees. Maybe years from now somebody will dig up his mummified remains, find an old-time rocker, and put him on display as one of the fiercer specimens of human attachment to place.

The Truman Effect, then, meant that professional worriers like Richard Aspin had to sell the possibility of genuine cataclysm to everybody they could, then do it again and again. For more than a year now, MVO staff members had visited every classroom on the island. They talked to hundreds of kids and their parents, and showed videos like the *Hazards* film that Maurice and Katia Krafft died while making. The result was that skinny ten-year-olds could toss off phrases like "phreatic eruption" and "earthquake swarm." (Swarm, as though the volcano were packed with angry bees!) They were probably the most volcano-hip kids on earth.

Still, Aspin fretted about the bitter-enders like Rock, hoeing away in his field with his back to the roaring mountain. Or the elderly dream home couple huddled in their living room while ash jimmied its way into their lungs.

And how would you quickly evacuate the very old and the feeble? Or the permanently befuddled, like the skinny guy with dreads I saw sitting motionless one morning by the side of the road, contemplating infinity or maybe just a hangnail? Aspin hinted to me that there were more than a few of that type on the island. You have to keep a handle on gossip, too, he explained. Hearsay gone wild is a plague that sweeps in after natural disasters anywhere on earth.

"Really, it's as if the old sugar mills have turned into rumor mills," Aspin said with a frown, making me think of Shirley. "We've got to overcome these suspicions that we're running a recolonizing plan. Believe me, it's expensive enough to keep the island going as is."

Aspin saw these things from two sides. He had moved here twenty-five years ago to teach electrical engineering at the tech college, fell in love with the place, married an islander, and had kids, then got interested in international charity work. He talked like he wanted to stay forever—he'd actually volunteered for this high-stress job—yet he knew how hard it was to keep the community running.

The medical school looked like it was gone forever. And a new airport, for instance, just wasn't going to happen. There was no safe place to put it, a dearth of flat land, and the cost of running it out over water would be absurd. So would be the cost of rebuilding most of the infrastructure, for who knew what fate.

People do keep on, though, Aspin pointed out when he saw me looking depressed. And often they help each other in beautiful ways, he said. A guy he knew owned a house nearby built on pilings. After the volcano woke up, he put in a downstairs apartment at his own expense. Since then it had housed, in turn, an early, interim volcano observatory, a school, a team of medical workers, and then a gaggle of the displaced. The owner never took a penny.

One night after I'd drunk some rum at Shirley and Lou's, I lay drifting on a raft in their pool. I stared for a long time into the blue-black sky. The stars looked so fat I half expected to hear them sizzle. The hills that piled up right behind the house kept me from seeing or hearing Soufriere Hills. I still had not glimpsed its most frightening face: the dome, pulsing in the night with blood-red cracks that revealed the lava within. So far I'd gotten only hints of its unruly life. A bruised tint to the sky in the late afternoon. A film of grit that I had to blow off my glasses and watch face every morning. And a scratchy feeling in my throat.

My throat had not felt like that since 1984, when SueEllen and I had lived in Xian, in northern China, teaching college English. Memory lives in more parts of the body than just the mind, I am convinced, and now that amazing year came flooding back in a new way.

Xian was hung with ghostly veils of coal smoke mixed with street dust stirred up by trucks and bicycles. That was bad enough most days, but one morning I awoke, with my throat doubly sore and my eyes uncommonly dry, to a world of fuzzy-yellow apparitions. The blocky, Soviet-style dorms across from our apartment looked soft and rounded-off, and fluorescent class-room lights glowed eerily purple. Dust was rolling down from the Gobi, I soon learned, talcum-fine loess arriving from hundreds of miles north. After class that day, one of my students told me that the Gobi blew in a little bit almost every day, but that you didn't notice because of all the other gunk in the air.

"But this . . ." My student paused dramatically. "This we call the Time of Yellow Wind." His eyes crinkled into a grin above a dust mask that made him look like the world's youngest surgeon. "Teacher John, they say that if it rains during this Yellow Wind, it rains blood."

"I see. But what exactly does that mean?"

"Unfortunately, Teacher John, I do not know."

The strangeness of that day and my student's Confucian puzzle stayed with me. Over the next few months, I began to notice how the field hands on the outskirts of town spent all day long knee- or elbow-deep in mud. How families in the Shaanxi countryside lived in caves they had carved out of loess. How the tiny, Mao-jacketed women who swept our campus breathed the clouds worked up by their willow-branch brooms. Feeling the scratchiness linger in my throat, hearing SueEllen break off coughing whenever she laughed, I came to think of China as a largely subterranean place. I began to imagine wormlike peasants working their way through the soil, much as it was working through them. As in the volcanic regions of the earth, the border between worlds started to blur.

It especially blurred whenever I bused across town to the tomb of China's first emperor, Qin Shi Huang-di. Under a gigantic Quonset hut, hundreds of life-sized terracotta soldiers had been dusted off and pieced back together to stand at attention in trenches, as they first had in 221 B.C. Each had been modeled after a real man, down to the smallest armor rivet and mustache hair. This was one of the world's great archeological sites, discovered by a well-digger in 1975.

But I was more drawn to the trenches that had so far been only partly excavated. Here was the handiwork of time and a changing landscape. Clay soldiers floundered waist-deep in packed dirt, a shoulder or an arm twisted or broken, armor plates cracked, bashed in. They seemed to be struggling for wholeness, contorting to pry themselves from the earth that had piled up over them thanks to floods, earthquakes, political insurrections, and, I suppose, a few thousand other Times of the Yellow Wind.

One day as I studied their faces through my binoculars, I began to imagine the human sounds of their struggles, a gargling in the throat. Then I began to hear a much more intimate struggle. It was my father, rasping for breath during the last few days of his life. A year before I left for China, I had sat exhausted beside his oversized bed in a Florida nursing home. My eyes and especially my throat ached as I pressed my forehead to the aluminum railing and listened to his breathing. Sometimes I found myself breathing for him. Other times I tried to will him from his week-long coma into a peaceful death.

But he labored on. Day after day my mom and brother and I sat around the bed, saying nothing, wrung out. Or we waited in pairs, whispering, or alone, taking turns letting each other slip home for sleep. Gradually his breathing grew more ragged, and one evening as I sat with him, just the two of us in the room, I came to think that this was the sound of the earth rising within him, reaching up for him because he refused to move down on his own.

The raft I was floating on bumped the side of Lou and Shirley's pool and briefly knocked me from my reverie. I got out, settled into a deck chair, and cracked open an Amstel. I looked straight up.

In her novel *Fugitive Pieces*, Anne Michaels writes, "Just as the earth invisibly prepares its cataclysms, so history is the gradual instant." And so my father, prepared by invisible cataclysms of emphysema and heart disease, moved in a gradual instant from air to earth, in the opposite direction of an erupting volcano, his fire diminishing. Alone in his room late one night, maybe half an hour after my brother and I had walked out together to our cars, he stopped breathing.

When we gathered back around him, my mom, looking tinier than ever, grew philosophical. His final solitude was fitting, she decided, since over the years he'd made all of his important decisions alone. So he'd outwaited us, independent to the end.

In Lou and Shirley's deck chair, I sipped more beer and thought about the gradual instants ticking away inside history and the earth, volcanic fire creeping to the surface: a hot mountain biding its time inside a cold one. Here at Soufriere Hills, even between eruptions, more subtle eruptions were occurring. Heat and fine ash wisped forth continuously, as my watch face and scratchy throat made evident. And I was just a visitor. For more than two years, Lou and Shirley and Mountain Man and practically everyone on-island had been inhaling fragments of the earth's interior.

Maybe volcanoes, which over the course of deep time had transported enough oxygen and water to the planet's surface to set the stage for life, just deepen or speed up a process that goes on all the time, everywhere. Ask any farmer on the drought-stricken plains of eastern Colorado, or migrant pickers in Florida, Idaho, and California. We literally inhale the earth, just as all of us swallow flecks of outer space, too: comet dust, spinning motes of Big Bang rubble.

The Buddhist teacher Thich Nhat Hanh talks about the folly of assuming that we exist independently of other living things or the universe. It is not that we "are," he says, but that we "inter-are." We are not just beings. We are inter-beings, exchanging breath, germs, minerals, energy.

The gritty plume of Soufriere Hills drifted invisibly in the night over my head and out to sea. The cold beer sliding down the back of my throat felt wonderful. I smiled, took another sip, and thought about interdependence, inter-beings: Montserratans and this volcano, the Chinese and dust, my father and the deep earth rising.

<hr>

If you'd lived or worked in Plymouth before the volcano swept over it, you could not have missed Gwen. She had a braying voice, and she used it to sell newspapers up and down the streets of the capital. You'd see her out there all day long, every day. You'd also have noticed that she wore no shoes, no matter how much the sun heated up the griddle of the pavement. At sunset, you might see her hurrying home. After that, however, nobody saw her.

"Gwen, I am afraid, was the victim of a spell. They say it was a curse put on her by a rival in romance." The teller of this tale was, of course, Shirley, who was sitting across from me at her kitchen counter. She was leaning in and speaking low, though not quite low enough to keep Lou, parked at the TV, from crossing his arms and mumbling, "Jeez . . ."

"They say that Gwen once stole a man from someone, so the spurned woman had a spell put on her." Shirley looked at me sharply, challenging me or any man to doubt what would come next. "And from that moment on, Gwen was forced to spend all day out of doors and barefoot, and every second of the night locked in her house. Do you know what would happen if she slipped up even once? She would burst into flames!"

I broke into a grin. I loved the fierce logic of this story, the curse forcing dangerous Gwen to stay in sight of the whole community by day and never again cat around by night. The sizzling pavement and the threat of spontaneous combustion were the spicy details that drove home the moral: *Mess with my man and you'll burn to cinders!* Later on, the more I thought about this weird story, the more I wondered about another of its possible lessons: that the changing physical world can affect the human psyche in more subtle and yet powerful ways than I had previously imagined.

Voodoo priests, juju wizards, obeah mammas, black magic masters who communed with the demented and the dead, sorcerers, red-eyed tree wraiths, snake devils, dolls run through with nails and bleeding mystical spells of revenge—these are the famous players of the so-called Dark Arts. From Miami to Haiti to Cuba (with its santería) and south through most or all of the Caribbean Islands, writers from Lafcadio Hearn to Jean Rhys to contemporaries like Christina Garcia and Martinique's Patrick Chamoiseau have made great drama out of their stories. And I'm sure the tales carry even greater weight in the repetitive, unrefined folklore and gossip of everyday people. The modern world has in many ways watered down some of these stories or pushed them into hiding. But while true believers may have retreated inland and up-mountain with the Caribbean's shrinking forests, juju apparently lives on, if you know how to find it.

Shirley knew how to find it. She had earlier told me about the night spirits of her old home, Grenada: "Lou Ligeroo," the red-eyed vampire you can appease only by inviting to dinner; Mama Malady, who steals babies. An unlikely anthropologist named Jay D. Dobbin also knew how to find juju. In the 1970s, Dobbin worked on-island as a Catholic priest, then went back to the States and wrote *The Jombee Dance of Montserrat: A Study of Trance Ritual in the West Indies*. When he wasn't conducting Mass or listening to confessions, Father Dobbin must have spent all of his time pumping his flock and their friends and neighbors for material. In town, along mountain paths, and probably on dozens of front porches, he learned about Emerald Isle rituals that were designed to invoke night spirits, or jombees. By the mid '70s, the rituals were becoming hard to find, one man told Dobbin, because " 'lectricity come, dee jombees die."

. But Dobbin discovered that back in the not-so-distant past, in the days of ordinary, dread-inducing darkness, the Montserratan universe was apparently as crowded with ghosts and superhuman beings as that of any other Caribbean island. For instance, there was the suckra, a skin-shedding vampiress who was often seen gliding along backcountry roads at night in a fiery glow. And jabless, a male or female malevolent spirit, about whom one person said, "Jabless blow you 'way like the whirlwind." And Jack-o-Lantern, or Jack Lantern, which another Montserratan described to Dobbin as: "Like big debil business . . . flame of fire, big, big. If it blows on you, blows you away and you can't be found."

And then *jombees,* a word that happens to rhyme with zombies. Jombees were uncommonly lively spirits who could work for either good or evil. According to one man, the evil ones were "dey who be jumble yo' up, mash yo' up." Dobbin never condescends in writing about these beliefs, which occupied what he calls a twilight region between magic and religion. He takes care, in fact, to say that he knows of highly educated Catholics (in the U.S., presumably) who cut up their Palm Sunday leaves and strew them into wheat fields to prevent lightning strikes.

The jombees that Dobbin studied floated up into the world from the graves of the recently dead. They'd do this on any of the "Rising Nights" that occur three to nine days after interment. The jombees were summoned via an exhausting, all-night dance put on by friends and family in somebody's home. It was a ritual that Dobbin got to observe once or twice. Thanks to hours of feasting and drinking, the subtle ministrations of a visiting obeah man or woman, and apparently tireless musicians called musikers, the dance gradually turned into a trance-like invocation rite.

Why invoke a jombee? For the usual struggles of the heart: to help a friend or relative out of trouble or into the arms of a worthy mate. Or for darker reasons like plain old revenge.

All of which, weeks after my Montserrat visit, helped me to understand what poor barefoot Gwen, the man-thief, may have thought she was up against. No wonder she was terrified.

After I finished Dobbin's book, I was struck by how many of these fiery and recently subterranean island spirits acted like the phenomena of erupting volcanoes. Murderous suckra glided along like lava glowing eerily in the dark. And the creature was "big, big." Like the searing winds of the Soufriere Hills pyroclastic flow that obliterated the farmers who kept sneaking back to their fields, Jabless and Jack Lantern could "blow you away" so you couldn't be found. There were any number of ways an erupting volcano could "jumble yo' up, mash yo' up." A human crisis tends to force the spiritual life into the open. Similarly, a volcano literally transports the inner earth to the surface. Thus, more geomythology.

It was true that Dobbin gathered his material two decades before Soufriere Hills rumbled out of its 400-year sleep. But Montserrat's juju folklore is widely thought to have traveled up the island chain from Martinique, where French and African voodoo influences are especially strong. From Martinique it jumped to Dominica, then to mountainous Guadeloupe, just fifty miles southeast of Montserrat. All three of those islands have been volcanically active during the last few centuries.

In fact, the more I thought about Montserrat's glow-in-the-dark volcano bulging with rising fire, the more I thought about the terrifying threat of jombees. During these last few difficult years, Soufriere Hills had indeed dabbled fiercely in the dark arts, and it could turn any night into a Rising Night. With little or no warning, it could make you burst into flames.

Early in my island stay, I found a hideaway I loved, a shady cove about a mile from Lou and Shirley's place. Late every afternoon I would hike down a crumbly macadam road to a beach park, chuck off my floppies, and wade into the surf. Or I'd sit and wriggle myself into the hot black sand that turned deliciously cool just below the surface.

Then I'd look out at a sea stack maybe sixty yards offshore, its cliffs crowded with frigate birds and pelicans. As the afternoon wore on, the birds struck various poses. They preened and craned their long-billed heads, and when the dropping sun fattened behind them, their silhouettes turned black and spindly. The birds turned into petroglyphs, and then they stretched their wings and flapped off in lines a half dozen or so at a time. They became sentences on the fly, antique language reconfiguring itself, rock code rewriting itself in the air. Where better, I wondered, to muse about such things than on the shore of a growing volcano?

The cove also was a good place to update my notebook. I could escape the late afternoon heat and sort out the half-formed ideas and stories I'd hurriedly jotted down each day. I needed these breaks. Except for the bananaquits flitting about and chirping in the bushes, and an iguana I once saw hauling itself through the sea grape and kapok trees, I had the place to myself.

Then late one afternoon a middle-aged man puttered in on a motorbike. He dismounted rather formally, peeled off his tie and white shirt, then everything else. He folded his clothes on the seat of the bike and sauntered into the water. He either didn't see me or didn't feel like acknowledging my presence.

Afterward, he stood for a long time under an outdoor shower. Eyes closed, smiling, he let the spray massage away his work worries and his volcano worries. Or so it seemed to me.

"This island of ours was *such* a Paradise!"

My notebook was loaded with statements like that. As I flipped through its pages, I noticed the motorbike man finally strolling over to a patch of grass. He lay down, the better to air-dry himself, I supposed. Fifteen minutes later he was back in his clothes, minus the tie. I guessed he was a teacher or government worker. As I watched him putter off, I found myself wondering if he had a home left to go to, and if the rhythms of island life had been as wonderful for him as they were for the people I'd talked to, before the magma indentured them to geologic whim.

Sometimes I dozed on the beach. Sometimes I looked past the sea stack and daydreamed about the trip I'd take to Martinique in a few days, or the journeys I might someday make to faraway volcanic islands. Réunion in the Indian Ocean, whose gushing lava fountains and meandering rock rivers had been a favorite subject of Maurice and Katia Krafft. Krakatau in Indonesia, rebuilding itself out of the Sunda Strait. Or a place I'd never heard of until I'd ferried here—tiny Saba, population 1,000 or so, which stuck abruptly up from the Caribbean a few islands to the north.

I'd read somewhere that Saba's dramatic silhouette inspired the image of Skull Island in the original *King Kong*. It seemed to me now that Kong clearly played a role on that fictional South Seas island that was analogous to the one enacted by volcanoes in ancient Hawaii, Sumatra, Latin America, and many other cultures. Kong was the beast in the garden, a volcanic force (who lived among smoking volcanoes) to be appeased with gifts such as albino goats, virgins, and children. Among the many things I was learning from my research was that the melodramatic clichés of volcano sacrifice were turning out to be more fact than fiction.

Near sunset one day, I watched a big roller come smashing up the beach. When it seethed back down it dragged along a thousand wave-polished cobbles under the surface. I'd heard these stones rumbling here before, vaguely. But today they seemed to vibrate in my chest, and I began to feel, or sense, the whole island filling with boiling rock, and then the dome of the volcano stretching thin enough in places to break open anytime and turn this cove into claustrophobic night.

This was what I couldn't feel when I drove with Rob and Beryl into the Exclusion Zone. But maybe by now Soufriere Hills had cast its spell over me. I was starting to feel wary. Exhausted, too, because I realized how weary I'd grown over the last few years of too many times of the volcano. I mean a lot more here than geology. I mean my Colorado up-canyon neighbor John, learning he had cancer and dying within weeks, in fact only three days after he'd chatted and laughed with me for most of an afternoon. Or my friend Carol, blindsided in a fatal car crash on her way home from church. Or my old Florida friend Doug, taking a nap after playing some basketball and never waking up. Only forty-eight, he was one of the strongest athletes I knew, and suddenly a wall had burst in his chest, flooding him with darkness.

And here I was, brooding in the shadow of Soufriere Hills. The nearest ash-mask hung in Lou and Shirley's living room, a long walk uphill. At least the pelicans stretching out their wings on the sea stack didn't look worried about any of this. But I noticed how twilight was starting to deepen the volcano's yellow plume, which was flowing directly over my head.

Yes, I was starting to realize, a volcano can fool you every time. Hell, it had even fooled Maurice and Katia Krafft. Sometimes a volcano just sits there for ten centuries while villages grow on its slopes and cultures fashion metaphors out of its immense stolidity, metaphors so common they can approach the level of clichés. Rock of ages. Rock steady. Granite hard. Bedrock values. On this rock I shall build my church.

A volcano poses as the generations-old landscape of home, throne of gods or devils, goal of pilgrims, eternal snow and cloud catcher. And then it changes so goddamn fast. It blows away nostalgia and sunlight.

Out on the sea stack, a few last birds were still preening and posing, but I pulled on my floppies, gathered my stuff, and started the uphill trudge to Lou and Shirley's place. Better not push my luck, I told myself. The sulfurous plume was growing thicker by the minute, or so the light made it seem. Besides, the Chinese had a saying: *If it rains during the Time of Yellow Wind, it rains blood.*

ORPHANS OF
THE STORM:
MOUNT PELÉE, MARTINIQUE

. . . in a story, which is a kind of dreaming,
the dead sometimes smile and sit up
and return to the world.

—Tim O'Brien,
The Lives of the Dead

By the time the ferry took me from Montserrat back to Antigua, this time minus a sea squall, I had spoken with a lot of people on the Emerald Isle. Not everyone mentioned it, but it became clear to me that the seed of their deepest volcano worries was the terrible story of what once happened in nearby Martinique.

One spring morning in 1902, on the northwest coast of this Caribbean slice of France, night overwhelmed the day. In a span of two or three minutes, 28,000 people were buried by permanent darkness. These were the occupants of Saint-Pierre, the largest and liveliest city on the island, a prosperous, musical, flower-bedecked place that was widely known as the "Paris of the Antilles." Twenty-eight thousand dead, and just a handful of survivors.

One of the survivors had the luck to be sitting in the most protected residence in town: the city jail. Tall and burly Ludger Sylbaris (also called *Sanson,* or Samson, for his great strength) was a habitual drunk who'd been sentenced to a month's confinement for wounding a man in a knife fight. The twenty-eight-year-old Saint-Pierre native happened to be the only prisoner in the jail that morning. It was May 8, 7:50 A.M.

As Ludger would later explain thousands of times, he'd been waiting for his breakfast, sitting in the grimy dungeon light, when his cell suddenly turned pitch black. A half second later, steam came whooshing in through the small metal grate on the cell door, his only window. The window faced away, or downslope, from Mount Pelée, which was the tallest and biggest mountain on the island—in fact, at 4,500 feet, one of the tallest in the West Indies. It was a mountain that Ludger's jail keepers told him had recently been emitting columns of smoke and blizzards of ash, a mountain that he himself could not see but occasionally heard giving off a deep rumble.

In a city crowded with thick-walled brick and stone structures, Ludger's cavelike cell was probably the sturdiest building of all. It was also sunk partway into the hillside. Nevertheless, the unexpected blast of darkness nearly cooked him alive. When the steam hit, he dove for the floor, curled up, and tried to breathe the searing air. For the next three days—days that he couldn't distinguish from nights, since an avalanche seemed to have plugged up the grate—he lay in agony while patches of skin on his hands, shoulders, back, and legs slid off like wet tissue paper. This imprisonment inside his other imprisonment must have been unimaginably frightening.

At last, though, Ludger heard the crunch of boots and the scrape of shovels. Then he heard muffled voices. He screamed like a madman. Rocks were torn away, the door was bashed open with a log, and he was nearly blinded by the daylight that flooded in. Two men took him gently by the arms and pulled him out.

Island of Flowers, or Madinina, as the Caribs once called their land, is a good description of Martinique today. As I discovered to my delight after I landed in the modern capital of Fort-de-France, the island was one of the lushest places I'd ever seen. Bougainvillea cascaded over walls and oleander lined roadsides and walkways. Mountain paths twisted through jungles that shone bright green between lavish afternoon showers. But when Ludger Sylbaris was helped to his feet in Saint-Pierre almost one hundred years earlier, he squinted hard against the light and saw nothing around him except Plutonian desolation—miles of smoldering gray rubble. Almost every hibiscus and moonflower bush, every palm tree and building in the city, including the Mouillage Cathedral with its massive stone walls and intricate crystal chandeliers, had been flattened, burned, broken, or blown away. Ludger could no longer even tell where the cobblestone streets had run. The few ships that he could make out in the wide, curving harbor lay smashed on their sides or had burned down to the waterline. They'd turned into black, oily hulks.

In Ludger's time, no one in the Caribbean lived without fear or a healthy respect for the power of hurricanes. *But this?* Ludger wondered. *What kind of storm could possibly do this?*

With the help of his rescuers, Ludger eventually managed to walk to the mountain hamlet of Mourne Rouge, four miles away.

There a parish priest took him in and tended his wounds with linseed oil, limewater, and phenic acid. By some miracle he did not die from infection. Eventually he healed—as much as one can from terrible burns—and was pardoned for his crime. And then, in another surreal turn of events, he was invited to tour the United States with the Barnum & Bailey Circus.

P. T. Barnum, who believed that an exaggeration was born every minute, billed Ludger as:

> The Only Living Object That Survived in
> The "SILENT CITY OF DEATH"
> Where 40,000 Human Beings Were Suffocated,
> Burned, or Buried by One Belching Blast of
> Mont Pelée's Terrible Volcanic Eruption.

Most of this, except for the number of victims, happened to be of little exaggeration, for even P. T. Barnum could barely overstate the impact that the earth had made on the "Paris of the Antilles."

During his years with the circus, Ludger shared a sideshow tent with Barnum's so-called human curiosities. There was a German family of dancing midgets. There was "Louise the Leopard Girl" and "The Man So Thin He Casts No Shadow." Several times a day in St. Louis and Philadelphia, in Atlanta and various points south, Ludger would peel off his shirt, revealing scars that had crumpled up like mountainous islands from the sea of his body. Spectators gasped at this sight or just stared. When they had had time to take it in, he would begin to recount, in halting English and sorrowful detail, the story of the disaster he felt but did not actually see.

One of the few other survivors of the Mount Pelée eruption was a young girl who must have seen far too much. Her name was Harviva da Ifrile, and her age, according to historians, was "unknown." So is almost everything else about her life. But during a brief hospital stay, Harviva told a visiting journalist just a few sentences about her ordeal. How she and her brother, on an errand to buy bread for their mother, had watched a dark smoke column shoot from the summit of Mont Pelée, which was more than four miles from their home in the city. How they had taken a shortcut past a kind of sinkhole in the woods, a brushy pit that filled up from below with a glowing rock foam that fascinated and then horrified them. How the foam soon boiled over like a kettle of rice, then transformed itself into a searing wave that chased them downhill toward the harbor. How Harviva, the faster runner, pulled ahead of her brother, jumped into a small boat, turned to see him get swallowed up by a monstrous black cloud, then pushed off and paddled for her life, scooting into a rock grotto just as the darkness caught up with her.

But that's it. That's all we have of her story. What happened to the rest of Harviva's family? Had they or their neighbors formed strong opinions about what the volcano might do? Had Mont Pelée given many hints of what was to come, or when? What were Harviva and her parents thinking and feeling in the weeks and days leading up to the tragedy? Any huge mountain that stands alone, as so many volcanoes do, tends to draw weather to its flanks—but what folklore and other stories does it also attract or transform?

I spent a couple of days poking around Saint-Pierre and its environs, wondering about that girl and her family, who seemed like they might speak for the lives of so many Pierrotins who had perished. A century after the eruption, the place had devolved into a sleepy little town of 6,000 with a couple of Creole restaurants and one hotel with five rooms. But it seemed smaller even than that. Perhaps this was because I knew how large and lively it once had been, or how everything on the northern half of the island was dwarfed by the long, forest-green flanks of Mount Pelée, which, as I looked at it from many angles, was giving off no smoke at all. Saint-Pierre also presented a huge contrast to the buzzing population and tourist centers in the south, near the airport.

And so I wandered around, trying to resurrect my high school and college French with the help of a pocket dictionary and a phrase book. I got by, and soon I was able to infer quite a bit from written and oral histories of the city and the island. Especially helpful were photographs and detailed newspaper accounts of Saint-Pierre's remarkable final days, which I pored over at the small but very fine volcanological museum built in the partly resurrected old downtown. A few miles to the south, I visited another museum, on a country estate where Paul Gauguin lived and painted in 1887, not long before he set sail for Tahiti and immortality. Later on, I read books and diary entries written by pre- and post-eruption visitors. But at a wonderful book and map store in Antigua, I had picked up a copy of *Two Years in the French West Indies,* by the great travel writer Lafcadio Hearn. Hearn sailed to Martinique in 1887 and found himself so bewitched, or "haunted," as he liked to put it, that over the course of two trips he stayed for months and months. This book especially, packed with drawings and photographs and vivid prose portraits, helped me imagine a Saint-Pierre just before and after the turn of the new century.

But none of this could tell me what might have happened to an individual survivor like young Harviva da Ifrile. Where did she go after the volcano orphaned her from the only existence she had known? What would any of us do if our home—as much a psychic as a physical place—had been blown from the face of the earth?

She had turned thirteen earlier that spring. At least that's what the story that I decided to imagine for her told me. As I walked around the town's cobblestoned streets and out to the ruins of the once-grand botanical gardens, I imagined that Harviva must have been a high-spirited girl, perhaps in love with everything. In love with her unusual name, which her brother and friends probably shortened Viva. In love with her handsome and broad-shouldered mother, her *Maman* in the Creole of the island.

And later, as I strolled along the black-sand beach of the almost empty harbor, the energy of the old city came alive for me. I could see her *maman* standing half a head taller than most of the women who crowded the waterfront market, milling around in their turbans and bright calico gowns amid huge stacks of cotton and flasks of molasses and rum. The molasses was made from the sugarcane that grew in so many places, including up and down the fertile slopes of Mount Pelée.

The city was usually crowded with French, Chinese, Indians, Senegalese, and Syrians: every shade imaginable of the planet's migrating people. "A population fantastic, astonishing . . . a population of the Arabian Nights," wrote Lafcadio Hearn.

At thirteen, the Viva I imagine had already gotten some of her mother's height, and she was learning to balance on her head ever-heavier baskets of mangoes, papaya, oranges, and laundry, as do the women in several of Hearn's photographs. Her *maman* did this with no hands as the two of them walked home past women and girls kneeling along the Rivière-Roxelane to wash clothes. Like all the rivers in the vicinity, the Roxelane ran down the slopes of the mountain. At home, her mother's forearms shone with sweat, her muscles rippling as she cracked open land crabs that Viva had caught for her in the jungle. As she stirred fish soup or fried up some conch, she'd chat with her daughter. And now and then she'd glance uneasily out through the window at the rain clouds shifting around Pelée's summit. As Hearn and others wrote, everyone called it "The Mountain."

Surely, Viva was also in love with her father with his bushy sideburns and white Panama suit, the kind so commonly worn by the middle- and upper class in photographs taken at the time. A slightly rumpled suit, too, because nothing in Martinique's submarine humidity could stay pressed for long. In the morning, she liked to watch him trot off on his horse toward his supervisor's job at the Guerin & Son Sugar Plant at the mouth of the Rivière-Blanche.

And sometimes after an early dinner, she'd hook her arm through his, and they'd walk past walls draped with morning glory vines and roses, then up through cane and tobacco fields. When the road entered the jungle, the air cooled suddenly, and parrots chattered amid royal palms, colossal ferns, a dozen kinds of bromeliads. Hardwood trees still dripped from blinding sheets of afternoon rain.

Chewing on a slice of guava or a chunk of coconut, Viva sometimes thought about the diamond-patterned fer-de-lance lying fat and shiny on the jungle floor, waiting to crawl onto the road, as was its deadly habit after dusk. As I noticed when I sat reading late one afternoon on the low wall of the botanical gardens, night dropped fast here, especially in among the trees. A hundred years ago, if you were Viva's age, oncoming darkness might fire your imagination with stories of backwoods things: not just the snakes and the biting, foot-long millipedes, but Catholic devils that are mentioned in written accounts of nineteenth-century island life. And *voudou* river spirits, tree goblins that swooped like bats, and island hopping shape-shifters like Damballa the Snake King. These *diables,* or devils, thrived especially in the minds of old women who traveled along roads or forest paths. Some of the older ones might carry a walking stick of *moudongue* wood, for snake protection and the dual arts of healing and casting spells. In 1902, quite a few of them could still remember their lives as plantation slaves, and they talked up a lively cosmology of evil—a hash of Yoruba and Christianity with neighborhood color and personal quirks most likely thrown in.

Viva's father, a city-bred man, might have laughed them off. Not so Viva's mother, who had grown up in the country and so paid the folklore a quiet kind of attention. Viva herself was probably still sorting things out. But when a breeze slid down off The Mountain, bringing with it a puzzling whiff of sulfur, she did sometimes wonder if she was smelling a kind of . . . breath. This raised the more troubling question of, *Whose breath?*

Today we can look back and say, *The breath of the volcano, of course. The geothermal exhalations of the world.* But it would not be fair to suppose that the average Pierrotin would know that. Like Montserrat's Soufriere Hills, Mount Pelée was a stratovolcano, meaning a volcanic cone built over the centuries by outbreaks of both lava and pyroclastic flows. The volcano had in fact erupted at least fifty times in the previous 9,000 years. But in 1902, only some people understood that the mountain was a volcano, and even they had little idea that it was such a long-lived or potentially violent one. In tropical regions throughout the world, heavy rainfall spurs revegetation that can quickly cover the evidence of even recent eruptions, sometimes lulling successive generations into a false sense of security. If you doubt this, look at how jungles in the Yucatán and Peru have smothered even massive stone pyramids to the point of hiding them for centuries.

Mount Pelée had erupted mildly in 1851, but not in any serious way for more than five centuries before that. If the Caribs who once lived here had incorporated that ancient violence into their folklore, the stories died with them long before Viva was born.

And so when dusk dropped over Viva's walks with her father, she had plenty to think about besides volcanoes. She probably leaned into him and made sure to keep her feet, and her gaze, fixed on the middle of the road.

One mid-April afternoon about three weeks before the disaster, Viva and her brother Michel took their small boat for a sail. From out in the harbor, she could see Saint-Pierre's cobbled streets and red-roofed houses climbing steeply away from the waterfront. She could see the ice plant, the opera house, the squarish cathedral, and behind all that, extensive botanical gardens thickening into crumpled green hills.

Michel was two years older, an outdoor boy who'd built the boat himself. As Viva would later tell the journalist who visited her in the hospital, she and her brother often fished or swam with friends, or edged the boat into a grotto they'd discovered not far offshore. In the shade of this natural cave, they caught black crabs and iguanas, and sometimes entertained each other with pirate stories.

On this particular afternoon, I imagine that they noticed something strange in the grotto: bubbles breaking the surface of the water and a stench of rotten eggs. Leaning over the gunwales, Michel studied the bubbles, then slipped into the water and made for the bottom.

Viva waited, listening to the slap of waves, studying the beaded green throat of an iguana, which seemed to study her in return. Then a cannon went off. The sound bounced around the grotto and sent the iguana scrambling.

"What was that?" Michel gasped when he broke the surface.

"Ship coming in. At least I think so."

At the turn of the century, freighters approaching the Saint-Pierre harbor fired a small cannon to announce their arrival. This booming often sent kids racing out in boats and canoes to beg the waving sailors to toss them money or souvenirs—a sport that several Saint-Pierre visitors noted in their books and journals. I like to think that Michel had once retrieved a small gold coin, then given it to Viva to wear as a charm around her neck. He could still see it flashing and tumbling down through the green water as he streaked ahead of other children to grab it.

Now, looking for the source of the detonation, they sailed farther into the harbor. Viva saw nothing unusual, just big-rigged ships and steamers already creaking at anchor. She shaded her eyes and looked west, scanning the indigo blue horizon. Nothing. She felt the pleasurable itch of saltwater baking into her skin.

Now came a much louder boom. Viva squinted at the cliffs where a huge white statue of the Virgin, Our Lady of the Watch, stood with arms outspread, looking out to sea. There were big black cannons mounted up there, some kind of memorial to war, and she wondered now if one of them was the culprit. But she couldn't see any artillery smoke.

A few seconds later, two frightful detonations.

"There!" Michel pointed at The Mountain.

A giant puff of black smoke, then another, emerged from the cloud-wreathed summit. They rose and expanded, merged, threw spooky shadows across Mount Pelée's lower slopes.

Michel leaned into Viva and said, "When I dove after the bubbles, I touched bottom and burned my fingers! Now our mountain's firing away. Do you suppose that our volcano is waking up?"

Viva only partly understood what this meant. She'd had no idea that a volcano, if that's what Mount Pelée really was, could be so green. When she thought about volcanoes at all, she had supposed that they were snow-capped and symmetrical things, like a photograph she'd seen of placid Mount Fuji framed by cherry blossoms.

Viva saw somebody in uniform on one of the nearby ships waving at them, but not in a friendly way. "Go on home!" he shouted. "Go! Home! Now!"

So they did. When they trotted into the high-walled courtyard of their home, they saw their mother emerging from her kitchen, carrying the broken pieces of a dish. She looked surprised to see them, as though she'd temporarily forgotten they existed.

"You know, children," she said dreamily, "this afternoon The Mountain roared. And then this dinner plate—well, look at it. It danced right off of my table."

She looked up and away at The Mountain, then at Viva. "What do you think of that? And what do you suppose that Vomit Devil is up to?"

Diable Vonmi is the way she would have put this.

Viva glanced at her brother. This was a devil that she didn't know. And this was a tone of voice she'd never heard from her mother.

When she was a child, Viva's mother had heard a story once from a *granme* who'd seen her gazing off at the V-shaped notch on Mount Pelée's oddly bare summit. Tapping her arm, then pointing to the notch with her *moudongue* stick, the old woman told her that a devil man lived up there in the mountain, a giant in the earth who now and then kicked and screamed to get out.

She said: "Little girl, someday this demon of roar an fire, he gonna jump right outta that montay! An when he do, he open up his black coat, his night-things coat, his dead-things coat. He open it so big it swallow the forest and sky and all them stars . . . An then, this world it start to shake and burn like you dont wanna know . . ."

Viva's mother ran off, thinking, *She's crazy as a goat.*

But then later that day she reminded herself that these backwoods grandmothers, who had been through so much in their lives, really did know a thing or two about the world. Their poultices of crushed cinnamon and clove leaves seemed to work. And she remembered taking a shortcut, once, across a cane field and discovering another kind of healing. She noticed a crowd and heard somebody moaning. She squeezed her way in between people's legs and saw that one of the cane cutters had somehow gashed his thigh with a machete. Blood ran in rivers. And then she watched a few of the *granmes* disappear into the woods. Soon they came trundling back with silky, luminous paste on their hands and forearms. Spider webs! They gathered around the injured man and bent over him like silver ghosts. They scraped the webs from themselves and packed them into his wound. His moaning kept on, but soon the bleeding slowed, then stopped.

And so Viva's mother had never been able to forget the story of the *Diable Vonmi.* Sometimes at night, when The Mountain was clotted with rain clouds, she saw how its great dark bulk really did swallow the stars, or half the sky, anyway. Over the years, especially after she'd had children, she'd occasionally wake up in the night and feel the house trembling slightly, the furniture rattling, and when she pressed her hand against the damp wood floor, it felt like the island was sweating with fever or a spell, shuddering in its dreams.

But she'd married a smart and sensible man who believed in a modern, sensible world, a man who didn't gamble his money away on the cockfights that were so popular on the island. "Baby earthquakes," he said about the shaking. "So what?" He didn't believe in demons or church miracles, and he refused to take off his hat when he passed any of the homemade religious shrines on the island's maze of footpaths.

She did *not* want her husband laughing at her.

After dinner on the day that The Mountain first boomed and coughed up black clouds, Viva's father motioned the family over to the dining room table and unrolled a map of the West Indies. I like to think that he'd acquired it as a young man working on ships sailing up and down the islands.

He pressed down the edges, and said, "See? All these islands? Volcanoes!"

He wasn't entirely sure of this statement, although in fact it was true over the long arc of geologic time. But he thought he'd better take charge and sound confident. His children and especially his wife were starting to look worried.

"Guadalupe, Antigua, Dominica—every green dot in the sea from Saint Croix all the way south to Grenada. Volcanoes!" He swept his hand over the scimitar curve of this archipelago of fire, a history of ancient and not-so-ancient eruptions, of islands that had risen from the sea entirely due to volcanic action.

Viva noticed that while he talked, her mother had picked up his rum glass and taken a sip. She usually drank only on holidays.

"In fact," her father went on, "my grandfather told me that he once saw Mount Pelée huffing and puffing with black smoke like we saw today. Now that must have been something!"

Viva's mother finished off the rum and stared at him. "And you never *told* me this?"

"Well, I didn't think it mattered. The Mountain's been dead our whole lives. It just twitches now and then like a fer-de-lance with its head cut off." He tried to smile. "It probably won't twitch again until we're rotting in our graves."

"Speak for yourself!" she said, and left the room.

At the time, even the world's best scientists could not have pieced together what many advances in technology and field-work have since revealed about Mount Pelée's history. In the short term, though, Viva's father seemed to have guessed right. Over the next few days The Mountain dropped back into foggy silence. Saint-Pierre's daily newspaper, *Les Colonies,* gave the explosions a light-hearted mention, as though Mount Pelée were somebody's loopy old uncle, grumbling a little as he passed through town. Today these all-too-real newspaper accounts make the saddest, most poignant kind of reading.

Then one morning, Viva opened her bedroom shutters and saw smoke streaming out of the mountain's notch. A long dirty plume rolled out over the sea. A few gray ashes came feathering in through the window. She wondered if snow ever looked as gritty as this.

That night at dinner Viva watched her mother drink a full glass of rum, then go out on the balcony, where she stood with her arms crossed, watching the smoke unfurl in moonlight: darkness lifting up against darkness. Her mother went to bed with hardly a word. Let's call this the last day of April.

The next day, exactly a week before the disaster, Michel showed Viva a book he'd found at school. "It says that some volcanoes rumble and smoke for centuries and hardly bother anyone," he told her.

"So Papa's right, then?"

"Well . . ."

He flipped some pages. Over his shoulder, Viva read from an account of the eruption of Krakatau, an island-volcano in the Dutch East Indies, today's Indonesia. Only a few years before she and Michel were born, in 1883, it had erupted on a massive scale, with the loudest sound ever documented, an explosion heard four or five hours later and up to 3,000 miles away. Almost two full days of fury discharged two cubic miles of material. The chaos of this displacement, in the Sunda Strait, pushed out tsunamis in all directions. Mounds of water up to 120 feet high ravaged the coasts of nearby Java and Sumatra, and in one case carried a paddle wheeler more than a mile inland, stranding it thirty-nine feet above sea level. Atmospheric waves circled the globe several times. In all, at least 36,000 people were killed.

Before she had finished reading, Michel said, "Viva, you can't even *visit* this place anymore. There's nothing left!"

"Don't show this to Maman."

She wasn't that worried for herself. Mount Pelée's smoking summit was several miles off, and their house was built of thick stone, not wood and straw like the huts that the poor Asians lived in near Krakatau. Besides, she told herself, perhaps The Mountain would soon calm down. What kind of God would ever allow such Hell to break loose in the world for a second time?

Having stood myself in the Belham River Valley of Montserrat, unable to truly imagine apocalypse roaring down on me from a distance of several miles, I got a decent idea of what someone like Viva might think.

On May 2, *Les Colonies* suggested that everyone enjoy the spectacle of the mountain's low-level eruption, which it called "surely temporary." It also urged its readers not to run away and to remember that the incumbent mayor would be needing their votes in the May 11 election.

"What they don't tell you is that he's part-owner of the paper," said Viva's father. "Politicians are the *real* devils. They'll shake your hand at the gates of hell and tell you to come in and enjoy the warm baths!" He was still trying to make his wife smile.

But he was growing concerned. At work in the sugar plant along the banks of the Rivière-Blanche, he'd felt an on-and-off trembling that he knew was not caused by any machine. And one of his workers who lived up on the mountain told him he'd heard a sound like a furnace roaring all night.

On the afternoon of May 3, Mount Pelée coughed up a huge black and gray cloud shot through with lightning. Viva saw it with her classmates at school, and minutes later pebbles began to bounce and clatter on the classroom's tin roof. Ash began to coat the magnolias and tamarinds outside the school windows. Like powdered cement, it piled up in the streets, eventually muffling even the giant wheels of ox carts. When Viva walked home, the city was weirdly quiet, ghost-gray. Her eyes burned and her throat felt sore.

All the next day, the sun was a dying coal. Strange things were happening all over town, and the newspaper reported many of them. Horses jumped and snorted without warning, throwing their riders. In the jungle canopies, parrots and macaws fell silent, and smaller birds, their windpipes apparently clogging with ash, began to drop from the trees.

Viva's mother kept the children home from school and asked her husband not to leave for the plant.

"Impossible," he said. "Life goes on."

But that day he didn't return until hours after dark. Viva, who was spelling her mother at the courtyard gate, watching for him, finally made out a lantern in the distance. Her father's silhouette gradually took shape. He was walking beside his horse—no, limping. Viva ran out to him and saw that his white suit coat was gone, his shirt just a gray rag. His face was monstrously swollen. He looked at Viva but said nothing. He just handed over the reins and motioned her to feed and water the animal.

When Viva hurried back inside, her mother was bending over him with compresses. He sat hunched forward on a stool, wheezing. Bare from the waist up, he was smeared with mud, oil, and dried blood, scarred by at least a dozen welts, as though he'd been beaten like one of the old-time slaves she'd heard stories about. Viva began to cry.

"Papa, who *did* this to you!"

"*Betes-ni-pie.*"

Beasts which are all feet: island slang for millipedes. The ones found in the Martinique forests could grow as long as your forearm and sometimes even enter the house, hide under a towel or in the laundry. They gave Viva the creeps, and not just because they bit like scorpions.

Her father said, "After lunch, The Mountain roared and shook again, very hard, and a while later the millipedes began to crawl out of the jungle and into the plant." He took a sip of water. "Not so many at first. We swatted them with cane stalks and shovels, but they kept coming. Ants, too."

Viva's mother daubed at his welts. She ordered Viva into the garden to gather herbs for more compresses.

"We tried crushing the millipedes under burlap sacks," he said as Viva edged to the door. "We tipped over barrels of lubricating oil to stop them. But there were *thousands*. They crawled up the horses' legs and up under our pants. They dropped from the rafters like rain . . ."

Outside, Viva held up a lantern with one hand and with the other shook ash from the plants. Even in daylight she couldn't always find the ones her mother wanted, these natural ingredients for remedies that doctors in town and at Viva's school had never heard of. Viva thought she saw something, a thin shadow maybe, sliding down a wall. She hurried inside with the herbs and bolted the door behind her.

They took turns watching him during the night. Soon he nodded off, his breath gradually becoming more regular. When it was her turn, Viva sat on the floor next to his bed and took his hand. It felt puffy and hot. She braided his thick fingers through her hair, closed her eyes, and soon fell asleep herself.

The snakes came about an hour after sunrise. They didn't enter the house, though Viva's mother flung a harmless racer back over the courtyard wall. They appeared mostly on nearby streets that bordered the jungle. You could hear shouting, the squealing of dogs and pigs, then gunshots.

Snakes were pouring off the mountain, they heard from a neighbor who sprinted by. Fer-de-lance wriggled out of the deep street-side gutters. They dropped over mossy walls. As though possessed, they squeezed their thick bodies under doors and through windows. The army was called out and began shooting. By the end of the day, more than a dozen people had died from snakebites. *Les Colonies* wrote about it all.

Poring over these dispatches that now hang on the walls of Saint-Pierre's volcano museum, which had been built on the foundation of the old opera house, I was reminded of the worst dreams of Poe or Kafka. Had these events really occurred here? Yes, just as tsunamis from Krakatau had actually grown to the height of ten-story buildings.

As I wandered through the museum taking notes, I thought back to the year that SueEllen and I had spent in China. Scientists there, I remembered reading in the English language *China Daily,* had long been interested in the potential benefits of using animals to predict earthquakes. Dogs and perhaps deer, they theorized, might help warn technology-poor communities in the countryside that something big was coming. Animals seemed to act nervously before major quakes, perhaps feeling tremors that people couldn't. It was also possible that their fantastic sense of smell could detect subtle ground emissions of gases caused by the deep and invisible stirrings of rock faults, of magma.

The Chinese had good reasons for their interest. Maybe the deadliest natural disaster of all time was the Hua-hsien earthquake of 1556, which killed at least 820,000 people. In modern times, the 1976 Tangshan quake, 7.8 on the Richter scale, killed almost a quarter million. When SueEllen and I visited a friend in Tianjin in 1984, we saw dozens of cracked apartment buildings from that quake, and those had apparently been just the ones worth saving. I wondered now if the Chinese researchers had ever heard of the millipedes and snakes of Martinique. Certainly these creatures knew something that people didn't.

That night, Viva lay sick in bed. Her throat hurt and she felt nauseated with fear. Nauseated, too, from the rotten egg smell that rolled down off the mountain—the wretched breath of the volcano. After a while she heard her mother come in and she felt the bedsprings give a little. She rolled onto her stomach, a habit from childhood when her mother would sing her to sleep while she rubbed her back.

"Viva," she whispered. "You should know that there are no serpents in the courtyard or the house. We're keeping watch." Then, "Lift your head. There, just a bit."

Viva did, and suddenly she was overwhelmed by the beautiful scent of oranges. The crushed fruit in her mother's hand, held just under her nostrils, was thrilling. She felt as if she were standing outside after a summer downpour, the clouds pulling apart and the whole world brimming suddenly with island light. It seemed possible, at least for a while, to remember a time before the volcano.

A volcano can erupt in many stages, not all of them cataclysmic, and in many ways, sometimes simultaneously. At Mexico's Parícutin, for instance, ash and cinders poured out of the crater right from the beginning, but it wasn't until weeks later that slow-moving lava broke out of its flanks. None of this tends to be very predictable in the life of any volcano, and it certainly was not in 1902. North of Saint-Pierre, on the morning of

May 5, a wall of boiling mud a quarter-mile wide came hissing down the corridor of the Rivière-Blanche. The Guerin & Son Sugar Plant stood in its path. A chocolate-colored torrent of boulders and muck, uprooted trees, scalded fish, and dead cows smashed open the doors and crushed the roof, burying everyone in it. More than twenty men. More would have died, including Viva's father, had they not stayed home to recover from the plague of millipedes.

For the next day or so, the volcano grew quiet, and then the afternoon rains began to wash the pale slopes green. Viva watched a parade of mule carts piled with furniture creak past their house. Children carried pets. Women swayed under wicker baskets of clothes, kitchen goods, and even, in one case, a sewing machine; many had pinned pictures of the Virgin over their hearts. Despite the exodus, the population of Saint-Pierre actually grew slightly, because families leaving for the capital of Fort-de-France, half a day's ride south, were more than replaced by refugees coming down off the flanks of the mountain and into town. Every living thing, it seemed, was rushing in a panic away from the *montay*.

While reporting this very bad news, *Les Colonies* also argued that the worst was over. The undersea telegraph cable to St. Lucia that had snapped, cutting off communication with the rest of the world, was being repaired. "Don't worry, Pierrotins," editorialized the newspaper. "Don't leave. And don't forget the election on the 11th!" Shortly after I read a framed account of this testament to denial, I noticed something odd in a corner of the volcano museum. It was the bell from the Mouillage Cathedral, bronze-green and weighing hundreds of pounds. If you stomped on a Dixie cup, you couldn't make it any flatter than this bell.

Viva's father wanted badly to believe the newspaper. But as he sat on his horse, taking in the ruins of the sugar plant, he found it hard to remain confident in anything. In the smoking slurry of mud and boulders, the only thing he recognized was the half-buried brick chimney, several stories tall. He'd ridden here to ground himself in the reality of the mud slide, which seemed like something you'd read about in Jules Verne, not on the front page of your own newspaper. Because the land itself had changed so thoroughly, he felt like the world of reason he'd grown up believing in had drifted away from him. In its place had swung a land of biblical plagues, hoodoo nightmares. So many of his friends and coworkers dead. And now he had no idea what to do for a living.

He dismounted and pulled out an old pistol. He pointed it at the sky and fired. For his friends. For his coworkers who were buried in the permanent night of the mud. Then he rode home.

Viva wandered downtown. Other youngsters did, too, since schools had been suspended and nobody really knew what to do. The city was a mess. In the cathedral, which was doing a brisk confessional business, the chandeliers faintly jingled, stopped, jingled again. Sodden ash spilled from roof drains and piled up in gray flower boxes. Snakes lay fat and rotting in the muddy gutters that once brimmed with cold water tumbling off The Mountain. People drifted by, coughing.

On the Rue Victor Hugo, Viva ran into school friends who told her a story they'd heard at the docks. A volcano had exploded on the island of St. Vincent, ninety miles south, killing a lot of people, although nobody knew how many. (In fact, it was at least 1,600.) As they sketched in what details they'd heard, her friends looked almost giddy. *But why?* Viva wondered, and said, "But don't you think a volcano that deadly is just another sign of doom?"

"Think of it this way, Viva," said one of the girls. "Let's say the volcano on St. Vincent is connected to ours by undersea plumbing. That's what people say, anyway. When it blows, it relieves pressure here. Therefore, shouldn't our own Mountain finally settle down?"

The answer came at four the next morning, on May 8, when thunder shook Viva from bed. She ran to her parents' room and saw them standing at the window, their faces flickering red-orange. She pushed between them. High on the mountain, two blast furnaces were roaring, sending up fire curtains that lit up the bottom of a giant, dull-red cloud.

Sparks arced out over the jungle. That's what Viva probably thought they were, but in fact they were probably burning rocks seen from a great distance, or lava bombs, some of them as large as ox carts, flying out of the throat of the volcano. She watched a far-off straw hut with a hole in its roof begin to burn. A palm tree on a ridge caught fire, then more palms, and the burning fronds began to wave like the arms of carnival dancers.

Viva held onto her parents and prayed. She stopped praying when it occurred to her that the statue of the Virgin that stood over the harbor, Our Lady of the Watch, had kept no kind of watch at all, had in fact done nothing for weeks but look blankly out to sea. What kind of wisdom and devotion and protection was that? Viva could feel her parents shaking.

By dawn, which was hardly dawn at all, so much ash had fallen that limbs on the breadfruit trees began to snap. "I don't know this place anymore," Viva's father kept muttering. He'd start packing a wagon with their belongings, then look at the stone walls of his house, then stop. Soon an image of the wrecked sugar plant would come to him, and the millipedes pouring out of the forest, and he'd pile more furniture on the cart. Then he'd think about the steep ravines and razorback ridges that stood between the mountaintop and their home, so many natural barriers. He also had to factor in the startling fact that Louis Mouttet, the governor of Martinique, had recently arrived with his wife from Fort-de-France to show the Pierrotins that there was no need for alarm.

Nowadays, when we consider the predicament of even someone as distraught and confused as Viva's father, it may seem insane that so many people would have chosen to wait things out. But when your lifelong home is suddenly threatened, it can turn into a magnet of unimaginable power, a phenomenon that disaster officials around the world have learned far too well. Besides, in 1902, no one knew much about the forces that were building inside Mount Pelée and what might happen if they finally broke out.

Even today, volcanologists can't predict most eruptions down to the hour or even the day. There's too much we still don't know, too much complicated voodoo operating inside the planet. On the other hand, if Gill Norton and her Montserrat crew were to observe the onset and sequence of similarly escalating conditions, I'm sure they'd try everything in their power to get the population packing.

At 7:50 A.M., Viva's mother was standing on her roof, shoveling ash. *I'm wasting my time,* she told herself. The family had been up for hours, packing, this time for real even if her husband mostly looked confused about it, and she'd sent the children running to her sister's pastry shop to get bread for the all-day walk to Fort-de-France. *On the other hand,* a small voice told her, *we might all be back in a week, The Mountain quiet and beautiful again.*

Then the world shook to its core. She almost lost her footing. Half a dozen roof tiles slid loose and smashed to the ground. She looked up at The Mountain and saw a colossal black column rising so fast it did not seem possible.

But then she saw that it was all too possible. *Oh yes,* she thought, *he's coming.* It was time, and he was coming just as the *obeah* grandmother had long ago predicted.

In seconds, it seemed, he stood a half-mile tall over the top of the *montay,* this *Diabe Vonmi.*

In a few more seconds he was a mile high.

And now *two.*

The demon grew taller than anything she had ever seen, his ink-black, dead-things coat wrapped so tightly around himself that he looked like a smoke pillar flickering with lightning, horrible and beautiful and venomous at the same time. But this was only a trick—she knew because she'd had so many years to think about it. And even now she could see that this wizard of roar and fire was trying yet another trick. He was splitting himself in two, not just shooting madly up into the sky, but smashing out of a mountain flank just below the notch.

Like night erupting into day, he swept down over the jungle, opening his dark coat. Out of its folds shot starbursts of lightning. He was the beginning of the world and the end. He was miles away but coming so swiftly that he would arrive in seconds, she could see that plainly.

Now he was sweeping over the rooftops on the edge of town, where the governor and his wife were staying. And now over the district where like a fool and a criminal she'd sent her children for bread. She saw trees splintering, houses just down the road exploding, and now he was so close and had opened his coat so wide that it blotted out The Mountain and the sky. A shadow flew over her courtyard, and the last thing Viva's mother saw was her husband sprinting from the house, looking up and shouting.

On their way to the pastry shop, Michel and Viva had jogged along a shortcut they knew that took them past a deep, weedy pit that everyone called the "Corkscrew." As they approached it, they felt a hot wind coming up from the earth. They looked down and saw a kind of red soup, or froth, boiling around in the pit, tinged with blue flames. Then the froth began to rise. We know the bare outlines of this and some of what comes next from what Viva told the journalist in the hospital.

"This place is going crazy!" said Michel, and they ran for it. In moments, the froth had spilled over the top and was chasing them down the street toward the harbor.

They ran like mad for Michel's boat.

Viva heard a tremendous explosion, but she didn't dare look back. She pumped her arms and flew over the cobblestones while the gold coin that Michel had given her slapped at her throat on its chain. The wharf seemed so far away, the ash-gray water beyond it another country. Viva flew faster. When she leaped into the boat, she turned to look for Michel but saw that he had dropped far back. Rushing up behind him and expanding everywhere was an inky hurricane. He had never been able to run very fast, and, she thought in a panic, he must have stumbled somehow.

"I heard him scream as the steam first touched and then swallowed him," she would tell the reporter from her hospital bed. And then she pushed off in the boat, paddling furiously. As the hurricane hit the water, there was an awful hissing and boiling, the first sound she'd heard it make. The water may have slowed it down a little—just enough, anyway. Somehow its tornadic force seemed to propel her toward the rocky grotto, then right into it. She saw that the space inside had shrunk, then realized that the water was rising fast.

Instant night.

A blast of steam.

Viva covered her face and balled up at the bottom of the boat. She thought, *This is the end of all things.*

———

News of the Mount Pelée tragedy spread quickly but incompletely. It appeared to be the world's greatest natural disaster since the 1883 eruption of Krakatau, and maybe the worst anybody had heard of in the Western Hemisphere. The death toll of 28,000 in Saint-Pierre was five times that of the prodigious hurricane with 120-mph winds that pushed waves and the tide across Galveston, Texas, in 1900.

At the same time, the very few eyewitness reports of this climax of Mount Pelée's eruption cycle were sketchy or observed long-distance. Thus, while the world quickly learned about the human cost of the tragedy, no one could explain how the volcano had managed to kill so many, so quickly. What exactly was the engine of all this destruction?

This scientific dilemma was oddly similar to the one that would be faced on a different, wider-ranging issue by German meteorologist Alfred Wegener about a decade later. Noting (as many others had over the years) how the coastlines of South America and Africa resembled a jigsaw fit of pieces separated by an ocean, Wegener had worked hard to build a case for a comprehensive theory of continental drift. The many lines of his argument included a similar distribution pattern of rocks and ancient fossils on opposite but apparently once-matching sides of the Atlantic Ocean. A key piece of his evidence was the fact that the 270-million-year-old fossil remains of a needle-toothed reptile, the mesosaur, were found only in Brazil and Africa.

In *The Origin of Continents and Oceans,* published and updated four times from 1915 to 1929, Wegener laid out his revolutionary and seemingly impossible theory. The continents, he argued, were giant sections (later called plates) of the earth's crust that *moved,* and always had. Sometimes they tore apart, as in the case of South America and Africa, or crashed together, or slipped over and under each other like prodigiously large rafts "drifting" or "floating" over the relatively liquid surface of the planet. But what mechanism or "engine" could make continents the size of South America and Africa move thousands of miles away from each other? Wegener had no satisfactory answer for this mechanical problem. Largely for this reason, his theory, while intriguing many scientists, was greeted with hostility and largely dismissed.

Wegener was long dead, having perished on a winter research expedition in Greenland, before his reputation was salvaged. In the 1950s and '60s, work by Princeton University geologist Harry Hess and many others provided an irrefutably plausible explanation for the mechanism of plate tectonics. The proof was made possible by the post–World War II discovery and study of midocean ridges, those ragged seams of seafloor mountain ranges, 5,000–15,000 feet tall, that we now know run beneath most of the world's oceans. The ridges, it turns out, are formed by tremendous volumes of lava rising from below in a supersized convection system of heated, rising rock. That constant movement pushes out or "spreads" seafloors.

Thanks to this and similar discoveries, roughly the first half of the twentieth century witnessed a great leap forward in our understanding of earth processes. What was learned on Martinique in the months and years following the Saint-Pierre disaster helped, in some small way, to spark this renaissance.

―――――

Six days after the Mount Pelée eruption, on the evening of May 14, the U.S. warship *Dixie* steamed south out of New York harbor. It departed under orders from President Theodore Roosevelt, who had pledged $200,000 in aid for the volcano refugees of St. Vincent and Martinique.

Some of *Dixie*'s American passengers, such as Harvard geologist Thomas Jaggar and U.S. Geological Survey scientist Robert Hill, had signed on specifically to discover what kind of deep-seated forces had driven Mount Pelée's murderous power. Narratives of the voyage published later indicated that *Dixie* was a crowded ship. Aside from 1,250 tons of food and medicine, it carried army officers and doctors, the Antarctic adventurer C. E. Borchgrevink, and reporters representing twenty-two magazines, press associations, and newspapers.

Among the media horde was a man who had never before written about volcanoes and who may never even have seen one. This was tall, gaunt, fifty-seven-year-old George Kennan, on assignment for *The Outlook* magazine. The intense-looking Kennan was easily the most famous man on board. A teenage wunderkind telegraph operator from rural Ohio (his mother was related to Samuel F. B. Morse), he had been turned down for duty on the front in the Civil War because of frail health. Yet by age twenty he found himself on a Western Union expedition to survey a cable route to Europe via Alaska, the Bering Strait, and Siberia. For two years he survived Arctic conditions of sometimes sixty degrees below zero. When the laying of the Atlantic cable made this dangerous venture abruptly irrelevant, he decided to stay behind and strike off on his own. Eventually, he crunched alone by dogsled across 5,000 miles of the Russian interior to St. Petersburg. The result was his first book, *Tent Life in Siberia,* an adventure-travel tale that made him famous.

His next book, born of a return journey, made him one of the most important journalists of his time. When he published *Siberia and the Exile System* in 1891, he became the first foreigner to expose the horrors of the czarist regime. The two-volume account of prison life and a nonexistent justice system was a kind of early, outsider's *Gulag Archipelago,* and historians credit it with helping to explain and contribute to the eventual overthrow of the Romanoffs. It's probably no coincidence that one of Kennan's distant relatives, George F. Kennan, should later have become the West's leading theoretician of U.S.-Soviet Cold War policy.

So crowded was the *Dixie* as it steamed 2,000 miles down the Atlantic Coast past South Carolina, Florida, and then Cuba, that Kennan and his fellow writers slept on hammocks on the berth deck, while the aroma of codfish wafted up to them from barrels in the hold. Time was more plentiful in 1902 than it is today—even this emergency trip, for instance, would take almost a week. In the first pages of the book that Kennan would eventually write about this experience, *The Tragedy of Pelée,* he fondly recalls how many of his shipmates would gather every night after dinner to hear talks from the men of science on board. They'd break out banjos and guitars and their favorite songs, then exchange stories about their many adventures.

Terra incognito was more plentiful a century ago, too, the blank places on maps that some of these men had visited or heard about through other travelers. How I'd love to have been onboard among them: so many raconteurs taking turns giving color and shape to the world's mystery places while the *Dixie* chugged through tropical waters past the exaggerated night silhouettes of Caribbean volcanoes, the ones that I like to imagine Viva's father pointed out to his family on his old map: Saba. St. Kitts and Nevis. Montserrat. Dominica.

On May 21, a couple of hours before dawn, the *Dixie* approached the northwest coast of Martinique where Saint-Pierre was supposed to be. By now the high spirits of the journalists had waned. The steam engine was cut. According to Kennan, they simply stood shoulder to shoulder at the rails, staring in silence at the black coastline. By starlight they gradually made out the still-intact silhouette of Mount Pelée, and then smoke rolling from its summit. Other than two orange glows along the harbor front that Kennan thought might be cremation fires, there were no lights at all. How could this ever have been called the "Paris of the Antilles"? There were no voices rolling out over the water, really no sounds at all, and nothing to suggest that a single flower had ever opened its petals on this part of the island.

Even the most battle-hardened of the journalists had not expected this; and the scientists on board were especially intrigued. In *Heart of Darkness,* Joseph Conrad writes, "Watching a coast as it slips by the ship is like thinking about an enigma." The enigma here was deep: what on earth, or *in* the earth, could have left the volcano looking relatively intact and still caused this level of destruction?

What nobody on board knew then was that less than a day earlier, a second black cloud perhaps as powerful as the first had burst from Mount Pelée and followed much the same downhill path over the city. Except that the only people who died this time were perhaps some of the looters who had entered the ruins of the city.

Meanwhile, two of Saint-Pierre's handful of survivors, Ludger Sylbaris and Harviva da Ifrile, were fighting off infections from their two-week-old burns. They were recovering, or at least managing to stay alive, on opposite sides of the island. Ludger lay in bed at Father Mary's parish in the northern mountains and Viva in the military hospital in Fort-de-France.

Viva could not tell the reporter who spoke to her what happened after the inky hurricane overwhelmed her in the grotto. A few hours afterward, the cruiser *Suchet* tried to approach the burning ruins of the city but was forced to turn back because of the intense heat. That's when its crew found Viva lying unconscious in her charred boat. The boat was drifting in grainy water littered with pumice, deck planks, shreds of sails, withered palm fronds, and human and animal bodies and body parts.

Viva and Ludger would probably not have known about each other, at least at first. He would have been too dazed by pain to notice much beyond his own body. She might have been told that a man had survived a direct hit from the death cloud. Like many residents of the island, however, she may have thought Ludger's story too preposterous to be true, a disaster myth. How could anyone have survived the full power of the blast when just one far edge of its shock wave had thrown the Lady of the Watch forty feet from its pedestal? That stone monument weighed three tons. A newspaper photograph that I came across in the museum shows the Virgin, whiter-looking than ever, her undamaged arms out-spread, lying face-down in black cinders, as though she were looking hard for a message from deep in the earth.

The *Dixie*'s scientists and journalists, plus other new arrivals, were soon doing their own kinds of looking. According to Kennan, there was a feeling in the air that whatever had happened here—so many thousands somehow not evacuated from an obvious danger zone—should never be allowed to happen again. These sentiments were among the first stirrings of modern disaster prevention.

Working their way along twisted roads toward Mount Pelée from the capital of Fort-de-France, Kennan and some of his colleagues passed hundreds of refugees straggling down from the northern half of the island. It had been more than two weeks since the May 8 disaster, and still people were coming. The reporters talked to everyone and gathered eyewitness reports from those few residents whose homes in the mountains overlooked the devastation zone.

When George Kennan finally entered Saint-Pierre, he noticed twisted girders and tangled telephone wires, melted iron crucifixes. He touched still-hot ash. And everywhere he saw ants—the first returnees, building tiny mounds of gray powder around their holes. *The Tragedy of Pelée* is worth reading for this level of observation alone, not to mention Kennan's careful speculation, in his final chapter, about what might have happened.

Meanwhile, Thomas Jaggar, who had studied the world's distribution of soils and rocks but never really volcanoes themselves, busied himself measuring ashfalls and noting the blow-down patterns of splintered trees. These activities drew him into more intense studies of volcanoes generally, and he became an advocate of studying what he called "splendid natural laboratories," noting, in 1925, that there were "more than four hundred more or less active volcanoes in the world not being continuously observed."

This career shift would eventually transform him into one of the pioneers of modern volcanology. Years after his Martinique time, he would found the Hawaiian Volcano Observatory, which today bears his name, and he would conduct pioneering lava-movement studies. He built a device to measure subtle changes in ground tilt, an advance in helping to record up close volcano behavior. For research in the volcanic Aleutian Islands, he would invent an amphibious vehicle that became a prototype of the World War II military "duck." Weirdly enough, he'd also become the first person to try aerial bombing to deflect or stop lava flows. His detective work at Mount Pelée was the start of all this.

Another detective soon arrived. Or maybe I should say two. Alfred Lacroix of the French Academy of Sciences stayed on Martinique much longer than *Dixie*'s passengers. With his wife (the daughter of his mentor in France) operating as his secretary and providing scale for his photographs, he spent almost a year studying and documenting subsequent eruption-avalanches from the still-hot and unstable mountain. By day these fast-expanding clouds that rushed downslope looked black or gray. But by night, he began to notice, they appeared to be lit from within, eerily incandescent as they raced down Pelée's flanks at 100 mph or more. "The moment it appeared," he wrote of one flow, "it looked like a compact mass of small size, but immediately it began to swell . . . lined with numerous convolutions with deep meanders, which grew ceaselessly . . . expanding . . . and advancing with a terrible majesty."

From these observations, he eventually inferred that they were debris- and boulder-filled blasts of superheated gas released suddenly from the pressure cooker of the volcano. Because of their nocturnal appearance and kilnlike interior temperatures, Lacroix called them *nuées ardentes,* or glowing clouds. Building on the observations of Jaggar, Kennan, and other eyewitnesses, laymen, and scientists, he would become the first person in history to correctly explain how they worked. The puzzle of Mount Pelée's horrific engine of destruction was finally solved.

Nuées ardentes are of course pyroclastic flows, or surges, and they're one of the main reasons why certain volcanoes the world over can morph so quickly into mass murderers. A Mount Pelée-like blast from any of the volcanoes that today simmer uphill of tremendous cities like Naples or Quito could kill a half-million people in three minutes. Recent studies reveal that some ancient pyroclastic flows, perhaps swallowing most of their own sound as they swept downhill, traveled up to sixty miles from their breakout point and carried *2,000 times* the punch of Mount St. Helens's famous blast.

A pyroclastic flow that bursts out high on a mountain flank isn't just fire from the earth. From the point of view of anybody and anything living on or downhill from that spot, it's fire from the sky.

It's also what I imagine Viva's mother called the *Diabe Vonmi.*

And what about Viva? Orphaned instantly from everybody she ever knew, exiled from home, scarred in several ways at once, she probably recovered from her burns. Then she lived the rest of her life—where? History hasn't the slightest idea.

I gave this some thought as I chewed on a piece of squid at a downtown restaurant, a Creole place that offered a nice view of the harbor. My young waitress had a bounce in her step and in her personality, and as I often do with my CSU students, I wondered what the future held for her.

If a story is a "kind of dreaming" in which the dead sometimes "sit up and return to the world," as Tim O'Brien puts it, then I like to imagine that Viva landed in New Orleans. It would have been a decent possibility. Ships from Martinique stopped in all the time, and at the turn of the century, Creole culture flourished there like nowhere else in the United States. One of the many schools run by the Dominicans or the Little Sisters of the Poor would happily have taken in a bright and spirited girl like Viva if, say, a sea captain or a businessman in Fort-de-France had taken pity and paid her way north. Besides, there wasn't any Saint-Pierre for her to go back to.

When I try to imagine her life after the volcano, I see Viva a few years later, at age eighteen or nineteen, living in the French Quarter. She's on her own, perhaps working as a domestic, not married, not "kept," and certainly no longer in love with quite everything. The dark joke of terra firma—the cruel if unconscious lie of ancient map makers that the world is a solid and unchanging place—has taught her some caution. She's grown tall and broad-shouldered like her mother, citified like her father. She thinks of them and her brother every day.

And I imagine her, one afternoon, picking her way through the long indoor alleys of the French Market, past the praline sellers, the bananas and plantains and mangoes piled as high as they once were in Saint-Pierre. I see her walking home past a brick wall plastered with bright new colors, which turn out to be circus posters of snarling gorillas, lions, and flying acrobats. And then, suddenly, there is Ludger Sylbaris, as large as life, staring down at her from his own poster. He stands barefoot in his prison rags (or P. T. Barnum's bright-white version of them—this poster exists today), looking sad and dispossessed and more than a little haunted, while behind him in the distance a shattered Saint-Pierre and Mount Pelée burn luridly.

Greatest Show On Earth

Greenville, Miss.—April 2–3

Greenville, in fact, is where the circus sometimes played during the years when Ludger toured with it.

I see Viva taking a train there, clacking north for hours while the brown Mississippi curves in and out of view through her open window. To Viva it must seem like such strange wide water, so much slower and browner than anything on Martinique, this earth-moving river sliding under a gray sky. And everywhere the flatness of the delta, and dead air.

In a cow pasture outside of Greenville, she slips into the sideshow tent with the matinee crowd, and suddenly she sees him shyly commanding a stage. He is telling his story in broken English, and then undoing the buttons of his shirt, peeling it back. Viva hears gasps and moans from the audience and perhaps from herself. From the back of the crowd, she studies his scars, the way they've hardened and thickened over the years, crumpling up into irregular lumps across his shoulders and back. They're like geologic relief, as separate and distinct, some of them, as the islands on that old map of her father's. They're terrible exaggerations of her own stiff scars, which she thought were bad enough until she saw this. Ludger's Pierrotin accent, though crude and uneducated, reminds her of Michel and her father, of the men she used to watch working on the docks, rolling and stacking hogsheads of sugar and rum.

The crowd thins, and she lingers, working on her courage. When she reaches the stage, she introduces herself, blurts out the bare details of her story. He looks down at her, stricken.

Smiling, she assures him that she is no ghost, then asks if he has time for a walk. She surprises herself by her forwardness with this burly, rough-hewn man whom she'd probably never have spoken to at home. But there is no home—only his island voice and hers, and what they remember together. To speak to him like this doesn't feel improper at all.

He has little time between shows but goes anyway. As they wander from the tent, he fumbles and stutters—still awestruck, she supposes, at the unreal fact of her existence. She doesn't know what to say, either. So they walk, one human curiosity moving beside another. This diaspora of two.

In a field near the river, she stops and turns to face him. With her index finger she nudges aside the gold coin at her throat, lets him study the round burn behind it. The brown river hisses by.

He nods. Tugs down his shirt over one shoulder. Up close, she studies the valleys and high ridges of his scars. The day is hot with no breeze, but Viva begins to feel trade winds stirring. She hears the papery clacking of palm fronds, the froth of tumbling streams. She closes her eyes, flies off, and fills up with island light.

WIRING UP
THE WORLD
REDOUBT VOLCANO, ALASKA

Suddenly you realize
the volcano is speaking to you,
and you understand the language.

—Bernard Chouet, *USGS scientist*

It wasn't until I flew to Alaska that I discovered and then began to feel how far the shadow of a volcano can reach. The effects of an eruption can travel hundreds or thousands of miles—and change the world in surprising and profound ways. In my case, it even changed the way I thought about flying.

But first, let's work up to the present by looking in some amazing new ways at the ancient world. Let's look at Atlantis. Thanks to recent work by anthropologists and volcano experts, it now seems as though Atlantis traveled far and uncommonly fast from its original site in the Mediterranean Sea, blown to dust and pebbles by one of the most gigantic volcanic eruptions of all time. This paroxysm made the great bulk of Thera, an island whose collapsed crater is today known as the Greek island of Santorini, disappear beneath the depths of the sea "in a single day and night of misfortune," as Plato once famously wrote. Thera, more and more, looks like Atlantis.

Locating the whereabouts of the Lost Continent has been one of the great puzzles of the ages. Another has been discovering the reason for the sudden collapse, in roughly 1600 B.C., of the apparently vigorous Minoan civilization centered on the north coast of Crete and nearby islands. Crete lies about seventy miles due south of Thera. Recent studies of volcanic ash deposits on land and from cores drilled into ocean floor sediments suggest that Thera's massive eruption occurred only a few decades before 1600 B.C. Basing their thinking partly on similarities with the 1883 eruption of Krakatau, which was also an island volcano, archeologists and volcanologists have concluded that the Thera blast could easily have spawned tsunamis large enough to destroy Minoan coastal cities and push the culture into a fatal decline. Thus the volcano may have killed two birds with one stone—one of them, within a few days, on its own slopes, and the other, over a few years or decades, to the south across the Sea of Crete.

The eruption illustrates two other points. One, that some volcanoes over the centuries have created unanticipated, long-distance effects on human cultures that are only now being comprehended. Two, that a key to minimizing the effects of future up close and faraway eruptions lies in realizing that volcanoes might be speaking to us before they erupt and that we need to understand their language.

The long-distance effects of volcanoes can be startling. In 1883, so much rock blew out of the eruption of Krakatau, in Indonesia, that rafts of pumice wandered the world's oceans for months afterward. One of them eventually washed up on Zanzibar, off the coast of East Africa, carrying the remains of trees and the sun-bleached skeletons of some of the volcano's human victims.

A century earlier, in May of 1783, a fifteen-mile-long series of fissures cracked open in Iceland, and for eight months out flowed a tremendous volume of lava. Poisonous gases, particularly sulfur dioxide and fluorine, rose from the fissures, creating a hanging blue haze that contaminated the island's grasses. This in turn killed thousands of livestock. In the resulting famine, up to 10,000 Icelanders died, perhaps one-fifth of the island's population. One thousand miles to the southeast, shortly after the eruption's onset, people in England noticed an unusually cool spring and summer. A horribly bitter winter followed.

Living in France as the American ambassador that same summer, Benjamin Franklin remarked upon a series of blue hazes, or "dry fogs," lingering over the countryside. When he took out a magnifying glass and ran into trouble trying to kindle paper, he began to wonder what could have so weakened the sun's rays. Eventually, he proposed that the temperatures in northern Europe might have been affected by widely diffused dust from the Icelandic eruption. He was the first person to link volcanic activities with climate and weather.

That link became much more obvious following the July 1815 eruption of Tambora volcano, which shot several million tons of sulfur dioxide gas into the Indonesian stratosphere. As volcanologist Haraldur Sigurdsson explains in *Melting the Earth,*

"The gas quickly condensed to form an aerosol, a cloud of sulfuric acid droplets that enveloped the earth and scattered solar radiation back to space, leading to a sudden cooling of the Earth's entire surface." The result in 1816, especially in the Northern Hemisphere, was the infamous "Year without a Summer." In Europe, mean temperatures dropped several degrees, severely shortening the growing season and causing widespread food shortages. In New England, snow fell every month of the year.

It's probable that Tambora's eruption influenced more than the world's climate. In the spring of 1816, Mary Godwin, eighteen years old and a reader of five languages, including Greek and Latin, accompanied her lover and future husband, Percy Bysshe Shelley, to the shores of Switzerland's Lake Geneva. There they shared a house with Lord Byron and his doctor, John Polidari. "The season was cold and rainy," she would later write, "and in the evenings we crowded around a blazing wood fire, and occasionally amused ourselves with some German stories of ghosts." Byron proposed a competition among the friends: who could write the best horror story. Out of Mary Shelley's hastily scribbled pages eventually grew her novel *Frankenstein,* which she published when she was twenty. The classic Boris Karloff movie and its many descendants offer no hint of the dark, polar landscapes that haunt her novel and provide an icy epitaph for the Monster.

Aerosols and airborne particles cause atmospheric light to shift toward the red zone of the spectrum—think of the lurid, blood-orange sunsets you sometimes see in cities full of air pollution. Even while cooling large regions of the planet, Tambora set sunsets aflame worldwide. And the glowing skies likely inspired another artist, the British landscape painter J. M. W. Turner. His renditions of spectacular seascapes at dusk began appearing at just this time, a major shift in his career. In a similar way, the tremendous eruption of Krakatau volcano in 1883 inspired William Ascroft to paint a series of almost unbelievably luminous sunsets over the Thames in Chelsea.

––––––

Flying to Alaska showed me how a surprising and potentially far more dangerous consequence of volcanic eruptions has come to light only in the last few decades. This consequence had to wait for the development of a seemingly benign piece of technology: the jet engine. Here's what I mean.

On December 15, 1989, an almost brand-new Boeing 747 jumbo jet took off from the Netherlands, bound for Tokyo. It didn't fly east from Amsterdam as you might imagine it would. It headed north, over the top of the world, following an arc over the frozen sea of the North Pole and then down toward Anchorage, Alaska, where it was scheduled to refuel and let off passengers before completing its run to Tokyo.

Look at a world map, a flat representation of a sphere, and this route at first seems to make little sense. But run your finger over a globe of the earth, and three-dimensional logic quickly shows that the shortest distance between Chicago and Hong Kong, or New York and Beijing, or Amsterdam and Tokyo (or at least the shortest route that also skirts spookily chaotic Russian airspace), takes you over or near Alaska. These are among the "great-circle routes" followed by thousands of international jetliners every year.

Add to them the local and regional flights that crisscross a mostly roadless state that's more than twice as large as Texas, and you have a lot of aircraft plying Alaskan skies. Puttering bush planes. Helicopters. Air Force jets and C-130s. FedEx, UPS, and other freight flights. Anchorage International Airport handles more international cargo, in dollar value, than any other U. S. airport. In all, at least 6,000 planes a day travel the Alaskan skies.

The Amsterdam jet, KLM Flight 867, entered northern Alaskan airspace around 11 A.M. The sun had just risen, slightly, over the absurdly brief Arctic day. There were 231 passengers on board, plus a crew of thirteen.

The jet was also beginning to pass over some of the most deeply unstable landscape on the planet. Thanks to the fractured geometry of plate tectonics, the northward-crawling Pacific oceanic plate creeps in a downward curve two or three inches per year beneath the North American continental plate. As the forward edge of this ocean-bottom crust grinds fifty miles or so below the Alaskan mainland, stresses and strains build up and are released in sometimes subtle, sometimes furious jolts, endless palsies in the earth.

The converging plates have crumpled up the Alaskan landscape into spectacular mountains. The plate movement has also helped give birth to more than forty of the fifty-four U.S. volcanoes that have been active in historic time. That's about 8 percent of all active above-water volcanoes on earth. Most of them are strung out, like beads on a necklace, along the 1,550-mile-long Aleutian Arc that runs west from Anchorage to Russia's Kamchatka Peninsula, which itself contains dozens of active volcanoes. The raw and windswept chain forms the northernmost portion of the Pacific Ring of Fire.

One of the most prominent mountains in this long arc is 10,197-foot-tall Redoubt volcano, a thickset triangle of ice and snow that hulks over Cook Inlet, in Lake Clark National Park,

about 100 miles southwest of Anchorage. The summit crater of
Redoubt has been fairly active over the years. Up until 1967, it
had gone off, moderately, six times during the twentieth century.

An hour or so before Flight 867 reached Alaskan airspace,
Redoubt, which had been rumbling seriously all day and threatening to blow for the first time in more than twenty years,
erupted explosively. It roared for forty minutes, sending up an
ash-rich plume that quickly grew to resemble a mushroom cloud
like the ones from those South Pacific atomic bomb tests. Soon
the cloud had climbed to a height of seven and a half miles above
sea level. At that altitude, which is higher than the summit of
Mount Everest and just past the point where the troposphere
thins out into the stratosphere, hurricane-speed winds are rou-
tine. Consequently, the top of the ash plume, ever widening,
began to race away from the volcano. The giant cloud bolted to
the northeast. Scalding hot subterranean rock had just turned
into "weather."

A modern jetliner is a wonder of technology. But all instruments have their limits, and the radar system on an ordinary passenger jet cannot distinguish an ash cloud from an ordinary
thunderhead. Before take off, 867's flight crew had been briefed
about the potential of a Redoubt eruption—although the exact
time and size would be only the wildest of guesses—so they'd
taken on 5,000 extra gallons of fuel in case they had to divert.

As they eased into their long descent to Anchorage, the pilots saw nothing in particular to divert from. They'd been informed by the Alaska Volcano Observatory, then in its first year
of operation, that Redoubt had indeed recently erupted. Yet they
were still more than 200 miles from the volcano. And if the cloud
layer the pilots were bearing down on looked a bit browner than

normal—a little bruised, maybe—they apparently felt no alarm. They barreled into it at about 500 mph.

There was instant darkness. Darkness, and then, for a few magical seconds, lighted particles zooming past the cockpit like a thousand fireflies, a million fireflies. It looked unworldly; it was a vision of the universe just seconds after the Big Bang—an incredible blast of stars. And then after a few seconds the crew saw nothing at all, for their acrylic windshields, the leading edges of the airliner, had been abraded as though in a sand storm. Fine brown dust began to swirl in the cockpit.

In the passenger cabin, the lights went out and a powerful smell of sulfur came through the vents. Passengers pulled out handkerchiefs and held them to their noses and mouths. Some of them saw coronas or eerie lights playing about the wings and engines. Generated by the supercharged ash particles grinding all around the plane, these electrical discharges were almost certainly Saint Elmo's fire, which during the Middle Ages had been named after the patron saint of sailors. Seafarers from Columbus to Magellan to the fictional, doomed crew of *Moby-Dick*'s *Pequod* reported seeing the saint's "holy body" glow briefly as an electrical discharge on the tips of their vessel's masts or yardarms. Sometimes the fire danced on harpoon points or the heads of spears. Many regarded it as a portent of bad weather.

By now, KLM 867 was definitely plowing through bad weather. The pilots noticed a "Cargo Fire" warning light blink on, but thinking that it was caused by what they were quickly realizing was volcanic ash, they decided to ignore it. Besides, there were more urgent matters to attend to. The gloom in the cockpit had become so thick that the pilot could find her copilot only by reaching out and touching his shoulder. The cockpit crew strapped on oxygen masks. Once she could breathe normally again, the pilot veered left and started a full-thrust climb to escape the ash as quickly as possible. At first the jet performed normally. But the more it climbed, the more it began to lose air speed.

"Ash" is a funny word. Unless you're a volcanologist, it usually brings to mind the gray, feathery remains of a woodstove, or dying campfire coals. But nothing soft or fluffy blasts out of the throat of a volcano. What shoots out is a magmatic mix of minerals and glass shards, fragmented and powered by violently expanding gases and steam. In other words, magma that's been blown to smithereens, blown into billions of pieces of fast-cooling, sharp-edged grit often smaller than the period at the end of this sentence.

Soon these particles were scraping the leading edges of the jet's wings and tail rudder. The finer pieces worked their way into the hydraulic system and fuel sump. They even seeped into the engine oil. More than seven tons of air per minute were being sucked through each of 867's engines, and the ash that now clogged that air began to gnaw away at the turbofan blades. In the combustion chambers, which operate at temperatures slightly above the melting point of ash, the particles cooked, then solidified as glass and coated the turbine blades in a ceramic skin. This fooled the jet's safety sensors into thinking that the engines were overheating. Then the sensors shut them down.

One minute into 867's diversionary climb, all four engines went dead. The jet was five miles above sea level, and three or so above the craggy, icebound peaks of the Alaska Range.

"ANCHORAGE," the pilot radioed, "WE ARE IN A FALL!"

When its engines fail, an airliner traveling at high speed doesn't just drop like a rock. It glides, at least for a while. KLM

867 had been climbing at a rate of 1,500 feet per minute. Now, in a great silence, it gradually leveled off and began to arrow slightly down, as though an enormous invisible rock had come to sit on its nose. The rock was gravity.

The pilots tried to restart the engines. Nothing. They tried again. Nothing. In a powerless glide, the jet dropped faster. Soon, pencils and pens began to float about the passenger cabin. So did thick novels, bags of peanuts, plastic cups, playing cards, pillows, and blankets, all floating in the dim, acrid air.

For five minutes the plane fell in silence, or at least a mechanical silence, because by now many of the passengers were screaming or retching or holding on to each other and praying. The pilots tried again and again to restart the engines. While they worked, the plane dropped out of the bottom of the ash cloud. The passengers could now see for themselves how close they were to the jagged peaks of the icebound mountains. On the eighth or ninth restart try, the now-cold glass that coated the turbofan blades in one of the left-wing engines fractured, and the blades bit into air. A moment later the other left-wing engine roared back to life. Three minutes later, the right-wing engines followed. With a few thousand feet to spare, the pilot managed to level off, then turn for Anchorage.

They landed without further incident, some in the cockpit crew leaning far to the side and squinting out of the slightly less frosted edges of the windshield. None of the passengers had been injured, at least not physically, but the engines were ruined. The jet suffered $80 million in damage and was grounded for months.

Meanwhile, the ash cloud kept moving. Although it didn't clog their engines, the ash scraped up two other nearby jets. As pilot and air control chatter filled the skies, rippling out over much of the Northern Hemisphere, the wandering cloud scared off many more aircraft. Growing ever more diffuse, the ash was pushed south by high wind currents toward Mexico. Two days later, as it passed over the skies of El Paso, Texas, it still carried enough particles to scratch up the wings of a Navy DC-9 that had no idea where the floating grit had come from. El Paso was 3,000 miles from the broken top of Redoubt volcano.

Lying within one hundred miles or so of Anchorage and the towns of Kenai and Homer, Redoubt had the potential to harm many people on the ground, as well. Nevertheless, the eruption caused no loss of human life—this time. But another "off-site," if not quite a long-distance effect of the blast, and following Redoubt eruptions, came close to causing an environmental disaster. Standing twenty-two miles from the volcano's summit, at the mouth of a river that meandered down Redoubt's very gradual lower slopes, was the Drift River Oil Terminal. It had been designed to transfer crude oil to massive tankers chugging up and down Cook Inlet, and it had a storage capacity of 1.9 billion barrels.

The eruption that almost pulled down KLM Flight 867 was followed by a few more during the next days and weeks. Some of them generated pyroclastic surges that helped melt millions of tons of ice and snow on the upper flanks of the volcano—the same process that scientists worry could occur some day at Mount Rainier. (This is also why Civil Defense officials have installed vibration sensors in the historical paths of Rainier's lahars.) On December 15, torrents of mud, boulders and ice blocks—some of them the size of two-car garages—began to seeth and tumble down Redoubt's Drift Glacier and into the river course below. The lahar of hot and cold debris was powerful enough to crush any storage tank in its path and send oil oozing into Cook Inlet, which is habitat to an Eden of animals, including seals, sea otters, orcas, porpoises, and pods of one hundred or more beluga whales. Tidal bores that move at 15 mph through parts of the Inlet would only deepen the catastrophic effects of an oil spill.

Shades of the *Exxon Valdez*. Fortunately, the Drift River flow crested just short of the terminal. Two weeks later, an eruption-generated lahar traveling the same course pushed floodwaters over the berm of the terminal and into some buildings, but did little other damage. Both cases were extremely close calls. They were also cautionary tales about human ignorance of geologic time scales.

It is sobering to think that all of this middle- and long-distance chaos (and potential disaster), on the ground and high in the air, was set in motion by a very ordinary-sized eruption. Redoubt volcano's blast might easily have gone unremarked a century or two ago, when the world was less technology dependent and not nearly as populated. But what if the eruption had been 10 percent more powerful? Or what if it had been anything like those eruptions in June 1912, that burst from a cluster of craters just another hundred miles to the southwest? Over a period of sixty hours, some of the the vents of the Novarupta/Katmai volcanic field sent seven cubic miles of material into the Alaskan skies, burying a nearby valley in up to 700 feet of hot ash.

One result of that eruption, the largest of the twentieth century, was an unreal and illogical landscape that extended for miles. A part of it was described five years later by a National Geographic Society expedition chemist, Mr. Shipley, as follows:

"Hot streams flow from beneath flanks of snow; extensive glaciers hobnob with steaming fumaroles, while icebergs and hot water are found in the same little lake." The Valley of Ten Thousand Smokes, as some of the transformed area came to be called, looked more like a part of the moon than Earth. Decades later, NASA would become aware of this and send astronauts there to train for the first lunar landing. They stomped around in spacesuits and drove moon rovers over its dust-choked surface.

Compared to Novarupta/Katmai—not to mention Washington's Mount St. Helens, Martinique's Mount Pelée, and dozens of other volcanoes that have erupted around the world during the last hundred years or so—Redoubt went off like a popgun. And it still almost dragged down a jetliner 200 miles away.

It's the mission of Guy Tygat and his many colleagues at the Alaskan Volcano Observatory to see that such terrifying near-misses never happen again. The AVO is headquartered in Anchorage but does much of its monitoring work 400 miles north, in the Alaskan interior, in a cubelike building on the campus of the University of Alaska-Fairbanks. The building sits atop a long ridge and is recognizable for miles by a huge satellite dish on its roof. One sunny May afternoon, eleven years after that almost-tragic eruption of Redoubt volcano, I walked up that ridge and visited Guy at work. I'd picked his name at random from the AVO Web site directory, and we'd hit it off over the phone.

But I have to confess something. I was a little reluctant to spend the day inside the AVO offices. Fairbanks, along the banks of the winding Chena and Tanana Rivers, happened to be on the verge of "greening-up." That's what I had heard some friends who taught at the university call the shockingly short time, maybe just three or four days, that it takes for birches, willows, and other deciduous trees to burst into bloom at this high latitude, which was starting to bask in sunlight for almost twenty hours per day. Like an erupting volcano, an Alaskan green-up seems to be another of the natural world's hurry-up moments in time, in this case a nano-spring popping up inside of a calendar spring.

But Guy's warm smile and willingness to explain complicated things to me made me temporarily forget what was about to happen outside the building. Very soon, he led me to a bank of slowly revolving canisters that I recognized as seismographs. They were hooked up to the twitchings of about a dozen North Pacific volcanoes, including Redoubt. Guy's major responsibility, he told me, was to oversee the mechanics of this vast monitoring system, and some of it was literally nuts-and-bolts work.

In the summer, he was frequently dropped off by helicopter onto a remote and sometimes unpopulated Aleutian island. (Unpopulated by humans, that is. The Aleutians provide homes for many enormous seabird rookeries, such as the nesting site of half a million northern fulmars on Chagulak Island.) Guy and sometimes one or two other AVO scientists or graduate students might camp at a work site for several days to a week. But if stinging rain blew sideways or fog rolled in, preventing the copter from safely returning, they might stay much longer. Their task, besides fending off hypothermia and loneliness, was to install or repair or replace monitoring equipment arrayed over the slopes of various volcanoes. Taking advantage of Arctic summer days, they often worked eighteen hours straight. The equipment needed constant attention not because of any innate delicacies or design flaws, but because of the awful natural conditions it endured year-round.

"And the bears," Guy said, looking suddenly exasperated, but smiling, too. "The bears can fool you."

I nodded, guessing that I knew what he meant. Guy was a sturdy blond man, forty maybe, with the air of a Viking. But he was no match for a bear that could stand seven feet tall, weigh more than half a ton, and outrun a horse. The Aleutians were home to Alaska browns, aka, far-north grizzlies, and they could be as unpredictable as they were large. Over the years, I had backpacked in Montana's grizzly country and hadn't always liked it. If I had to work all day and then sleep in a pup tent on the treeless slope of an Aleutian volcano, I'd be damn wary, too.

But it turned out that Guy wasn't talking about personal danger. Nope, he was talking about *data*. A brown bear trudging across a rocky Aleutian slope can make footfalls heavy enough to fool a measuring device and screw up the numbers. A ground monitoring sensor, for instance, can mistake a bear walking by for a series of shallow earthquake tremors, which in the absence of other data can suggest that magma and gases are migrating toward the surface, cracking rock above and preparing to blow. Guy told me he also worried about the bears' maddening habit, shared by a number of smaller creatures, of gnawing at the power cables of the sensors, silencing them until at least the next summer.

And like apparently everyone who works outdoors in the Aleutians, he fretted about cold rain, spitting snow, and wind. Especially wind. Storms that sweep over the Aleutians sometimes blow so hard they can make the stony surface of a volcano actually vibrate, also messing with the data.

Guy grabbed a photo album from the top of a file cabinet and opened it to a shot of something that might have been a Port-A-Pit for children. It seemed to be bolted into a dark rocky slope.

"It's a cover we designed," he said. "To give the instruments a chance. The conditions out there are unbelievable." He closed his eyes and shook his head. I reminded myself that this is a man who lived year-round in Fairbanks, where winter temperatures plummet to forty and fifty below and can freeze shut your eyelids. This actually happened to one of my CSU graduate students, who before she retreated south to balmy Colorado once tried to walk across the UAF campus in January. So I wondered what a *normal* person would think of Aleutian Islands weather.

"Let me show you something about the elements," he said. He flipped the album pages to a shot of one of those three-sided, ladder-like antennas made of steel tubing. It seemed to have been trampled by outraged bears. Bent completely back on itself, it looked like a Möbius strip cut from paper. But it was wind that had done this trampling. Wind also shortens the lives of solar panels and the hard-sided instrument and battery covers by zinging pebbles and ice chunks at them for days at a time.

Because Aleutian volcanoes are socked in by clouds, sometimes 300 days a year, visual observation of their pre- and post-eruptive behavior is out of the question. Still, potentially turbulent volcanoes anywhere on the planet and especially near busy air corridors need to be watched constantly. I was not happy to learn that what Redoubt almost did to KLM 867 had not been an isolated incident. Not at all.

At least eighty times in the last two decades or so, geology has reminded pilots that the skies they fly are sometimes far from friendly. In 1982, ash from Galunggung on central Java, made a British Airways jet drop for six miles before its engines restarted. Japan's Sakurajima volcano once spit pebbles five miles into the sky, and one of them cracked the windshield of a passing 747.

There have been no disasters so far. But every year more aircraft crowd Alaskan skies, and more pilots fly over or downwind of dozens of active volcanoes in Japan and the Kamchatka Peninsula. It doesn't help that a new, hotter-burning generation of jet engines may be capable of melting drifting ash even more quickly than before, making the turbines more prone to shutting down in midair.

Only 10 percent or so of the world's 1,500 potentially dangerous volcanoes have been wired up so that ground instruments can beep up their growls and hiccups to stationary or orbiting satellites. The satellites shoot the electronically coded data back down into dishes like the one on the roof of the Geophysical Institute in Fairbanks, the building that houses the AVO.

That's when Guy and his colleagues pore over seismographic scribbles, spectrographs, and other printouts. They concentrate like scholars bending over the Dead Sea Scrolls, but without the luxury of time. If a volcano is "popping," as they like to say around the AVO, they must measure and analyze it fast, factoring in reports from other volcano observatories, like those in Russia and Japan. A jetliner might be zooming toward an eruption cloud at eight or nine miles per minute. Ever more refined mathematical models help scientists project the path of ash clouds that high-altitude winds have whisked away from their sources—although variables such as cloud density, size, and shape, as well as wind speed and direction can be daunting. (The acronyms for monitoring systems, technology, and agencies can also be daunting, especially to amateurs like me: MVIRI, VISSR, VAFTAD, PUFF, SIGMET, PIREP, and lots more.)

At each step of a tracking activity, warnings are shot out to the National Weather Service and the Federal Aviation Administration. The FAA in turn alerts air traffic controllers and all nearby and approaching aircraft.

Information gathered by the AVO may also help caution coastal residents as far away as Hawaii about another kind of long-distance threat: tsunamis that may have been spawned by undersea earthquakes or by avalanches caused by volcanic eruptions. Although it doesn't seem possible, a tsunami can race with the speed of a jetliner across a harbor or the entire length of the ocean. (Thus, in roughly 1600 B.C., the seventy-mile-long frontal assault of the Minoan empire from ancient Thera probably took just ten or fifteen minutes.) Because it is really a packet of energy moving almost entirely below the surface of water, a tsunami may barely disturb oceangoing ships in its path. But then, slowed down and forced upward finally by shallow coastal waters, the wave can rear up to create deadly havoc. Anchorage's Good Friday Earthquake of 1964, the largest ever recorded in the Western Hemisphere at 9.2 on the Richter scale, shook loose a series of waves that even 1,600 miles away, in the northern California town of Crescent City, destroyed several blocks of homes and commercial buildings. Alaska needs to worry about both launching and getting slammed by tsunamis because it has more coastline than all of the other U.S. states combined. The AVO trades information with tsunami warning centers like the one headquartered outside Honolulu, where scientists on duty never stray far from the office, even sleeping within sprinting distance of their monitoring equipment.

After my first full day of shadowing Guy and walking around the AVO, I began to understand how important and difficult it was to wire up the world.

The next day I discovered that Dörte Mann had understood this for some time, despite her youth. Blonde, graduate-school-trim, and German-pale, she struck me at first as a quintessentially indoor person. I thought this even after I learned that she first fell in love with volcanoes by hiking among stunning Andean peaks when she was in college. But maybe she was pale because she was wrapping up a PhD at the University of Alaska, I finally told myself. Or that she did most of her hiking these days in overwhelmingly gray weather. Like Guy Tygat, she had spent much of the previous summer trying to wire up Aleutian volcanoes.

She and I had been talking for a while, sitting across from each other on the floor of an AVO administrator's office that had been taken over by coils of wire and bright yellow power packs. I was holding in my lap a gizmo that resembled a high-tech pizza tray. It was a GPS antenna. In her very soft voice, Dörte was telling me how she customarily bolts it to a tripod on an active volcano. Soon, if everything worked right, it would catch and return signals beamed down to it from some of the thirty-five GPS satellites above the earth. These space eyes, I learned later, are only a fraction of the 10,000 satellites that have been rocketed into deep space or sent in orbit around the planet since the very first Sputnik, in 1957.

Other antennae that Dörte and her coworkers have so far planted on the slopes of about twenty Aleutian volcanoes operate with similar goals. When the ground under any of the sensors bulges or sags by just a few millimeters, suggesting rising magma, the stirring of a possible eruption, the AVO knows it almost instantly. Thanks to an airplane- or ground-mounted instrument called a correlation spectrometer (COSPEC), the volume and chemical composition of gases emitted by a volcano can also be measured. When the numbers are crunched by high-speed computers, the patterns of these often subtle ground and gas changes can help predict what's cooking below the surface, and when and where on a volcano's slope or summit something may crack open or boil up.

Remote sensing also allows the AVO to observe eruption clouds and, far below them, "thermal anomalies" or hot spots on or near the surface of a volcano. This is often the only way to look at a volcano that has not been seismically wired, and at this high latitude it also takes advantage of frequent satellite coverage as orbits converge and overlap near the North Pole.

In short, like their compatriots at other observatories around the world, the AVO crowd tries to observe the inner planet much as certain modernist painters once looked at vases, landscapes, and French women—from as many angles as they can, simultaneously. The painters let you take your time and fend for yourself among those views. But given the potential consequences—a flood or rushing tsunami, a jetliner falling out of the sky—volcanologists act fast to try to synthesize and interpret their views for possible answers.

Tom Simkin, of the Smithsonian Institution's Global Volcanism Program, likes to compare the range of monitoring approaches to that of medical checkups, both examining what really can't be seen by the eye. Studying a volcano's chemistry is like taking blood work and a urinalysis, seismology is akin to listening to the heart via stethoscope and EKG, measuring deformation compares to checking the head or torso for lumps, and so forth. No one exam tells you everything you need to know. And,

Simkin adds, "Let's not forget that all-important history that a doctor extracts from a patient. History is extracted from a volcano mainly by careful and often arduous fieldwork—mapping, dating, and analyzing older deposits to gain the personal history of that particular volcano."

Studying the deposits from past eruptions helps understand the long-term behavior pattern, or character, of a volcano. As in people, volcano character varies widely: some degas wildly just before an eruption, some don't; some, like Mount St. Helens bulging out toward Spirit Lake and stubborn old Harry Truman, deform big-time before erupting, some hardly do at all. Thus the value of old-fashioned, rock and hammer fieldwork, the sort that just about every geologist thirty-five or older remembers in his bones starting in the first summer of graduate school. The nostalgic pull of this dusty, precomputer activity was underscored for me when I spoke one afternoon with Jon Dehn. Jon is a skilled volcanologist, but he also seems to be one of those all-purpose technical wizards everybody in a place like the AVO likes having around. Several times in three or four days I saw him called over to fix a miscommunication between a laptop and an overhead projector, or some other annoying glitch. He'd stare at a computer screen for a few moments, frown, and then type in commands at light-speed. Done!

But when I asked him how he got interested in volcanology, he leaned back in a chair and smiled broadly. "When I was a kid, somebody told me that when you whack open a rock, you're the first person to ever look inside that world. How cool was that? I don't think I ever got over it."

Volcano prediction science is exciting science, some of it using "eyes" that orbit dozens or hundreds of miles above the ground to read the earth's various languages. This in turn can potentially save thousands and thousands of lives. And yet, as I left the AVO for the last time, I felt a bit gloomy. The culprit, I suspected, was the proliferation of just that high-tech looking. Monitoring remote and formerly inaccessible islands, filling in so many blank spots on a map . . . is there no place anymore for shadows in the world? Call me a Luddite or a romantic, but it all seemed to leave less and less room for mystery, even though I know very well that innovations like the microscope and then the electron microscope have probably led us to more and deeper mysteries than we ever knew existed. I worried that satellite mapping might soon make the ordinary human senses obsolete and regional knowledge of place irrelevant. Did a sailor still need to memorize the subtle compositions of clouds? If we know a volcano's about to roar up out of the sea, will there ever be another day, like the one in 1706, when a band of surprised and awestruck Aleuts might shout "Bogoslof!" God's Voice! as they watched Bogoslof Island rumble into existence?

When I got outside and headed back down the ridge, I noticed that the UAL campus had indeed greened up. "Bogoslof!" I wanted to shout.

I walked past the wonderful anthropology and art museum that the university had built on the ridge. Beside it stood an old totem pole set among birches, and nearby a reconstructed hexagonal log cabin with a sod roof. They were such fine handcrafted expressions of intimate local knowledge, and they got me to thinking about the life and death of Maurice and Katia Krafft.

With all of their equipment, scientific training, and unsurpassed knowledge of eruptions, why had they kept throwing their bodies in harm's way? Of course, only they knew. But I bet it had a lot to do with the allure of fieldwork, especially when the field was changing fast. Maurice and Katia thrived on the up close and the visceral, the need to not just hear, but *feel* the monster roar of magma.

On the other hand, I reminded myself of something that Dörte Mann had told me as we sat among GPS telemetry gadgets on the office floor. After patiently describing the intricacies of an Advanced Very High Resolution Radiometer (AVHRR!), she allowed herself a little smile. With the understatement of a true scientist, she said, "I think perhaps we can learn a lot with this technology."

I thought ahead to my flight home. If the pilots were given the best information available, the engines on our jet would suck in nothing but sweet, uncluttered Arctic air. I'd have satellites and the men and women tinkering on Aleutian volcanoes to thank for that.

Well, Dörte, here's to learning everything you possibly can. Here's to deep seeing made deeper by wiring up the world.

VOLCANOES OF THE MIND
THE CASCADES AND MOUNT SHASTA

When I first caught sight of [Shasta] over the braided
folds of the Sacramento Valley I was fifty miles away
and afoot, alone and weary. Yet all my blood turned to
wine, and I have not been weary since.

–John Muir, *The Mountains of California*

Hokusai did not complete his *One Hundred Views of Mount Fuji* until late in his life, until at least his mid-seventies. I was surprised to learn this at first. But then, the more I thought about it in the context of several trips I took to the Pacific Northwest and to northern California, the more the shape of Hokusai's career began to make sense to me. It's hard enough to understand the physical characteristics and ecological relationships of landforms as complicated as volcanoes because, for all their visible bulk, they lie mostly hidden from view beneath the surface of the earth

211

or the ocean. But what about the challenge of trying to understand volcanoes of the mind, mountains of the human imagination gone wild?

I'm still far from my own seventies, but I have definitely
pitched over into the second half of my life. And only now am I
starting to understand, as Hokusai did, how it might take years
to see that a single thing can be viewed from so many sides.

During the summer of 1998, half a year after I'd explored the islands of Montserrat and Martinique, I flew out to Seattle to track
some of the bigger Cascade peaks south and to rendezvous, finally, with California's Mount Shasta. I was interested in Shasta
for several reasons. First, I wanted to see how people from my
own culture, speaking my own language, thought about a volcano. I also wanted to explore the slightly odd reputation that
Shasta had acquired in recent years as a spiritual or New Age
center. What exactly did that mean? Finally, a long time ago, on
my first trip through the American West, Shasta had seized a part
of my imagination and never really let go.

After I tossed my duffel bag of camping equipment into a
rental car at Sea-Tac Airport, I traveled in wobbly fashion down
a three-state-long Avenue of Volcanoes. These eye-catching
summits and broken craters—fifteen in all, from British
Columbia's Mount Garibaldi to California's Lassen Peak—were
formed by two tectonic slabs, the Juan de Fuca and Gorda plates,
grinding underneath the massive North American plate. The result was the northwestern U.S. section of the Pacific Ring of Fire.

Mount Rainier, at 14,411 feet the tallest of the Cascade
peaks, is also one of the most dramatic. That was underscored

for me as I got out of my car at the base of the mountain and hiked up to Paradise Meadows, where melting snow had recently nurtured bursts of blue lupine, purple asters, and Indian paintbrush in a dozen shades of pink and red. The meadow climbed away from me, tilting up steeply into conifers where magpies glided from tree to tree. Here began the world of snow. From here up, except for outcroppings of dark jagged rock, everything was brilliant white snow, glaciers, and ice fields, spiraling up to infinity.

Although it is not old as volcanoes go—it has been building for about 500,000 years—Mount Rainier long predated any human habitation of west-central Washington. It so dominated the landscape that it inspired creation stories from just about every Native American tribe that could see it. The Nisqually called it Ta-co-bet, meaning either "Where the Waters Begin" or "Nourishing Breasts." And the Yakima, who called it Ta-ho-ma, meaning the same two things, refused to climb it because they believed they could not survive the power of the spirits living on its summit.

I had had no such worries myself back in 1990, when I found myself preparing for a Mount Rainier summit climb with a group of friends who had gathered from all over the country. Since none of us had ever been on the mountain, we had hired a guide service to help us with the adventure. I had never even put on a pair of crampons. In fact, until the day before one of the guides handed me an ice ax, I had never laid eyes on Rainier.

It's only a fourteener, I had told myself back in mile-high Colorado, home of fifty-four mountains that rise above 14,000 feet. And so I had prepared somewhat casually and late, strapping on a backpack weighted with rocks and water bottles and striding up and down some of the foothills near my home, but not doing much else.

Of course, the Colorado fourteeners I had in mind were not volcanoes. Hardly any of them stood alone, as Cascade volcanoes tend to, having been built from below by one explosive eruption at a time. This subterranean creation meant that Rainier in its glorious isolation caught the full force of wind- and snow-storms ripping in from the Pacific. Its proximity to the coast ensured that that happened frequently. Over the centuries, more than one cubic mile of ice and snow had accumulated on the volcano's enormous flanks, creating twenty-five glaciers and thousands of shifting, unworldly blue crevasses. When I got my first close look at the mountain, I actually gasped.

And yet, I had little problem trudging up through sun-blasted snow from the bottom of Rainier to a sleeping hut at 10,000 feet. To my surprise, the crumpled ice fields near the hut did make me think of Tibet, a far cry from the wildflower meadows that SueEllen and I often strolled through at similar elevations in Colorado. I had to remind myself that this was late June and not December.

But only after we were awakened at midnight for the summit "assault" and I heard an ungodly roaring, did I start to worry. I stepped outside into a steady, fifty-mile-per-hour wind. Ice chunks whistled past my head, and the guides ordered us to put on our glacier glasses. Since this was already the middle of the night, it was hard to see more than ten feet ahead, even with my headlamp. Wind gusts that roared in from some far corner of the universe shook me so hard I thought I might fly right off the mountain, especially after I watched one of the guides, a guy who had once summited Mount Everest, get knocked flat. The fact that we were being roped up into teams of five wasn't all that reassuring. Climbers did die on this mountain. *Will we all go down together?* I wondered.

But we didn't. And gradually, as we climbed toward morning and the summit, the winds abated. Sunrise was glorious, offering an incredible view above the clouds of the crisp white triangle of Mount Adams, a volcano fifty miles to the southeast. Not far to the west of Adams stood snow-capped Mount St. Helens, beautiful, too, but no longer looking very symmetrical. Until its famous eruption of May 18, 1980, it had been called the "Mount Fuji of America." Far below me, in a Rainier meadow, sat SueEllen, uninterested in this macho climb. Later on she'd tell me that she talked to a guy who'd been standing on Rainier's summit on the morning Mount St. Helens erupted. He told her he thought the entire mountain was exploding. The blast came rushing in his direction, and even though the violence was unfolding fifty miles away, it terrified him.

As we trudged higher, kicking steps into the ice-glazed but crunchy snow, various climbers turned back, complaining of dizziness or cold. I felt strong and not cold at all. But during our last rest stop, at about 13,500 feet, I noticed one of the guides looking me over.

"I dunno," he said, studying my eyes. "You look a little funny to me. The altitude's getting you, maybe. I wonder if you should skip the summit. But I'm going to leave it up to you."

So I tried to think about it. That's when I realized that I couldn't. Think clearly, that is. I could move around just fine, but I felt slightly sedated, a little removed from myself, loopy. I knew these were possible effects of the altitude. *Well,* I rationalized after a while, *I've had my fun, plus I've never been much of a peak bagger, anyway.* And so without much more thought, I turned around.

But now that I had returned to Rainier, now that I was studying its incredible steep slopes from flower-packed Paradise Meadows, I rued that decision not to try the summit. I was still not much of a peak bagger, but I did wish that I had climbed on to glimpse the summit crater that I'd barely thought about then, before I'd started viewing the world with volcano eyes. Photographs show a gigantic sag in the snow that apparently gives off steam from several fumaroles. I recalled that one of the guides on our adventure told me that a party of climbers had once gotten stranded up there by a blizzard. They were stuck for days and had avoided freezing to death by taking shelter near those warm vents.

The vents were visible proof of what deep-earth studies have confirmed about Rainier. While it has not erupted in any significant way since 1825, it has blown with great violence at least ten times in the last 8,000 years. And it will certainly erupt many times again.

Standing among the wildflowers, looking up at that cubic mile of frozen water, I wondered what might happen someday when large parts of the upper mountain inevitably heat up from the inside. I had learned recently that the Boeing aircraft factory complex outside Seattle had been built over ancient mudflows that had slid at least sixty miles downhill from Rainier. Tens of thousands of people now live in the path of that one lahar alone, though most don't know it. As a Seattle native once put it to me, before she realized that Rainier was still a living volcano, she thought of it as "Just there, big and beautiful, but not something that could play an active part in my life."

White, white, white! That's what I thought as I squinted up through my sunglasses. How could anyone's imagination *not* be charged by such an imposing presence? "Some say the world will end in fire/Some say in ice," wrote Robert Frost. Yakima people who refused to climb Ta-ho-ma because their sensibilities had been haunted by this mammoth house of the spirits would have known exactly what Frost meant—and maybe more. For they would have had their entire lives to ponder and maybe witness a third kind of Armageddon: a world that could end by fire *and* ice.

After Rainier, I stopped briefly at Mount St. Helens. As I drove and hiked around the national monument, I noticed a surprising amount of greenery poking up between the shattered trees in the eighteen-year-old blast zone. A ranger I talked to mentioned that the new growth was luring back elk in big numbers, a somewhat unexpected benefit of all the destruction.

Farther south, I caught some fleeting views of Mount Hood from Vancouver, Washington, where I stopped to talk to some scientists at the Cascades Volcano Observatory. With Mount Hood fading in and out of clouds in the distance, I felt as Hokusai might have as he moved about nineteenth-century Edo doing preliminary sketches of Fuji framed by the high arch of the Ten Thousand Years Bridge, or as the volcano loomed over the garden of Ryuganji, a pine-shaded Zen temple. For two days I watched wide and symmetrical Mount Hood slip behind its cloak of sky, disappear, and then reappear like magic, like grace.

But it was Crater Lake in southern Oregon that I found the trickiest of all to see. I don't mean the lake itself, six miles wide and shining sapphire blue against jagged crater walls more than one thousand feet high. That's one of the great sights of the world, and the deepest blue I have ever seen. What was difficult to see was the shape of the volcano that formed the lake roughly 6,900 years ago.

Mount Mazama, as it was posthumously named by people who once lived in southwestern Oregon, had grown to a height of 12,000 feet when a series of explosive eruptions started tearing it apart. As with all Cascades volcanoes, the magma beneath Mazama was high in silica content, meaning that it tended to clump up and explode violently rather than burble out as, say, highly basaltic lavas in Hawaii usually do. The violence here culminated in a blast that by volume was many times the size of Krakatau's and more than forty times that of Mount St. Helens. But the caldera where the lake now shimmers did not have its top blown off as you might assume. Instead, the bulk of the mountain collapsed into the void from which perhaps twelve cubic miles of magma had spilled out or shot into the sky.

Since then, almost seventy centuries of rain and snow melting from Crater Lake's meandering, thirty-mile-long rim have formed the deepest lake in the United States. It's also an unusually closed ecological system: water does not flow in or out and apparently never has. There is no evidence of fish having ever lived in the lake until several species were introduced by humans beginning in 1881. Although the National Park Service stopped that practice in 1941, kokanee salmon and rainbow trout still survive. In 1989, scientists in a small submarine explored the lake bottom 1,900 feet below the surface and discovered warm springs, suggesting that this, too, is a living Cascades volcano.

It was not until I had driven about sixty miles south, to Lower Klamath Lake, just over the California border, that I looked back north over a horse pasture and saw the true dimensions of the old volcano. My God, there was no mistaking it. On the distant horizon was a great bulge in the earth, the lower slopes of Mount Mazama rising toward each other before breaking off into air, suggesting the complete outline of the enormous, pre-eruption volcano.

I had been traveling for almost a week now and had begun to notice that from the vicinity of one Cascades volcano I could always see the bright, ice-bound top of another—weather permitting, of course. Soon I would drive partway up Mount Shasta, and in places where the road broke out of the forest I could look south and see the thick white bulk of Lassen Peak—a thrilling sight. The landscape in between was unimpeded by any evidence of towns, roads, logging cuts, or other trappings of the modern world.

Lassen is the southernmost big volcano in the Cascades chain, a place some Native Americans called *Broke-Apart Mountain*—geologic truth since it has erupted at least half a dozen times in the last thousand years. If I were one of the old-time poets of China or Japan, I'd say my Avenue of Volcanoes journey was a dream of pine-scented mountains in which every day I was offered a glimpse of heaven from heaven. How amazing that the earth's sizzling subterranean heat had built mountains high enough to catch and hold prodigious volumes of snow and ice. More to the geomythological point, if I were a member of one of the Indian clans that once lived between Seattle and northern California, I would know many of the legends of warrior-heroes, demons, and lovers who lived in the form of virtually every Cascade volcano. Many stories, for instance, recount the exploits of the brothers Wy'east (Mount Hood) and Pahto (Mount Adams) who battled for the favors of the maiden La-wa-la-clough (Mount St. Helens). At times Wy'east threw rocks out of large holes, shot forth streams of liquid fire, and clogged great valleys with rocks—more apparent geologic truths. The connection of extraordinary landscape to story was palpable. I felt this now as strongly as when I sat in that boat rocking in the Tyr-rhenian Sea, watching Stromboli throw lava into the night.

The legendary battles of two great gods arced across the skies between Mount Mazama and Shasta, 125 miles apart. According to a Klamath Indian myth that suggests the 4900 B.C. creation of Crater Lake, Llao, the Chief of the Below World, who lived under Mount Mazama, did battle with Skell, the Chief of the Above World, who descended from heaven over Mount Shasta. In their conflict over a beautiful young woman (of course), fires poured out of Mazama, burning forests for miles and turning the skies bright red. Then darkness fell over the land while the earth convulsed wildly. In the end, Llao's mountain collapsed, leaving the beautiful lake we see today while Skell continued to visit the white throne of Mount Shasta.

Just as that throne tends to draw the human eye from every direction, it also gathers a wide variety of Native American legends. One of the wilder stories is that thirteen lizard kingdoms lie stacked up over Mount Shasta, an idea possibly inspired by the meteorological fact that some of the most spectacular lenticular clouds on the planet form over that summit. Often these lens-shaped apparitions pile up like a stack of celestial pancakes, a sight of unearthly beauty. Another legend comes from the Modocs, who lived east of Shasta in the burnt-looking, cinder-cone-strewn landscape that today is Lava Beds National Monument. The Modocs told tales of a Great Spirit who lived inside a mountain in a lodge whose top, like Shasta's, was a smoke hole.

One of Shasta's origin stories goes like this. Before there was ever a mountain, a local Karok chief led his people every year on a pilgrimage to the Pacific Ocean one hundred miles to the west. Eventually, he grew too old to travel, but wanting to see the blue waters once more before he died, he had his people scoop earth into baskets and build him a great mountain for an outlook. This is Shasta.

The baskets of earth used by the Karoks suggest the incremental growth of the volcano, which has been building one eruption at a time for 200,000 years. It's not true, though, that you can see the Pacific from its summit—the Pacific Coast Ranges get in the way. Thus, this legend's truth operates mainly on mythic levels, especially in its suggestion that Mount Shasta affords remarkable, even supernatural, vision.

Shasta, when I first laid eyes on it during the summer of 1971, certainly looked like a vision to me. Like John Muir as he hiked north through the Sacramento Valley, I too was weary and ready to have my blood transformed into wine. Boy, was I ready. Muir was thirty-eight as he approached Shasta. I was only twenty-three or twenty-four, but my journey had been hard enough. I had recently finished college in Florida, and to make a short and painful story shorter, let's say that I had become by then a thoroughly lost soul. And so hitting the road had begun to sound good to me—the road to California, more specifically. The Golden State: deserts and cool mountains, the air clear enough to let me see a long way, maybe even into my future.

On a hot and muggy Tampa morning, I hopped into my little green Datsun and took off. Except for flying to L.A. once on a family vacation, I'd never seen anything west of New Orleans. After several days of driving, I noticed that the deep south humidity, normally powerful enough to soften a stone, had begun to dissipate in the high, wide, almost interstellar spaces of west Texas. In downtown El Paso, I found an Army-Navy surplus store and bought a bright orange pup tent and a bright orange polyfill sleeping bag. Together they cost $36, which was about twice as much as I'd spent on gas—at thirty cents a gallon—to that point. I already had an Igloo cooler, a wool blanket, a rope hammock, a box of books I had skipped reading in college but meant to get to, and a Swiss Army knife I'd been carrying around since I was twelve. I was set. I think I was planning to live on sunshine and metaphors.

And over the next few months, I just about did—even though my first night out in the New Mexico wilderness, at 8,000 feet in the Mogollon Mountains, turned out to be one of the coldest of my life. I woke up to wind-whipped flurries, and I shivered in my blanket inside my all-but-useless bag. The idea that it could snow anywhere in June had never entered my head.

Lots of other things I soon experienced had never entered my head. That space on this planet could brim with such sublimely brilliant light, more than the New York sun I grew up under ever gave off. That you could drive fast for half an hour without once having to turn the steering wheel. That you could feel the bread on your sandwich dry out in your hand, its surface turning as rough and stiff as lichen on rock. The world really did change from place to place, and if I were lucky, the same might be true of me.

I saw and felt the West one laser-sharp valley and mountain at a time. Not far from Carson Pass in the Sierra Nevada, I found myself a campsite along a tumbling creek, far down from where I parked my car. It was so hidden that I was never bothered by anyone, not even the Hell's Angels who rumbled through the campsite loop on weekends in packs 100 strong. Swinging in my hammock, I read about a book a day—*Sons and Lovers, Siddhartha,*

Moby-Dick (a two- or three-day immersion), *The Heart Is a Lonely Hunter.* Books packed with yearning and transformation. Talk about interstellar spaces. I lived in the woods for three weeks.

Moving northwest through California, I camped at the mouth of the Russian River. On the beach at night, the glow from wind-splashed bonfires played over driftwood huts that seemed fashioned from the bleached bones of mastodons. Bearded, broken-veined old men ducked in and out of them. They were probably in their forties, but they looked to me like ancient pilgrims—mountain-wandering poets or the mad saints that Jack Kerouac and Charles Bukowski wrote about.

In a bar somewhere up the coast, I talked for most of an afternoon with a woman who had had a hard life, lots of bumpy relationships with men. She'd moved in finally with the guy who wrote and sang that strangest of '60s songs, "They're Coming to Take Me Away, Ha-Haaa!" He sang under the name Napoleon XIV.

"And they did," she said slowly, picking at the label on her Budweiser. "They finally did take him away . . ." I had no idea if any of this was true, but she had sad eyes and a kind voice, so I bought her another Bud. Then she told me about growing up nearby as an only child raised by a mother who dabbled in religions full of chanting, and who ate vegetarian when that was a sign of kookiness even in California. She turned into a lonely child, afraid to bring friends home from school.

Except for one time. They were studying the planets in class, and suddenly she raised her hand and said that she knew a place where, crazy as it seemed, you could see the stars in the middle of the day. The next afternoon the whole class was standing in her backyard.

"I pulled back the root cellar door and we went down a few kids at a time," she told me, or words to that effect. She'd often sat down there for hours, playing with her cat or reading, and she'd discovered that if you angled it right at a certain time of the afternoon, you could shade out the effect of the sun, look up from that dank cellar, and faintly see the stars.

"Imagine that," she said, starting to smile at me. "All those stars twinkling in a light blue sky! It was like heaven shining through heaven. Then everybody saw them! My classmates and finally my teacher took turns sitting down there with me, talking and trying to make out the constellations. I moved around like a hostess, pointing out things. I explained how to look, how to do it right."

She took a sip of beer and stared out the window at the ocean, and I wondered if what she'd told me was even possible, to see the night stars poking through the afternoon sky. I wondered what kind of looking that would take. "You know," she said finally, "I think that may have been the high point of my life."

After that I zigzagged inland to Sacramento, then headed north on I-5 to check out the deep green forests of Oregon, Ken Kesey country. It was on my way there, driving a route roughly like the one that John Muir once hiked, when I saw flashes of Mount Shasta coming up on me from the north—a brilliant white peak. As the highway climbed out of the furnacelike, tabletop flatness of California's Central Valley, dark pines began to speckle the foothills, and I watched the mountain grow into the most gorgeous chunk of landscape I'd ever seen, a tremendous cone of ice, all the more massive for standing completely alone. It seemed to stand for everything that the Florida part of my life was not. I had not known the mountain was coming and I did not know its name.

I pulled over, got out of the car, and just stood by the side of the highway as traffic whipped by. I couldn't take my eyes off the thing. Two vertical miles of earth and rock wrapped in ice and snow, heavy as the world, and yet somehow the entire mountain seemed to float. It was a kingdom of light, and it shone more brightly, I thought, than all the West's big-sky valleys and high plains combined.

Of course, imposing heights, the world over, have for centuries engendered the sacred. Mount Olympus, Mount Sinai. Mount Ararat, Turkey's Holocene-era volcano reputed to be the final resting place of Noah's Ark. Indonesia's smoldering Gunung Agung, which let loose a tremendous eruption in 1963 and which the Balinese have for generations worshipped as the "Navel of the World." For miles in every direction, they honor it by sleeping with their heads toward the summit. Tibet's Everest and Kailas, and lower Himalayan peaks and ridges snapping with prayer flags. Japanese summits that have given birth to Shinto mountain-worship. China's T'ai Shan alive with immortal beings who yoke dragons to their carriages and then climb the floating clouds. Not all of these are volcanoes, but because "mountains alive" tend by their nature to stand magnificently alone and also often act with great violence, they evoke the mystical even more often than "ordinary" striking mountains.

And so it was for me during those first few minutes that I took in Mount Shasta. A would-be writer, I was just beginning to comprehend how narratives can cluster themselves around not just people but places, certain places, anyway, and how stories can shout themselves down from high rocks and snowy summits. While I was taking in the mountain, it's possible that it was also taking me in.

Now I was approaching it for the first time in twenty-seven years. It was nearly sunset when Shasta swung into view. I was instantly struck, once again, by how packed with light it looked. But I also looked on with my recently acquired volcano eyes. The ancient, internal fires that burned up and down the Cascades—the Earth's rising forces, great subterranean mysteries—seemed to be gathering inside this volcano. Shasta, I knew now, had not erupted since 1786. Nevertheless, it seemed almost to tremble with life and movement: a vortex or convergence point of geothermal power.

The odd reputation that Mount Shasta had acquired over the years had something to do with another kind of convergence—the two-day Great Harmonic Convergence of 1987. At the time, I had read some newspaper stories about the gathering, which seemed to be a kind of New Age Woodstock held simultaneously that summer in what the faithful called "sacred power points of the world." These places included Sedona, Arizona; Machu Picchu, Peru; the pyramid-shaped Temples of the Sun and the Moon near Mexico City; and Mount Shasta. The idea was to affect a shift in consciousness for the entire planet. I vaguely recalled a blip on the evening news featuring aging hippies standing in a mountain meadow, holding hands and humming. It was just the kind of scene that SueEllen and I loved to laugh at.

Hold the cynicism, I told myself as I now drove into the city limits. The main drag of Mount Shasta City at first offered little to ridicule. The streets were wide, as befits an old Western town. There were coffee shops and restaurants with hand-painted signs, a health-food store, and lots of little mining-town homes with rock gardens of columbines and asters. The place reminded me of Crested Butte, in southern Colorado, which SueEllen and I love. I assumed it was full of U.S. Forest Service retirees and hard-body kayakers, rock climbers, and rafting guides—the leathery ectomorphs who often showed up in my writing classes at CSU, looking for meaning.

I got out of the car in front of a cozy-looking bookstore called the Golden Bough. Just off the sidewalk was an outdoor, wall-sized bulletin board plastered with dozens of flyers. When I got close enough to read them, the day quickly turned strange.

If I wanted a *Shower of Angel Energy,* whatever that meant, it was just a phone call away. The same for *Clairvoyant Lightwork,* a baffling phrase I loved. Same for *Kundalini Counseling, Hathor Sound Healing, Cranial Therapy,* and *Etheric Surgery. Divine Tune-Ups* were also available, plus the channeling of former lives, or conversations with 50,000-year-old masters, many of whom, according to the small print, happened to live inside Mount Shasta itself. And on and on.

Soon I found myself reading the bulletin board as though it were a postmodern novel, full of disconnected paragraphs that made sense only in the occasional patterns I managed to impose on them. The magical beings who supposedly lived inside Shasta were often referred to as "Them" or the "Ascended Ones." At least a dozen Personal Transformation Coaches offered to guide me through these and other golden realms. The coaches had names like Shastina Free Bear, Ixthara, Andraleria, Vlasta Bramah, Mary Ma McChrist, and RA-MA-AA. (If you don't believe me you can look up their Web sites.) All of them seemed to live in town or in the nearby, foot-of-the-mountain communities of Dunsmuir, McCloud, and Weed. Or they were coming soon.

Of course I had glanced at an occasional flyer like these in the windows of crystal shops and organic food stores across the Rocky Mountain West. I'd seen them from Fort Collins to the dinkiest mountain hamlets to those twin Meccas of the New Age tourist trail, Santa Fe and Sedona. But the Golden Bough's menu of metaphysical options contained *everything*, an exaltation of strangeness!

Tearing myself away finally, I drove deeper into town. Soon I passed Bruno's Brakes & Tires, then Darlene's Salon of Beauty, a place that looked capable of sculpting and laminating a foot-tall beehive if anybody were still around to ask for one. But what was this? Between the two businesses was a stucco storefront with a large white banner running across the top of the building.

The Archangel Michael's Soul Therapy Center

Ah, I thought, *the New Age standing hard by the Old, the ethereal bumping up against the blue collar. How could I not drop in?*

When I did, I discovered almost right away that Joa Dolphin-Play was in pain. I knew this because I heard him say so to a woman in the loose white gown who nodded at me when I walked through the door. She had smiled at me in a way that made me want to call out, "And the Force be with *you*, too!"

I was standing across the room from her, pretending to read a deeply weird pamphlet. Really, though, I was trying to eavesdrop on her and Joa Dolphin-Play. I had slipped into my sly-reporter mode.

Joa, who looked about thirty, sounded like a tremendously nice guy, his voice a soft wind. Now and then he shook his dark, shoulder-length hair with a slight duck of embarrassment, as though he realized that anybody with a name like his, anyone who looked so comfortable in a tie-dyed T-shirt full of sunbursts, shouldn't have to admit to unhappiness.

But he *was* in pain, he told her. Stressed out. He was an astrologer and free-movement coach, he explained, showing her one of his flyers with his picture and name, which I recognized instantly from the Golden Bough's bulletin board. He said that he had come to Mount Shasta, one of the great power points of the universe, to codirect a "Three Days of Bliss" workshop. Unfortunately, though, he had sunk too much money into advertising, especially given the number of people who'd signed up and the condition of his bank account. Now the caterer was threatening to pull out. He wondered therefore if the Woman in White could cut him a deal on the standard donation for Etheric Healing. He could really use a dose.

The woman closed her eyes and nodded, shaking a tangle of curls that was almost as white as her gown. *Of course,* she seemed to say. *Isn't that what this place is for?*

I began to notice that harp music filled the room. Had the Woman in White somehow cranked up the volume? She led Joa Dolphin-Play to a well-padded, sunken bed that lay under a four-sided pyramid frame made from what looked like elegant PVC pipe. A glance down at the pamphlet in my hand corrected this impression. The thing Joa was settling himself under, removing his sandals, lying back and closing his eyes and letting loose a massive sigh, was in fact an "Ascension Meditation System," a "7 ft. Cheops Copper Pyramid" painted white.

The pamphlet had pictures. Employing "phi ratios," it explained, the pyramid "aligns the individual to the Planetary Soul." The English usage I know and teach to my writing students doesn't permit you to align anything "to" anything else. But here in the shadow of Shasta, the rules of grammar, like the laws of the physical universe, were perhaps made to be broken.

Even during the most lost of my lost-young-man days, I would not have been drawn to anything as strange as *Etheric Healing*, despite the loopy poetry of the language. Back in 1971, if I'd met any of these seekers and true believers, or realized how many fantastic stories the mountain inspired in them, I might have shrugged or laughed and called them Cultural Grab-Bag Artists. Or Shastafarians—a word SueEllen would coin after I got home and told her about my trip. "Good one, SueEllen!" I would laugh. Yes, Shastafarians.

I wandered around and looked at a bunch of other pyramids. They had price tags. $495. $795. Not exactly for the homeless. In fact, the pyramids shone like cars in a showroom, interdimensional sports coupes, shiny starmobiles. I seemed to have stumbled into a high-tech, New Age dealership.

Minus, however, any high pressure sales pitch. Indeed, the Woman in White now stood over Joa, smiling calmly down at him and waving over his long toes a baton wrapped handsomely in copper wire. She could have been stirring lentil soup. The pamphlet called the thing in her hand an "Etheric Weaver." That or a "Sacred Geometric Vajra." It depended on the shapes of the chunky crystals strapped on each end, which I couldn't quite make out from where I was standing. Either way, it was one of the "Metatronic Angelic tools" originally created for the "Himalayan Masters of Wisdom." It occurred to me that "Metatronic" was a word built from a preface and a suffix but with nothing in between—a kind of doughnut word. I liked the sound of it anyway.

The pyramids, said my pamphlet, had been designed by:

The incarnation of
Archangel Michael 'Lama Dorje'
The Buddha Maitreya Jesus *Babaji* Sanat Kumara.

In other words, the guy who apparently ran this place, wherever he may have been. Or whenever. Snapshots of him were framed on the walls. In most of them he sat cross-legged in yellow Tibetan robes, wearing a tall pointed hat. He looked about my age, with a dark beard going gray in places. In fact, the Archangel Michael looked a lot like *me,* though with many more pizzas under his belt. I'd have bet money that he was originally from Brooklyn or New Jersey.

Meanwhile, the Woman in White ran her stick in the air back and forth over the length of Joa's body. Joa was taking deep, blissful breaths and looked ready to drop into sleep, which was surely a dimension removed from his waking world of financial stress. I was happy for him, I really was. He seemed so well-meaning, and earlier, on the outskirts of town, I had noticed him getting out of his van followed by a black dog, a big galumphing thing, and I could tell right away how much he loved it.

Now Joa was beaming. He seemed to have gotten himself aligned with the Planetary Soul. After a while, he opened his eyes, blinked, and sat up. He fumbled with his sandals and climbed out of the pyramid. Thanking the Woman in White, he forked over a ten.

Well, I told myself, *it sure beats the price of a shrink.*

Never mind that every time Jean, my haircutter in Fort Collins, tilts me all the way back in her chair, I end up feeling a lot like the way I suspected Joa did here. Jean eases me back into her sink and shushes warm water through my hair. Then she massages her soapy hands over my skull and asks, in her beautiful Trinidadian accent, "So how you been, eh?"

"Oh, so tired," I want to say as I suddenly realize, in the middle of the afternoon, how much stress and how much bad news of the world I've been hauling around. I realize, too, how these few moments of lying back in Jean's Intergalactic Shampoo Therapy Chair are worth ten times the price of my haircut, and how there are days when I just want to stay here with somebody hovering over me, massaging my soul forever.

Sometime after Joa left, the Woman in White drifted over. She asked if I had any questions. She seemed very kind. She was maybe a couple years older than me, almost certainly a '60s earth mother. Up close, I was struck by how handsome she was. Smooth skin. Teeth like fresh snow. Light gray eyes—though tinged gray, I suspect, by divorce; or divorces, and maybe years of struggling to raise kids alone. That's what I thought, even if I was jumping to conclusions. She reminded me of the woman I had talked to years ago in the bar along the coast.

I did have some questions for her.

Tell me, I wanted to ask, *What combination of griefs and raptures have conspired to bring you here? Why has a reasonable-looking person like you come to work in this den of archaic babble?*

Of course, I didn't ask. I didn't have the heart to, or the arrogance. After all, I could see through the windows that the California sky over Shasta's high snows was a gorgeous cobalt. It was an afternoon sky that hid a dome of shimmering stars. And besides, who was I to question whatever helped this very nice woman glimpse bright bits of heaven shining through?

In September of 1999, slightly more than a year later, I returned to the foot of Mount Shasta. At first I told myself that I had come back because I knew the mountain and the countryside would look stunning, the autumn leaves glittering gold, the enduring bounty of this one-time gold mine country whose veins had long ago been sucked dry. Say what you want about the Shastafarians, you can't knock their taste in scenery.

But I was also back, I realized, because I still couldn't figure out what to make of all the New Age stuff, which was starting to drive me a little bit crazy. "Some of us are so alone we have guardians that talk to us . . . that teach us things we've long forgotten," said a local resident on a video I'd come across, *The Many Faces of Shasta.* For no reason that I could fathom, she called herself Sister Thedra. I suspected there was a lot of truth in what she had said about extreme loneliness and Shastafarian beliefs, but I didn't entirely understand it, either. For instance, while I doubt that anyone on the national psychic hotline holds much old-time shamanic knowledge, I can see why you might want to dial one up, especially if you'd recently become unmoored from a relationship or a career and were about to plunge into a blind date or a job interview. The same for visiting an astrologer. To talk to a psychic guardian is to request not just advice but human contact, friendship, compassion: *Oh, you DO understand the depth of my yearning, don't you?*

But what was I to make of the Mount Shasta woman I had talked to on the phone recently? A lively woman with an easy laugh, she told me—perfect stranger conducting an interview— that a Lemurian she met while on a camping trip to Shasta advised her to sell her business on the coast and move here. She described his height, his Asian features. She spoke with such simple conviction that I listened in silence, unable to ask, *How can you possibly expect me to believe this stuff?* And, *Why do so many of these stories seem to converge at Mount Shasta?*

When SueEllen drove me to the airport shuttle in Fort Collins for my flight to Sacramento, she had looked me over and said, "You're sure you need to do this trip?"

"Yup."

"You still don't have enough material?"

"Nope."

"Then why are you being so tight-lipped and defensive?"

I joked about riding off with Joa Dolphin-Play to meet the Ascended Ones inside the mountain. Then I said that if she didn't hear from me again, she could always send out a rescue team—say, our most cynical writer friends, men and women so hard bitten by the world of publishing and rejection that even the "Ashtar Command," which Archangel Michael's Web site claimed was the "Airborne Division of The Great White Brotherhood," couldn't knock them off my trail. SueEllen laughed. But only a little.

One of the first things I did when I got back to town was head to the Soul Therapy Center. I wouldn't have minded running into my doppelgänger, Archangel Michael himself. But mainly I wanted to talk some more with the Woman in White.

No, not to hear any more Metatronic hoo-ha, but to figure out what some of the doughnut concepts and other Shasta stories *really* meant. All those golden rooms in Mu and Atlantis crowded with astral-traveling sages, all this going-to-the-mountain insight, had to add up to something that I could make sense of. It seemed to me that like volcanoes, stories that loom large in a particular place couldn't have gotten that way without major *oomph* from below.

Also—I might as well admit this—I was starting to chafe a bit inside my straitjacket of logic, what could at times feel like a cult of rational thought. This was underscored for me one Saturday afternoon when I had lunch with the Rocky Mountain Skeptics Society, on the CU campus in Boulder. I had no problems when they skewered showbiz spoon-benders like Uri Geller or shook their heads at the literal Creationists who, terrified by notions of incomprehensibly deep time, still can't forgive Darwin or leave the rest of us alone. Or when they tore apart "quantum healing," a so-called alternative medical treatment that has borrowed loonily from quantum mechanics and been talked up, apparently, by New Age megastars like Deepak Chopra, who appears on my PBS channel even more often than Yanni. All or most of this criticism I happily agreed with. What got to me during the after-lunch discussion was a tone I didn't like, an accumulating smugness and complete lack of irony. *Can you BELIEVE how many dopes are out there?* the skeptics seemed to be saying as they egged each other on, grinning.

Dopes!

Slaves to religion!

Wackos!

Hey, I told myself as I played with my dessert, I think there are too many squishy thinkers out there, too. I think we need rational alternatives to pseudo-science and extraordinary evidence for extraordinary claims.

But on the other hand, I found myself thinking, what about all those people who seem to hear or feel things that my own senses don't quite catch? Stars that I can't see really *do* flicker behind the afternoon sky, every day of my life. The gravitational pull of the sun and moon is so powerful that it bends the rocky crust of the planet—it even has a name: "earth tide"—yet none of us notices a thing without the help of high-tech instruments. The same goes for the great restlessness below and inside of volcanoes.

More and more often, when I sit at home in simple meditation, just following my breath, I sense the enormity of so much that I miss, the subtle physical relationships that swirl around me all the time. I sit quietly with my eyes closed, breathing in and out, trying to smile, and soon enough I hear wooden floor beams and joints creaking, adjusting to gravity and tiny changes in temperature, as though the house were an old man stretching. And then maybe SueEllen opens a window two rooms away, and I feel the air pressure microscopically shift, a fluttering of tiny wings on my cheeks.

And this is just the potentially verifiable stuff.

What about whatever may lie beyond measuring? What about whatever caused the novelist Reynolds Price to say on NPR one afternoon, as he concluded a commentary about walking down a hallway and meeting a relative who happened to be long-dead: "The world is not only strange, but stranger than we're capable of knowing."

And what about the mysterious, middle-of-the-night world in which, years ago, my grandmother, my mom's mom, let me know exactly when she died, nudging me to wake up suddenly in my apartment fifty miles from her hospital ward? My Grandma Ritterbusch had played and laughed with me throughout my childhood, and it's true that during her last few days it was obvious she would die soon, shrunken by fast-moving cancer, comatose in her huge metal bed. I'd visited her in Brooklyn that last afternoon with my mother, who at first did not even recognize her, having to double-check the name on the bedside chart. Then I'd driven back to my small apartment on Long Island. I was twenty-two or so.

On my dresser that summer sat an old-time clock radio with glass tubes, some family hand-me-down from the world before transistors. That night I fell into a troubled sleep, and then, deep toward morning, I awoke to find myself sitting up and staring into the darkness. Across the room, through the plastic grillwork of that old radio, the tubes began to glow. They glowed more and more brightly, yet the radio never made a sound. Then they dimmed, they slowly faded away, and I knew that my grandmother had, too. I said good-bye.

I also made note of the time, and later on, when it was confirmed as the moment of her death, I just nodded.   •

I've never believed in ESP, UFOs, spirits, channeling, astrology, the Virgin birth, or other nonrational, unverifiable phenomena. I've always trusted the laws of science, the assumptions of a provable reality. For years I've regarded that night message from my grandmother as perhaps the one mystical experience of my life, the one incident that I can't explain away through coincidence, probability, or the kind of deep yearning that can drive the soberest among us through some invisible wall and into another world.

All of which is why I was growing excited, and nervous, as I cruised once again down Mount Shasta Boulevard toward the beautifully named Soul Therapy Center. For whose soul, after all, couldn't use at least *some* therapy?

But, wait! It was gone! The old stucco building was empty. A FOR RENT sign was taped to the window. Then I noticed a tiny scribbled note on the door. When I got up close, I learned that Archangel Michael's was to reopen in a month, down the street in a house that the Marine Recruiting Office would be vacating.

The Marines?

I stood around for a while on the sidewalk, feeling deflated and a little bit lost. Then I caught myself grinning. The Marines! Oh, how I'd love to stroll by that recruiting office on moving day. How I'd love to watch the buzz-cut and well-pressed young men snapping shut their laptops and wheeling out their file cabinets while the Soul Therapy folks squeezed past with their clunky Cheops pyramids and their armfuls of Sacred Geometric Vajras!

Said the English scientist Michael Faraday, "Nothing is too wonderful to be true."

That afternoon I walked over to the Siskayou National Forest headquarters to get some hiking maps. Leaning on her elbows behind an information desk was a friendly looking young woman whose name tag said Cari. When—unable to stop myself—I asked her about the influence of Mount Shasta on town life, she pondered a moment. "You know," she said, "there *is* something about this mountain that I can't explain. Some kind of pull."

Cari was no Ixthara or RA-MA-AA, and not just because she was wearing a National Forest Service uniform and looked at home among topo maps and posters of chipmunks and bears tacked to the walls. She was clearly a no-nonsense type whom I could imagine climbing down from a 4x4 to tell some hunter to douse his campfire, now: "Drought conditions, pal. You got that?"

She'd lived in sight of Mount Shasta all her life and seemed both irritated and amused by the growing "alternative community," she explained. There was a first-rate mountain shop in town and a lively climbing fraternity, but she had noticed that New Agers rarely summitted the mountain. They weren't serious outdoor types, although some of them, trust funders, she guessed, seemed serious enough about money. Dreadlocked Rainbow Families who had stopped by for years added spice to the Shasta mix. So, once, did followers of the free-love guru Bhagwan Shree Rajneesh, from nearby Antelope, Oregon. The Bhagwan—now that was a name I hadn't heard in a long time. Cari said his contingent had roared into town in a fleet of BMWs and Mercedes painted the colors of sunrise.

Cari's coworkers had found homemade altars burning unattended on the mountain, and huge medicine wheels and pentagrams laid out from cobbles pried from meadows. These ecological and cultural transgressions also outraged the Wintu and Ajumawi people, who had been performing sweats and healing rituals on Shasta for generations before the forty-niners swarmed here. I would soon read about an Ajumawi woman who hiked to a favorite hot spring to pray, only to find it clogged with store-bought crystals.

The previous summer, a neatly dressed man showed up at Cari's counter. He'd left his job in Chicago one day because a telephone psychic had told him to look up Shasta in the encyclopedia, and there it was, an image that had been haunting his dreams since childhood. "Like the Devil's Tower thing in *Close Encounters*," Cari told me. Later, he hung around for days downtown, asking people on the sidewalk if they had a message for him. Nobody did.

"Really, he was just so polite and nicely dressed," she said, sighing. "Every season we get a few like him. Also, the ones who actually ask for topo maps with the secret entrances to the mountain marked on them. You know, for the subterranean worlds?"

All that I ever wanted to know about Mount Shasta's subterranean worlds, and much, much more, I soon discovered in two places. One was a wonderfully wry and comprehensive annotated bibliography of Shasta literature compiled by Bill Miesse. Bill, who lives in Mount Shasta City, is an independent scholar, lecturer, and avid windsurfer whose work deftly summarizes more than 1,200 scientific monographs, Native American tales, sci-fi and literary novels, memoirs, and poems. The second source turned out to be my favorite library collection ever, the Mount Shasta Collection at the lovely College of the Siskayous, in Weed, just a few miles northwest of the mountain. There, with the cheerful and skilled help of curator Dennis Freeman, I skimmed through shelves and shelves of the stuff that Bill Miesse's bibliography had helped Dennis collect. I wondered whether there was a larger storehouse of one mountain's literature anywhere, or a sampling so imaginative and wild.

Dozens of the Shasta collection's works are devoted to essentially the same thing—their authors' personal, usually transformative encounters on or inside the volcano with alien or magical beings, including UFO pilots, talking animals, Tibetans, and Venusians. One frequent Mount Shasta visitor, Frederick Morrison, claimed in a 1945 letter to the *California Folklore*

Quarterly that inside the mountain lies a great city, Yaktayvia, whose galleries and tunnels have been hollowed out and illuminated by the vibrations of gigantic bells. How the bells do this is unclear, but the Yaktayvians are the world's greatest bell makers, Morrison explained without a shred of irony. And their greatest bell of all, humming constantly from mountain winds playing over it, keeps the entrance to their Secret Commonwealth invisible—unless, that is, you happen to stumble to within eighteen inches of it.

Other writers have frequently described encounters with tall and slender sages from the ancient lost continents of Atlantis, Lemuria, and Mu. The continents seem to exist independently of each other, yet all fit inside the volcano. The Lemurians have the habit of lounging about in gold-lined or jewel-encrusted chambers. Now and then, wearing spotless white robes, a few of them come to the surface and appear in one of the human towns on the edge of Shasta's forests, where they've been spotted buying salt and lard. They pay for these supplies with gold nuggets and don't ask for change. Nobody explains why these seven-foot-tall ascended beings need lard.

Immersing myself in the lives of these California dreamers soon pushed me to try something new. As twilight fell during each of the next few days, I strapped on my boots and packed two flashlights, a wool sweater, a water bottle, and some sandwiches. Then I hiked off along one of Shasta's trails or up a nearby mountain. My goal was not really to pick my way back to the car by starlight—although I did, and very carefully, since I was alone. It was to move through the trees during the witching hour.

This is the very still, darkening time when doorways between worlds can seem to open a crack. It's a time—or a time out of time—when the chatter of a squirrel can sound like somebody calling to you, or the rasp of a crow's wings against fast-cooling air makes you wonder if a spirit is swooping in from another planet or maybe your own distant past. As Nathaniel Hawthorne, Sarah Orne Jewett, Washington Irving, and the Brothers Grimm were aware, witching hours can drop over good-sized forests anywhere (which is reason enough to save them from the blade!). Thanks to their history full of strange encounters, the slopes on and near Mount Shasta suggest a much more fruitful darkness.

Twenty minutes into my first hike I was cursing myself for not having taken walks like this most of my life. The air was cold blue and beautiful, a perfect conduit for the hooting of what I thought might be a great horned owl. I trudged up through a Shasta meadow, then wound through red firs 150 feet tall, their mossy trunks growing taller and wider, it seemed, as they darkened. Soon they'd turned into gigantic robed beings: *my* kind of Ascended Masters.

I walked slowly back down by flashlight—couldn't risk breaking an ankle when nobody knew where I was. Then I stopped and clicked off the light, sat quietly on a log, and let my eyes try to become animal eyes. Before I headed on, I looked back upslope. There was the summit; unbelievably high, still gleaming from a sun that had long ago pulled its light from the forest floor. I felt like I was watching the last light in the world. Or yesterday's light, a different time zone.

All of which made me wonder: not far north of here lay Klamath Lake and Tule Lake, migratory stops for thousands and thousands of snow geese, white pelicans, and cranes. These were flocks I'd stopped to see a year earlier on my Avenue of Volcanoes tour. And so I wondered, to look up from this darkening forest during the witching hour, and to see flights of sandhill cranes floating past the summit, their wings flashing white or gold . . . well, what a sight that would be. Or to have looked up a century ago when you were prospecting, hungry, cold, and aching in mountain shadows, desperate for a sign from heaven, a sign from anywhere that told you that you weren't cursed or a fool, doomed to die shivering and broke and alone in the wilderness. Maybe it's no wonder that so many guardian angels and spirits had come streaming out of the high snows of Mount Shasta.

The next evening, hiking up a nearby mountain, I made out Shastina for the first time. This is Shasta's most recent vent, thousands of years old but geologically speaking still a kid, which bulges out of the western flank of the volcano. Over the centuries it has sent pyroclastic flow deposits over sites on which Mount Shasta City and Weed were built, and it could well do it again. From my forest viewpoint it looked completely tranquil. Shastina stands a few thousand feet high, a mountain in its own right. But from many angles, especially after new snow, you can hardly see it at all. White against white, a volcano on a volcano, it can seem to disappear into Shasta, as though it has temporarily ducked back inside the mother ship, the mountain that it's still growing out of.

Vision, perception, tricks of time and light—the kind of looking it takes to see what's subtly standing right in front of you or all around—wow, what a complicated business this can be.

On my second to last day in Mount Shasta City, I picked up my research pace. I breezed around poking my head in here and there, window-shopping for revelation.

A door or two away from an Italian restaurant, I stopped at a storefront with a neatly lettered sign that I had passed many times: St. Germain Foundation. It looked like a Christian Science reading room.

I gripped the door handle, then froze. Had I reached my daily or even lifetime limit for weirdness? It mattered around here, where the bland seemed to walk so casually hand in hand with the bizarre.

I reminded myself that a woman at the chamber of commerce this morning had told me that the St. Germain folks ran one of the town's most respected spiritual outfits. For fifty years they'd put on a summer passion play under the stars. She showed me photos of Jesus and crowds of angels standing around in bright pastel robes, under hokey lighting. Very Oberammergau and Cecil B. DeMille, but by Shasta standards not strange at all.

I opened the door.

Harp music washed over me. At first I thought it was the same tape that I had heard at the Soul Therapy Center almost a year ago. But soon an old-time organ joined in, though not with that woofing exuberance you'd expect. In fact, if it were possible for an organ to play tepidly, even *obsequiously,* this one was doing it. The music swelled slightly, ebbed, swelled again, but not by much. Any angel that had tried to fly to the sound of this stuff would never have left the ground.

Soon I'd wandered into a room plastered with yellow and purple posters depicting flames and long-robed beings. Tables and magazine racks displayed brochures that were mostly yellow or purple, too. One of them looked oddly familiar: a close-up of George Washington, the same purple likeness that I remembered from the old three-cent postcard stamp in my U.S. album.

"Hi there!"

I looked around but didn't see anybody.

"I'm over here!"

Sitting at a desk right in front of me, laughing heartily at my spaciness, was a chunky woman with short white hair expensively done up. She wore designer frames. Two handsome crystals hung from her neck by slender gold chains. Despite this stylishness, she reminded me instantly of Aunt Bea, from the old Andy Griffith Show.

Soon enough, she was leading me affably through the St. Germain philosophy: "The Mighty 'I AM' Presence," the "Old Age of Jesus Descension," the "New One of Violet Flames," the "Sixth Golden Age," the concept of "So-Called Death," and so on. I didn't understand it all, of course, but it seemed well meaning enough—a bunch of metaphors, arcane though they may have been, designed to help you get by in this vale of tears.

And Aunt Bea seemed sober enough, too. She told me she had been trained as a nurse and lived in Chicago with her husband before they joined "the Activity." One day he brought home a book and said, "Honey, you're really gonna love this one!" Then he read it out loud to her, cover to cover.

The book was *Unveiled Mysteries,* by Guy Ballard, a mining engineer, who wrote it after a remarkable encounter he had one afternoon in 1930 on the slopes of Mount Shasta. Out hiking alone, he recalls in the book, he stopped to drink at a spring, felt an electrical charge run through his body, and looked up to see a beautiful young man in a white jeweled robe standing before him. "My Brother, if you will hand me your cup, I will give you a much more refreshing drink than spring water," he said. The drink was astoundingly delicious and revivifying. It came from "the Universal

Supply," from Life itself, the man said. And then he revealed himself to be St. Germain, the Beloved Ascended Master and Lord of
the Seventh Ray to the Earth. Eventually he instructed Ballard to
start "the Activity" to help mankind achieve happiness. I had noticed some of Ballard's books at the College of the Siskayous library, but they hadn't made much of an impression.

Somewhere in here Aunt Bea's phone rang.

"Hi hon," she said. "What? Um, y-o-u-t-h-f-u-l-n-e-s-s. You
could look up the others in the dictionary. We have one, you
know." She gave me a *Teenagers!-what're-you-gonna-do?* look.
"Listen, hon, gotta go. I've got a customer here."

This gave me pause. Customer? I braced myself for a big sell.
Back in high school in New York, I had wandered one day into
the Billy Graham pavilion at the world's fair, and pretty soon
some guy with a pompadour and a cheap suit had cornered me
in an inner sanctum and kept asking me to accept Jesus. I'd been
wary of God salesmen ever since.

But Aunt Bea just yakked away. She drew my attention to a
black-and-white photo on the wall. An elderly man with a 1930s'
Bela Lugosi air: hair slicked back, white cape, a very stagey pose.
Next to him stood an equally stagey woman in a long white gown.

"Mr. and Mrs. Ballard," said Aunt Bea, pausing to let this sink
in. "Mrs. Ballard, who had a background in vaudeville, played the
harp at Mr. Ballard's talks around the country, which drew thousands. She composed the music you're hearing now, in fact. I listen to it at home all the time."

I couldn't imagine what that would be like, so I checked out
Aunt Bea's eyes. They were large, alert, and very clear. If I were
lying in a hospital bed, I'd still be thrilled to have her be my nurse.

I pointed to the George Washington brochure. "Why's *he* on there?"

She looked at me curiously, as though I should have known better. "Mr. Ballard *was* George Washington. In previous incarnations, he was many great men, which he discovered that day on Mount Shasta. He was Shakespeare, too, for example. You know, he *will shake* his *spear* against the bad things in this world?" She broke into a big smile.

I smiled back. I didn't know what else to do about this California voodoo. Keep smiling, I guess, thank her, and edge my way to the door.

A few minutes later I was about halfway out when she said, "Gosh, I almost forgot! Want to see the Violet Flame Room?"

"Oh, why not?"

I followed her down the hall to a tiny room with two or three folding chairs that faced what looked like a window-sized Etch A Sketch screen. On a little table sat a boom box and a cassette. That was it.

"I'll do the lights and crank up the flame, and you pop that tape in if you want—it enhances the effect. I've got paperwork to do, so stay as long as you please."

The lights dimmed and the door clicked shut behind her. The cassette label said "I AM Music of the Spheres," so of course I didn't touch it. I straightened in the chair as though I were preparing to meditate, but I kept my eyes open. Very open, since I figured, half-seriously, that this was one of the ways that cults started roping you in, and even though I'd always thought I was immune to that stuff, a place like Shasta does makes you wonder. The screen began to glow violet.

Volcanologists have a nice name for the route followed by molten rock that rises over millennia from deep in the earth, the heat-driven new earth that bursts through the crust eventually as a volcano. A magmatic plume. That's what they call it, a plume: billions of tons of hot rock ascending in a feathery current through cooler and denser rock.

I mention this because it's exactly what I was struck by when glowing shapes on the screen arranged themselves into violet plumes. It was immensely soothing, this slow-motion fire rising silently as I sat and watched, and after a while I found myself wondering what Aunt Bea might see in it. Maybe, in the eternal, upward-feathering light, she recognized a bountiful life force. Or maybe antique wisdom ascending through the generations, that Shakespeare to George Washington to Guy Ballard business. Who was to say?

But I knew what *I* saw, or felt. I felt the energy from the world beneath me being channeled into this one; the crater of young Shastina pushing up out of the flanks of Mount Shasta; a mountain morphing from within, transforming itself again and again to the music of the spheres.

My time with Aunt Bea drove me back for a closer look at the Mount Shasta Collection. As I told Dennis Freeman, I was getting more and more interested in the early encounter stories. He turned into my research angel. Within minutes, he had me sitting in a private room with a stack of books in front of me. As I leafed through them, he kept coming back with more books fluttering with Post-it notes, and saying, "I think you might find these of some interest."

One that I found of very great interest was among the oldest in the collection, *A Dweller on Two Planets* by Frederick Oliver, published in 1895. Surveying his family's mining claim on Mount Shasta one day, seventeen-year-old Oliver took out a pencil to jot down some measurements. Suddenly, he began to scribble uncontrollably, writing everything that he heard from a voice that came to him, somehow, from deep within the mountain. The voice, he said later, belonged to a Lemurian spirit named Phylos.

Over the next three years, in short bursts of automatic writing, Oliver transcribed the wisdom that Phylos had picked up in previous lives, his vast journeys through space and time. Prominent was the knowledge of how to avoid becoming "tinged by the dead black shadow of materialism." After Oliver published this advice as a novel that he called *A Dweller on Two Planets,* it quickly became one of the earliest American occult classics. From what I could gather, it also seemed to be the foundation text for the vast Shasta canon of genuinely underground literature.

The Shasta Collection also gave me some illuminating views into the white-caped Guy Ballard, founder of the St. Germain "I AM" Foundation, and his wife, Edna. For instance, after completing *Unveiled Mysteries,* Ballard wrote many more books, most or all of them in the same endlessly repetitive style. I learned that the hard way, trying to plough through a few. Also, after claiming to meet St. Germain in a Mount Shasta forest, Ballard apparently forever after abstained from eating onions and garlic because he believed that their odors were repugnant to Ascended Masters. Finally, I confirmed that his "I AM" rallies really did draw thousands during their heyday in the late '30s, just as Aunt Bea had told me.

Typically, after Edna, the old vaudeville hoofer, warmed up the audience with some harp and organ numbers, Guy would bound on stage, white cape flying, in a wash of colored lights. Waving his arms, he'd lay out some of the philosophy, then exhort the crowd to reject unbelievers. He also railed against labor agitators and Communists, for during this time the movement was apparently growing more right wing by the week. Finally, Edna would lead the singing of "America the Beautiful" while assistants in white suits handed out envelopes for "I AM Love Gifts."

You get the picture: a Jim and Tammy Faye Bakker show decades ahead of its time, with elements borrowed from Mussolini, who was rising to Fascist power at the same time. Mail fraud charges apparently dogged the Ballards for years, though if kindly Aunt Bea knew this, I'm sure she didn't believe it.

I also discovered that Ballard's *Unveiled Mysteries,* like so much Shastafarian-speak I heard around town, borrows heavily from two best-selling books that initially helped popularize New Age thinking in the United States and especially in California. Theosophy guru Madame Blavatsky's *Isis Unveiled* and Ignatius Donnelly's *Atlantis, the Antediluvian World* had been published in the 1920s, not long before Ballard rose to prominence. I'm not surprised, then, that Ballard may have "channeled" some of these books' ideas; "borrowing" to the point of serial plagiarism seems to be as prominent a characteristic of New Age literature circles as wretched writing.

In my opinion, Ballard also lifted more than a little from Frederick Oliver, the teen-aged surveyor and scribe to Phylos. But then, young Oliver is *worth* stealing from, at least by Shastalit standards. After reading the first couple of chapters at the College of the Siskayous library, I stopped by the Golden Bough bookstore and bought my own copy of *A Dweller on Two Planets.* As I sat reading under a tree, Oliver's book began to hit me like a revelation. This was not just because parts of it (but *not* the parts where characters say things like "Thou art right, Zailm, my son") are vividly written.

I think I came to *A Dweller on Two Planets* at just the right time. For when I considered it in context with the witching-hour hikes I had taken in the evening and my encounters with the Woman in White and Aunt Bea's Purple Flame Room, not to mention my own lost-young-man pilgrimage through deep-woods California, I think I finally began to understand a few things about Mount Shasta's last hundred years or so of stories.

For starters, I began to notice how many early Shasta authors or their protagonists were miners or gold prospectors. Before he hit a different kind of pay dirt with St. Germain, Guy Ballard worked for years as a mining engineer; before that, he'd apparently bombed as a land and mineral-rights speculator. And when Phylos broke in to change his life, seventeen-year-old Frederick Oliver happened to be staking out his family's mineral claim on the mountain. In other words, like swarms of other northern California men of their day, Ballard and Oliver and a host of other Shasta storytellers spent a huge amount of their energies scratching at mountains to uncover vast hidden riches.

I suspect that Oliver wrote *Dweller* in response to all that mountain-scratching, writ large—insanely large. I mean the California gold rush. Frederick Oliver grew up in the midst of its devastating cultural and physical consequences. The frantic search for gold dealt a final blow to the forest-dwelling Indian communities that his parents and grandparents probably knew. Rivers and mountains had been literally ripped inside out by placer mining and blasting, then ripped further by the terrible erosion that followed. Trees had been sawed down by the millions for railroad ties, mine shaft beams, and planks for shanty towns. Tumbling brooks were stained garish yellow and red, while human nature became stained green with envy, violence, and greed: what Frederick Oliver, after all, called "the dead black shadow of materialism."

Oliver writes movingly about roaming through forests and sleeping under the stars, of climbing high on Mount Shasta and feeling his heart thud like a pile driver. If only we'll look for it, he implies like an untutored Henry David Thoreau, we'll find riches in nature beyond those other, more profane riches. "On [Shasta's] stony, stratified pages Nature's students may read the doings of the gnomes, mother earth's treasurers," he writes, revealing both his youthful idealism and an eye that knows how to read both geology and deep time.

A Dweller on Two Planets is certainly a young man's book, full of nostalgia for the recently departed Edenic past. Dedicated "to progressive thinkers everywhere," it's a book that yearns for decent living and tolerance, one that also reminds me happily of my own youthful and uncomplicated time in the California woods. In one important scene, the sage Phylos tells Oliver that only a generation earlier, in one of his previous lives, he worked in nearby gold mine country as a coolie named Quong. When he was noticed at all, Quong was reviled by other miners as a Chinese heathen. One day, though, a grizzly bear came charging out of the forest. Drawing upon his mystical, Far Eastern powers, Quong stepped into its path, commanded it to stop, then made the grizzly lie down. Soon Quong's grateful and impressed coworkers came to recognize his humanity, and even, in one case, to rue their own racism. If you learn how to truly *see*, Oliver suggests in this tale, you'll discover in the chambers of the heart treasures greater even than the gold and jewels that line the chambers of Lemuria and Atlantis, the kingdoms where Phylos began to learn what he would eventually pass down to humanity.

Writes Oliver: "The one who first conquers self, Shasta will not deny."

For years this book was called a clairvoyant classic, and a recent reprint plays up the same elements. New Age marketing, I suppose. But *Dweller,* unlike so much cover-to-cover literary tripe that followed, *announces* its own metaphors, thus lending its author a bit of ironic distance from the material. Like good writing and like a genuine understanding of science, irony is also hard to find in New Age lit. And the parts of *Dweller* that speak most passionately to me seem to brim with basic ecological awareness, commonsense environmental ethics years ahead of their time, not to mention moral lessons drawn from close observation of volcanic landscapes. Oliver doesn't urge you to get your Kundalini going by sitting in front of some many-named guru like Archangel Michael "Lama Dorje," et cetera. Rather, he asks you to simply go to Mount Shasta—wherever your Shasta may be—and look hard into it, past human time and mortal concerns. That's how you'll learn how to live with and in the world. *This* world.

And if that's not wisdom of the ancients, what is?

I think Oliver's *Dweller* is an intriguing and overlooked book. But why have so many other Shastafarian stories, written and spoken, made such a geographical and space/time hash of the mountain?

Beyond the possible reasons I've already implied and the fact that the lenticular clouds that often pile up over the mountain resemble not just celestial pancakes but flying saucers, here are two hunches.

Hunch Number One. A deep nostalgia much like Frederick Oliver's has been operating collectively in Shasta stories for decades. I mean, you can't spend much time in California without realizing how incredibly, amazingly beautiful and wild the place once was, and not all that long ago. Consequently, as pretty as the Golden State still may be, it's hard not to see loss everywhere: through smog, under Malibu beach mansions and acres of freeway concrete, beneath the manufactured, miles-long rows of artichokes and orange trees and suburban houses. I'd call this a California subset of what biologist E. O. Wilson, discussing our modern awareness of the extinction of species, calls the "Age of Loneliness."

If you spend any time at all in rugged Shasta country, you feel lonely for the loss of people, too. I mean the many different Indian cultures that knew how to see and touch parts of the world, or other worlds, that we at the turn of the millennium can't or won't. So you become aware of the recent extinction of not just people and their languages—Wintun, Maidu, Chimariko, Yahi—but the very nature of their dialogues with the natural world: their collective dreams, their myths. Gone, gone.

In other words, you see all too well the broken rungs in the sky-ladders that native people once climbed to bring back traditional, sacred knowledge. Consequently, I suspect that Mount Shasta, with its inner kingdoms full of time-traveling, ancient robed beings, has come to replace those ladders for new tribes of seekers. The mountain is the connection to better times in the past and, you hope, the immediate future. And so Shastafarians climb *into* the mountain for transcendent wisdom. Unbearably lonely, shunned or ridiculed by a more rational world, they prospect for the gold of companionship and the sound of some-body's—anybody's—caring voice.

The upper two-thirds of Mount Shasta also provides spectac-ular views of Lassen Peak to the south. Lassen's dense, brushy foothills—the eroded crenellations of old lava flows—happen to have been the final hiding place of Ishi, a Yahi hunter who became famous as the "last wild Indian in North America." In 1911, poor Ishi emerged starving and terrified from a once-viable Stone Age existence, the absolutely final member of his tribe. He died only five years later, of tuberculosis, on the campus of the University of California at Berkeley, where Alfred Kroeber and others had cre-ated a place for him to live in the anthropology museum.

I suspect that whatever wisdom so infamously died with Ishi—and by extension, all native people in the region—has haunted Shastafarian tales, in exaggerated fashion, ever since. After all, as-cended masters, the sages of Mu, and UFO pilots tend not to die, not for keeps, anyway, and this means that their arcane and ele-vated wisdom, unlike that of the very real native California Indians, is eternally reclaimable. In a sense, then, Shastafarian authors may be retelling the Ishi story in their own strange tales, then often tacking on happier endings. In these ways, Ishi lives again, trans-formed into a Lemurian, an Atlantean, a Yaktayvian bell ringer.

Hunch Number Two. Like far-traveling Mu and Atlantis, an ancient continent veined with gold *really did* once exist beneath the sea, and then it moved to California. This is yet another geologic truth wrapped inside local mythology. Thanks to plate tectonics, continents, and the eventual additions to present continents, migrate great distances over and under the surface of the earth. For instance, a seafloor packed with fossils can drift along an inch or two per year for millions of years, eventually rising, drying out, and buckling up into a mountain range like the Sierras. In *Assembling California,* John McPhee describes this planetary restlessness about as well as it can be described. Then he sums it up in one sentence: "The summit of Mt. Everest is marine limestone."

Here's part of how McPhee describes what you might call the Origin Tale, and then the journey, of central and northern California's Mother Lode country:

> In or close to the magma chambers under oceanic spreading centers, seawater, which has descended through fissures, dissolves metals (copper, silver, iron, magnesium, gold); it carries the metals upward and precipitates them on top of new rock. If the new rock, in its migration, happens to end up on a continent, the metal comes with it. In the suturing process, faults form. Deeply circulating groundwater redissolves the metals and redeposits them in quartz veins in the faults.

In other words, and especially when volcanoes grow in such country: *pay dirt.*

And thus have California's treasure-packed subterranean chambers literally come riding in from afar: a Great Harmonic Convergence that eventually spurred the gold rush. In general, economists believe that fully half the world's gold deposits are associated with ancient volcanism.

But what about the fact that none of the old-time Shastafarian authors and few of their later interpreters would have known anything of plate tectonics, which emerged only in the 1960s? I think it probably doesn't matter. The point, as far as myth goes, is that mountains move, the world can change on a grand scale, and in doing so it can change people, too. The natural world can revolutionize the human heart.

And the world *is* packed with riches. As I once read somewhere, the desire of the ancient alchemists was not just to turn lead into gold. It was to become golden themselves.

———

But what was my excuse? Only three months after buying the cassette tape from Aunt Bea, I found myself returning to Shasta yet again. Was it the effects of Edna Ballard's wretched harp and organ numbers, which I had played (partly as a joke, I thought) until SueEllen thought I was going nuts? Or was it that I still did not fully comprehend the mythic power of a landform as charismatic as Mount Shasta?

Stealing most of a day from a literature conference in Reno, I drove west and then north for three hours through spitting snow and rain, toward the volcano. The sky hung low, a dirty sheet that I hoped would tear open any minute to reveal a brilliant blue. It never did, though.

As I approached the town, I kept looking between foothills and through bare, wet-black trees for a glimpse of the summit, which I assumed was poking through the clouds, sparkling with snow miles overhead, visible to airline passengers and sandhill cranes and Ascended Masters. But no dice down here. The mountain was socked in and I couldn't see a thing. Wrote Basho:

> Misty rain,
> can't see Fuji
> —interesting!

Plenty interesting, because I wondered if I was already starting to feel it. To work the car-rattle out of my legs, I decided to
walk fast through town, and with every step I felt *something* ex-
erting a pull. I swept past the Golden Bough bookstore, past
Bruno's Brakes & Tires and Darlene's Salon of Beauty. I did not
slow down at the "I AM" reading room, which in any case was
not yet open for business. But I was only a few long strides past
it when I heard the slam of a car door. I turned my head, and—
how to explain this to SueEllen?—saw a very short man, a dwarf,
I'd guess, middle-aged and bearded and wearing a gray three-
piece suit, shuffling with a briefcase toward the St. Germaine entrance. *Just keep walking,* I told myself.

I did, but a few blocks later, I found myself standing in front
of the relocated Archangel Michael's, peeking through the windows. There was no trace of the Marine recruiters, and the new
Soul Therapy digs did look nice. I stepped inside. The ascension
pyramids shone, incense floated, but there was no Woman in
White. Instead, a tall, handsome young man in yellow Tibetan
robes, though he was no Tibetan, came out from behind a curtain and shook my hand. He spoke with an English accent and
effortless charm, and soon, for no reason that I could see, he was
telling me about aliens.

A little-known fact: during the Harry Truman administration, in 1950, maybe '51, flying saucers landed briefly in the
Maryland woods. Aliens stepped out and gave humanity a plan
for world peace. When he heard them out, a grateful President
Truman was all for it, but military bigwigs convinced him to keep
everything hush-hush, and so nothing was done. Soon the woods
were fenced off and the encounter erased from history. Today we
call this area Camp David.

"Ah-h-h," I said, nodding as the young man smiled broadly.

And I thought: *so many Shastas!*

In fact, too many Shastas, and as soon as I got out on the side-walk, I told myself that I had to drop this stuff right now. Then I ambled back to the car in a steady drizzle, which felt quite wonderful. Plain old wet rain, just falling down.

The sky was hanging lower than ever, and I still couldn't see Mount Shasta. But I could feel the volcano close at hand, tremendous in its invisibility, erupting not with ash or magma but *meaning* for so many different kinds of people. It loomed for me like the image that Dr. Atl had created of roaring Parícutin, a bridge between the deep earth and the stars, our grounded life and some of our most compelling desires. Shasta pulled on the countryside for miles around, on northern California and Oregon and the whole Cascades chain. It pulled on the cosmos, drawing in Atlantis, Lemuria, and Mu, offering as many Ascended Masters and stories as anyone desired: lost continents swept through time, hauled over huge distances through the generous and expressive earth.

ACKNOWLEDGMENTS

For accompanying me on so many trips physically and in spirit, for the gifts of a wonderful mind and heart, my wife SueEllen Campbell.

For leading me into temptation down the path to Volcano Land, Randy Jorgen. For keeping me on that path and away from bone-headed mistakes and misunderstandings: Robert I. Tilling, of the U.S. Geological Survey, for serving as technical editor of my children's volcano book; and Tom Simkin, of the Smithsonian Institution's Global Volcanism Program, for early advice and especially for reviewing this manuscript in great and inspiring detail. Any mistakes that remain are mine. For inviting me to write a natural history column for *Coastal Living* magazine and for many kinds of friendship over the years, Ben Brown; for later assignments that helped fund travel, Susan Haynes and Steve Millburg. For further travel moneys, the Professional Development Program of the College of Liberal Arts at Colorado State University.

Aside from the many kind and patient people I mention in my text, these scientists and other experts gave me valuable time in the office or out in the field: John Eichelberger, Henry Heasler, Richard Hoblitt, Lazlo Keszthelyi, Arnold Okamura, Lee Siebert, Cindy Lee Van Dover, and the support crew of the submersible *Alvin*. For a wonderful day of rock-whacking on the slopes of Mount St. Helens, Ed Wolfe. Mount Shasta bibliographer William C. Miesse and librarian *extraordinaire* Dennis Freeman.

For reading and commenting on work in progress: Jonathan Cobb, Valerie Cohen, James D. Houston, Ian Marshall, Robin Martinez, Lauret Savoy, Scott Slovic, and my CSU writing group of Gerry Callahan, Pattie Cowell, Sue Doe, Mark Fiege, and David Mogen.

Friends, family, and acquaintances who helped or inspired me in so many other ways: Roy Bird; Chip Blake; Donna Braginetz; Doug Brinkerhoff; Douglas Campbell; Bill Calderazzo; my dad, John Calderazzo; Mary Calderazzo; Maria Calderazzo; my mom, Wilma Calderazzo; Christopher Cokinos; Marcia Deines; Carolyn Duckworth; Tracy Ekstrand; Joel Fishman; Stephanie G'Schwind; Emily Hammond; Luana Heikes; Parker Huber; Walter Isle; Jon Luoma; Dawn Marano; Vance Martin; Richard Messer; Carol Mitchell; David Quammen; Tom Ranieri; Helen Ritterbusch; Steven Schwartz; Bart St. Armand; Bill Tremblay; Steven Trimble; Laurence Wiland; Susan and Ann Zwinger.

My hard-working and confidence-producing agent, Jane Dystel and her colleagues at Dystel and Goderich Literary Management. My editors at Lyons Press, Ann Treistman and Christine Duffy.

NOTES

During the writing and research of this book, I discovered that places where the earth begins are also places where a wide variety of disciplines often converge in happy confusion. As an amateur blundering into the many worlds of the earth sciences, not to mention anthropology, art, history, philosophy, and sociology, I needed all the help I could get. The help came in a series of conversations, as I came to think of them, with the following particularly illuminating works, among many others.

IN GENERAL

Robert Decker and Barbara Decker, *Volcanoes* (New York: W. H. Freeman & Co., 1979).

————. *Volcanoes in America's National Parks* (New York: W. W. Norton, 2001).

Richard V. Fisher, Grant Heiken, and Jeffrey B. Hulen, *Volcanoes: Crucibles of Change* (Princeton, NJ: Princeton University Press, 1997).

Stephen L. Harris, *Agents of Chaos* (Missoula, MT: Mountain Press Publishing, 1990).

Maurice Krafft, *Volcanoes: Fire from the Earth* (New York: Harry N. Abrams, 1993).

Edmond A Mathez, ed., *Earth: Inside and Out* (New York: New Press, 2001).

Haraldur Sigurdsson, editor-in-chief, *Encyclopedia of Volcanoes* (San Diego: Academic Press, 2000).

————. *Melting the Earth: The History of Ideas of Volcanic Eruptions* (New York: Oxford University Press, 1999).

Tom Simkin and Lee Siebert, eds., *Volcanoes of the World* (Tucson: Geoscience Press, 1994).

Dorothy B. Vitaliano, *Legends of the Earth: Their Geologic Origins* (Bloomington: Indiana University Press, 1973).

Thomas L. Wright and Thomas C. Pierson, *Living with Volcanoes* (U.S. Geological Survey Volcano Hazards Program, 1992).

Many outstanding volcanology Web sites run links to dozens more. Young readers may enjoy the Electronic Volcano. For wonderful public service information and detailed, clearly explained science, see especially the Smithsonian Institution's Global Volcanism Program and the U.S. Geological Survey's many Web sites.

PROLOGUE

Audrey DeLella Benedict, *Sierra Club Naturalist's Guide: The Southern Rockies* (San Francisco: Sierra Club Books, 1991).

John Calderazzo, *101 Questions about Volcanoes* (Tucson: Southwest Parks and Monuments Association, 1994).

SueEllen Campbell, *Even Mountains Vanish: Searching for Solace in an Age of Extinction* (Salt Lake City: University of Utah Press, 2003).

Paul R. Ehrlich and Anne H. Ehrlich, *One with Ninevah: Politics, Consumption, and the Human Future* (Washington, DC: Shearwater Books, 2004).

Robert B. Smith and Lee J. Siegel, *Windows into the Earth: The Geologic Story of Yellowstone and Grand Teton National Parks* (New York: Oxford University Press, 2000).

Special Publications Division, National Geographic Society, *Our Awesome Earth: Its Mysteries and Splendors* (Washington, D.C.: National Geographic Society, 1986).

Cindy Lee Van Dover, *Deep Ocean Journeys: Discovering New Life at the Bottom of the Sea* (Reading, MA: Addison-Wesley, 1996).

Julia M. White, Reiko Mochinaga Brandon, Yoko Woodson, *Hokusai and Hiroshige* (San Francisco: The Asian Art Museum of San Francisco, 1998).

ANCIENT FIRES: VESUVIUS, STROMBOLI, MOUNT ETNA

Elio Abatino, *Vesuvio: A Volcano and Its History* (Naples: Carcavello, 1989).

Barbara Grizzuti Harrison, *The Islands of Italy* (New York: Ticknor & Fields, 1991).

Athanasius Kircher, *Mundus Subterranus* (Amstelodami: Apud Joannem Jarssonium and Elizeum Weyerstraten, 1665).

Pliny the Elder, *Natural History: A Selection* (London: Penguin, 1991).

Susan Sontag, *The Volcano Lover* (New York: Anchor Books, 1992).

Lawrence Weschler, *Mr. Wilson's Cabinet of Wonder* (New York: Vintage, 1995).

INTO THE RING OF FIRE: KILAUEA AND UNZEN

Pam Frierson, *The Burning Island* (San Francisco: Sierra Club Books, 1991).

James D. Houston, *In the Ring of Fire: A Pacific Basin Journey* (San Francisco: Mercury House, 1997).

W. Jacquelyne Kious and Robert I. Tilling, *This Dynamic Earth: The Story of Plate Tectonics* (U.S. Geological Survey).

Maurice Krafft, producer, *Understanding Volcanic Hazards* (IAVCEI: International Association of Volcanology and Chemistry of the Earth's Interior, 1995). Videocassette.

Gail Willumsen, Teresa Koenig, producers, *Volcano: Nature's Inferno* (Washington, DC: National Geographic Society, 1997). Videocassette.

FROM EARTH TO THE STARS: PARÍCUTIN, MEXICO

Fred M. Bullard, *Volcanoes in History, in Theory, in Eruption* (Austin: University of Texas Press, 1963).

Constance Classen, *Inca Cosmology and the Human Body* (Salt Lake City: University of Utah Press, 1993).

Todd Downing, *The Mexican Earth*, 2d ed., (University of Oklahoma Press, Norman: London, 1996).

Beatriz Espejo, *Dr. Atl: El Paisaje como Pasion* (Coyoacán, Mexico: Fondo Editorial de la Plastica Mexica, 1994).

James F. Luhr and Tom Simkin, eds., *Parícutin: The Volcano Born in a Mexican Cornfield* (Tucson: Geoscience Press, 1993).

Johan Reinhard, "Peru's Ice Maidens," National Geographic Magazine 189, no. 1, 1996, 62–81.

Ian Thornton, *Krakatau: The Destruction and Reassembly of an Island Ecosystem* (Cambridge, MA: Harvard University Press, 1996).

Patrick Tierney, *The Highest Altar: The Story of Human Sacrifice* (New York: Viking, 1989).

TIME OF THE VOLCANO: SOUFRIERE HILLS, MONTSERRAT

Arrow, "One Day at a Time," from *Ride De Riddim* (Arrow Music Ltd., 1996). Audio cassette.

Michael Bernbaum, *Sacred Mountains of the World* (Berkeley: University of California Press, 1998)

Jay D. Dobbin, *The Jombee Dance of Montserrat: A Study of Trance Ritual in the West Indies* (Columbus: Ohio State University Press, 1986).

Thich Nhat Hanh, *Miracle of Mindfulness: A Manual on Meditation*, trans. Mobi Ho (Boston: Beacon Press, 1987).

Anne Michaels, *Fugitive Pieces* (New York: Vintage, 1998).

ORPHANS OF THE STORM: MOUNT PELÉE, MARTINIQUE

Lafcadio Hearn, *Two Years in the French West Indies* (Philadelphia: Harper & Brothers, 1890).

George Kennan, *The Tragedy of Pelée: A Narrative of Personal Experience and Observation in Martinique* (New York: Negro Universities Press, 1902).

Thomas A. Lewis, ed., *Planet Earth: Volcano* (Chicago: Time-Life Books, 1982).

Tim O'Brien, *The Things They Carried* (New York: Penguin, 1990).

Stephanie Ovide, *Creole-English, English-Creole Dictionary (Caribbean)* (Hippocrene Books, 1996).

WIRING UP THE WORLD: REDOUBT VOLCANO, ALASKA

Alwyn Scarth, *Vulcan's Fury: Man against the Volcano* (New Haven: Yale University Press, 1999).

Nancy Lange Simmerman, 2d ed. *Wild Alaska* (Seattle: The Mountaineers, 1999).

VOLCANOES OF THE MIND: THE CASCADES AND MOUNT SHASTA

Cecelia Svinth Carpenter, *Where the Waters Begin: The Traditional Nisqually Indian History of Mount Rainier* (Seattle: Northwest Interpretive Association, 1994).

Col. James Churchward, *Cosmic Forces of Mu*, vol. 2 (New York: Ives Washburn, 1935).

John Einarson, ed., *The Sacred Mountains of Asia* (Boston: Shambhala Publications, 1993).

Jane English and Jenny Coyle, eds., *Mount Shasta: Where Heaven and Earth Meet* (Mount Shasta, CA: Earth Heart, 1996).

Walter Kafton-Minkel, *Subterranean Worlds: 100,000 Years of Dragons, Dwarfs, the Dead, Lost Races and UFOs from Inside the Earth* (Port Townsend, WA: Loompanics Unlimited, 1989).

Theodora Kroeber, *Ishi in Two Worlds: A Biography of the Last Wild Indian in North America* (Berkeley: University of California Press, 1961).

John McPhee, *Assembling California* (New York: Farrar, Straus, Giroux, 1993).

Frederick Morrison, "California Bell Legends: A Survey," *California Folklore Quarterly* 4, no. 1 (1945).

John Muir, *The Mountains of California* (New York: Century, 1894).

Phylos the Tibetan (Frederick Spencer Oliver), *A Dweller on Two Planets* (New York: Harper & Row, 1886).

Michael Zanger, *Mount Shasta: History, Legend, and Lore* (Berkeley: Celestial Arts, 1993).